Politics Backstage

POLITICS BACKSTAGE

Inside
the California
Legislature

Michael J. BeVier

Foreword and Afterword by
Eugene Bardach

Temple University Press
Philadelphia

Library of Congress Cataloging in Publication Data

BeVier, Michael J
   Politics backstage.

   Includes index.
   1. California. Legislature. 2. Legislators—
California. I. Title.
JK8767 1979.B48   328.794   79-1021
ISBN 0-87722-150-2

Temple University Press, Philadelphia 19122
© 1979 by Temple University. All rights reserved
Published 1979
Printed in the United States of America

To Lillian

He who enters politics concludes a pact with devilish powers, since it is a realm where alone power and violence are valid means; yet from good may come evil and from evil good.

—Max Weber

Contents

Foreword

Eugene Bardach

DIFFERENT READERS WILL APPRECIATE THIS BOOK IN DIFFERENT ways. It will appeal to many people's natural curiosity about the mysteries of the legislative process, for BeVier was an insider who not only saw more than any outsider could have seen but also understood more than most similarly situated insiders would have understood. Secondly, for that minority who wish to improve their own skills in political gamesmanship, BeVier's book will be instructive as well as illuminating. BeVier and his colleague Bob Klein are the dramatic center of this fascinating story, and we watch them learning and practicing the craft of policy entrepreneurship from their position as staff "consultants" to the California Legislature Joint Committee on Community Development and Housing Needs. Although Bevier draws very few explicit inferences about "how to do it" from the experiences of Klein and himself, it will be easy for any reader thus inclined to do so. Better still, the do-it-yourselfer can simply allow himself to be infected by the entrepreneurial spirit and enthusiasm that pervade the book. Yet a third level on which the book can be appreciated is that of an adventure story. The plot is rich with melodrama, suspense, and surprise. The scheme, described in the last chapter, to make off with the governor's airplane is one of the boldest plans, as well as one of the funniest stories, in the written annals (though not in the oral lore) of legislative politics.

Finally, and most importantly, *Politics Backstage* will be valuable for scholars concerned with analyzing the dynamics of the legislative process. Although this book is not itself a work of scholarship, it should be of immense value to scholars; for it contains a rather unusual record of the process as seen through the eyes of one of the two central participants.

In my afterword, I attempt to clarify some of the conceptual and methodological issues that have long bedeviled students of the legislative process, and to suggest why participant-observer records such as BeVier's are likely to be a necessary, or at least very helpful, preliminary step toward further analytical progress.

Jerusalem, Israel
September 1978

Preface

THIS BOOK IS A NARRATIVE OF THE TWENTY MONTHS I SPENT AS a staff consultant to the California Legislature. During this time I was concerned solely with the passage of a single package of legislation comprised of several bills and a proposed amendment to the California Constitution intended to create a new state agency to finance housing for low- and moderate-income families.

Before arriving in Sacramento, I thought I possessed a sophisticated understanding of legislative process. Prior to law school I had majored in government and even spent a semester in Washington, D.C., writing a thesis on lobbying activity in Congress. I soon realized, though, how remarkably ignorant I was of the way legislative decisions are really made. As a student I had suffered no lack of texts which formally described and analyzed how a bill becomes law, but none evoked the emotional fireworks and pervasive negotiative context which are the living flesh on the otherwise dry bones of legislative procedure.

I wrote this book in the hope of conveying not only the formal structure of legislative decision-making, but also the aroma and texture of it which I found equally, if not more, important to its outcome. The book is not intended to expose the shortcomings of individual legislators nor to debunk the legislature as a whole. There are, no doubt, places where some disillusionment with individuals or the legislative process is expressed or implied, but this disillusion reflects at least as much on my own naivete as it does the performance of individuals or institutions.

That the book deals with a state as opposed to the national legislature is significant for at least two reasons. One is that state legislatures are, in their own right, worth considerably more attention than they get. Bernard McCormack, in *The Sometimes Government,* expresses the popular view of state legislatures through a conversation with the "typical" citizen:

"Do you know your state representative?"
"Nope. We got somebody up there."
"Do you know your state senator?"
"Yeah, you know his name. Delworth's kid."
"Do you know what they do up there?"
"They don't do anything."
"How would you sum up the legislature?"
"A bunch of thieves."

The casual recrimination is, I think, of less concern than the obvious indifference. State legislatures are said to suffer from a poor public image, but they suffer even more from having no public image at all. In some states this belies the amount of authority they actually possess; in every state it prevents them from becoming as vigorous and effective as they might otherwise be.

Many political scientists believe state governments have exciting potential. They have been called the "keystone" of our federal system. Midway between national and local government, they can avoid both excessive centralization and the extreme localization from which the other two governmental levels often suffer. California, generally considered to have one of the best legislatures in the country, is an ideal place to assess this potential.

A state legislature also provides what is possibly the best forum in which to study the dynamics of legislative politics generally. The more common studies of Congress suffer from an inability to portray all of the different influences which bear on major bills. The Congress is so very large, the interest groups surrounding it are so numerous and diverse, the executive branch with which it deals is such a labyrinth, that to portray the decision-making process as a whole is extraordinarily difficult. The smaller size of the state legislature and its greater informality result in a more concentrated, more personal forum and give the opportunity to provide what is perhaps a richer view of the legislative process.

This is, necessarily, a personal account. I have written almost solely in accordance with my own recollections and the extensive notes I compiled. Others may recall the same events differently. Most of the quoted conversations have no better source than my memory. I have quoted conversation, however, only in those cases for which I retained a specific recollection of what was said and also felt that there was an important flavor to the conversation which could not be conveyed in any other way. I have tried to be fair in describing the individuals involved, but cannot claim to be either wholly disinterested or completely objective. I was a parti-cipant—an active advocate—not an impartial observer. I have described events and people the way they appeared to me.

My only regret in adhering to such a method is that it tends to understate the role which others played. This is especially true of my partner, Bob Klein. Circumstances frequently required that we be at work simultaneously on different parts of the legislative puzzle and it was not possible for me to describe all that he did. Bob has his own story to tell.

Politics Backstage

1

Calamity Breeds Inspiration

ON MONDAY, JANUARY 8, 1973, GEORGE ROMNEY, SECRETARY OF the Department of Housing and Urban Development (HUD), was in Houston, Texas. There, at a convention of the National Association of Home Builders (NAHB), he made a stunning announcement: As of the previous Friday, January 5, the Nixon administration had cut off all funds to subsidize housing for low- and moderate-income families.

Romney's speech made both the *New York Times* and the *Los Angeles Times* the next morning. Reaction to the impoundment of housing subsidies was quick and fierce. The NAHB president immediately denounced the action as "disastrous and a catastrophe," a deputy mayor of New York City called it a "grossly irresponsible act," and harsh congressional criticism soon followed from major figures in both parties: William Proxmire, Wright Patman, Jacob Javits, Robert Taft, Jr., and Charles Percy, to name a few.

For me and my partner, Bob Klein, the effect of the impoundment was devastating. Since graduating from Stanford Law School less than two years before, we had struggled to establish a business, the sole function of which was to build housing for low-income families. To produce housing which such families could afford was possible only with government subsidies, which were the lifeblood of all our housing developments. The federal government was the sole source of such subsidy funds in California and without them we were finished.

When we began the business in 1971, the concept of working in tandem with the federal government to provide decent housing for the poor seemed not only a worthwhile activity but a business with considerable potential for growth and, certainly, stability. The United States had been providing housing assistance to low-income families since 1937. That program, still in use today, provides subsidies to local public housing authorities which are created and authorized by state law to construct, own, and manage low-rent housing. For almost a quarter century, public housing remained the only source of housing assistance to the poor. By the 1960s, however, there was growing dissatisfaction with the program. The public bureaucracies created at both the federal and local levels to administer the program were criticized as being slow and expensive. Most of the structures built were large multi-story buildings, whose architecture encouraged no sense of community among the occupants. Concentration of poor families in these publicly owned and managed high-density apartment houses often exacerbated the problems of vandalism and delinquency which better housing was supposed to alleviate, and the living environment frequently offered little improvement over the slums these housing projects replaced.

During the Kennedy and Johnson administrations a number of experiments were undertaken to develop alternative ways of subsidizing housing. Most of these alternatives were designed to substitute private initiative for management by public bureaucrats. One of the more ambitious of these attempts was the enactment in 1965 of a new section to the 1937 act which provided local housing authorities with funds to lease privately owned housing units. Under this new "Section 23 Program," local housing authorities could lease privately owned apartments at market rents and then sub-lease them to poor families at low rents. The difference between the rent paid by the housing authority to the owner of the apartments and that paid by the low-income tenants was made up through federal subsidy payments. This new program obviated the need for much of the cumbersome bureaucracy which was required to build and operate conventional public housing. It also helped to disperse some poor families throughout a community instead of concentrating them in large housing projects.

Among those in California who became interested in using Section 23 were Sam Oschin, president and chairman of Empire Financial Corporation in Los Angeles, and Bill Glikbarg, who was a senior partner in a Beverly Hills law firm and who specialized in real estate and mortgage financing. Both men had spent time in South America under the auspices of AID, attempting to help several Latin American countries solve the monumental problems of housing their vast and rapidly growing numbers of urban poor. They became increasingly intrigued with the problems of housing the poor and decided to devote full time to these problems in this country. After the Section 23 Program was created, Glikbarg left his law practice, Oschin resigned as president of Empire, and the two men formed a company for the purpose of developing and owning housing subsidized under Section 23.

In the spring of 1970, Glikbarg taught a course in housing policy as a visiting professor at Stanford Law School. There he met Bob Klein, a classmate of mine, who later introduced Glikbarg to me. During 1971, Bob and I formed a partnership with Oschin and Glikbarg's company. Instead of expanding the volume of Section 23 housing which they were doing in southern California, Bob and I sought to broaden the business geographically by developing housing in northern California under two new subsidy programs that had been created in 1968. One of these had been established under Section 235 of the National Housing Act. It authorized HUD to provide mortgage insurance to those lenders who financed the purchase of homes by low- and moderate-income families. It also allowed HUD to provide monthly subsidy payments to lower the effective cost of home financing for these families down to one percent. The second program, established under Section 236 of the same act, provided mortgage insurance and one-percent financing to developers of new rental housing, requiring them, by means of rent and profit control, to pass on the benefits of that low-cost financing to their tenants in the form of lower rents.

Bob and I developed housing under the Section 235 and 236 programs for just over twelve months. It was a year of furious activity and of exhilarating successes. By the end of 1972, Bob

and I had put together a number of subsidized housing developments worth several million dollars. Although all the units were to
be for low- and moderate-income households, our buildings were
not monolithic high-rise barracks but single-family homes, two-
story garden apartments, and, in one case, a hotel which we rehabilitated to make apartments for the elderly. We had several
hundred units under construction in various locations, both urban
and suburban. They provided many families with their first opportunity to live in decent housing. We put much of our expected
profit into additional amenities for these developments and into
counseling programs for the occupants, but we still expected to
make something for ourselves and had great plans for future expansion.

I was in our offices in Palo Alto, California, that Monday
afternoon when I received a telephone call informing me of the
substance of Romney's speech. After several confirming calls to
the HUD offices in San Francisco and Washington, Bob and I were
convinced that our business was shattered. The most we could do
was complete the projects for which we had already obtained irre-
vocable subsidy commitments.

Bob and I were certainly not the only ones to suffer from
the impoundment. The volume of housing subsidies flowing out
of Washington following passage of the 1968 housing act was immense. Hundreds of thousands of units per year were being built
with federal subsidies, in some years exceeding a fifth of all housing production in the country. In the four years 1969 through
1972, over one and a half million units were committed for subsidy, as many units as had been subsidized for low-income families during the previous forty years. The potential impact on
labor and the construction industry of stopping this massive flow
of money into housing was considerable.

Within two weeks of the Romney speech the construction
industry and the construction trade unions, along with local
governments and representatives of the poor and minority groups,
were organizing a national coalition to protest the termination of
housing subsidies. Congressional action seemed imminent. Suspen-
sion of the housing subsidies was only one of several impound-

ment decisions by which the Great Society was being dismantled. Congress was affronted by these refusals to spend appropriated funds, and on January 16, Senator Sam Ervin introduced a bill which would prevent presidential impoundment of funds without congressional consent. Before the end of the month subcommittees of the Senate Judiciary and Government Operations Committees had commenced joint hearings on impoundments. Many claimed that Nixon's actions were unconstitutional, a violation of the separation of powers principle, and law suits against HUD were contemplated to require that it spend appropriated housing funds. Many believed that one or a combination of such actions could force Nixon to rescind his impoundment decision.

Bob and I had little confidence that any of these efforts would be successful. We surmised that Nixon had anticipated the extent of criticism his action would bring and had acted in spite of it. He had just won a landslide victory, and at that moment he possessed what seemed to be an unshakeable political mandate. The president was not going to change his mind. Nor did we believe enough support could be generated in Congress to override a veto of legislation which outlawed presidential impoundment. And, from our point of view, the possibility of getting such action overturned in the courts was no more promising. Even if presidential impoundment of appropriated funds were eventually determined to be unconstitutional, a final adjudication to that effect would take a year at the very least. We could not keep our business going for that length of time without the availability of subsidies for new development. Besides, our faith in the commitment of HUD to provide housing for low-income families had been irreparably damaged. Even without formal impoundment, and entirely within the letter of the statutory language, HUD could, if so determined, render the subsidy programs almost totally unworkable. If Nixon did not want low-income housing to be produced with federal subsidies, we were confident that by one means or another he would see to it that little or none was built.

Even after writing off the possibility of continuing subsidies from the federal government, we were still loath to abandon our own commitment to low-income housing. Neither of us was ready to settle into a law practice, and we had spent long, hard hours acquiring some expertise in the field. But the only other governmental entity large enough to commit the amount of money necessary to subsidize any substantial number of housing units was the state and we could hardly expect California's Governor Reagan to be, any more enthusiastic about subsidized housing than Nixon.There were, however, some political advantages to pursuing the idea of government subsidies for housing at the state rather than the national level. We judged the governor to be more accessible than Nixon to interests which were, or might be persuaded to be, in favor of state housing assistance, and the coalition forming to protest the federal impoundments offered an excellent springboard for political action. If we could direct some of its energy toward the state government, and possibly add to it the force of other interests which might have a particular concern with state as opposed to federal involvement in subsidized housing we might be able to amass such formidable political support for state housing assistance that Reagan would not be able to resist.

Besides the political advantages of working to establish a subsidy program at the state level, we were attracted by the opportunity to design a housing subsidy program from scratch. From our experience with HUD we had formulated very definite ideas of our own as to how government housing subsidies should, and should not, be administered. Since we could not continue producing housing for the poor, the next best way of using our knowledge would be to help create a state program through which others eventually could. We decided to try to obtain sponsorship from some part of the state government to research and draft legislation which would create a state housing assistance program.

2

A Foot in the Door

BOB AND I WERE QUITE CERTAIN WE WOULD FIND NO ENTHUSIASM in Governor Reagan's administration for funding of state-assisted housing and therefore decided to focus our efforts on obtaining a sponsor in the state Legislature. To approach a legislature, though, is a peculiar undertaking as no single individual or office speaks for it. We were faced with 120 offices representing 40 senatorial and 80 assembly districts throughout the state. It was difficult to know where to begin.

Bob found the clue we needed in an article in the *San Francisco Chronicle* describing a contract under which the Assembly had engaged two engineering research firms to construct two steam-powered prototype automobiles. Of the $3 million cost of the contract, $500,000 had come from an Assembly contingency fund to finance this step in California's quest for cleaner air. The article identified for us a potential source of research money under immediate control of the Legislature: an Assembly contingency fund which was apparently available to fund research projects of statewide interest.

We were encouraged because we not only believed that housing constituted a more important and more immediate need than improved steam engines but were confident that housing was an issue with greater political attraction than steam engines. Furthermore, we estimated that it would cost considerably less than the half million dollars just committed for research on steam-powered automobiles to do the necessary research plus draft legislation creating a housing program.

After making several phone calls, we knew that use of the contingency fund was controlled by the Assembly Rules Committee and that the staff arm of that committee was the Assembly Office Research. We arranged an appointment with Bill Hauck, the director of the Office of Research, and it was in order to meet him that we made our first trip to Sacramento in January 1973.

We prepared ourselves for this interview by learning what we could about both Bill Hauck and the office he directed. A description of the office's role is comtained in the publication *California's Legislature,* which is published each session by the Legislature as an official guide. The 1972 edition stated:

[T]he Office of Research maintains a professional staff with a wide range of research skills to respond to the requests of individual Members of the Assembly and to the requests of committees for in-depth studies of major legislative problems. . . .

The duties of the Office of Research should be distinguished from the duties of the majority and minority consulting staffs, in that the former provides services exclusively for all members of the Assembly on a nonpartisan basis, while the latter provides services for the respective parties in the Legislature.

We learned, however, that the office was anything but nonpartisan. It is controlled by the Assembly Rules Committee, which, in turn, is controlled by the majority party. Since the speaker of the Assembly is leader of the majority party and controls committee appointments, he has considerable influence over the Rules Committee and therefore over both the staffing and operations of the Office of Research. That control is in fact so firm that there is inevitable temptation for him to appropriate some or all of its capacity for purposes that serve his party or his personal political ambitions. The value of this control is considerable, for staff is always critical to the effective running of a political organization or an individual campaign.

Before he became director of the Office of Research, Bill Hauck had been Speaker Bob Moretti's chief legislative aide. Moretti is a Democrat, and his appointment of Hauck to direct the Office of Research, which occurred only a few weeks before our trip, was interpreted as an important move by Moretti in building the foundation of a campaign staff for his expected gubernatorial race in November 1974.

Political reality convinced us that Hauck would be more receptive to our proposal if we were recommended to him by members of his party. Bob had taken a year off from law school to work in the successful campaign of Democrat John Tunney for the U.S. Senate and knew a number of individuals who were still active in the California Democratic Party. He called several of these before we left for Sacramento.

We arrived on a bright, cool January day and found the Assembly Office of Research in the Library and Courts Building, a six-story structure built forty years ago of light grey granite. Located across the street from the Capitol on the Ellipse, it is distinguished by two large white statues that flank the front steps, one of a deific-looking male and the other of a severely chaste but bare-breasted woman; both are seated and gaze rather vacantly toward a fountain which splashes enthusiastically a hundred feet away. We met Hauck in his fifth-floor office—a slim, intense man in his mid-thirties. Hauck introduced us to Leah Cartabruno, one of his staff who had previously done some research in the area of housing and community development. I was immediately encouraged by the fact that Cartabruno was there. If Hauck had intended to tell us he wasn't interested, I thought, there would be no reason for someone on his staff to attend.

Bill Hauck was already informed of the purpose of our meeting. During the previous week we had sent him a letter which summarized our proposal to design for the Legislature a program by which the state could subsidize housing for low- and moderate-income families. Bob and I had said very little about our credentials in the letter, believing we could sell ourselves more effectively in person. We assumed that Hauck knew nothing about us, so after the usual civilities of greeting, instead of describing our proposal we began reviewing those portions of our academic background and experience with low-income housing which we believed would give us some credibility. We then described the moratorium on federal housing subsidies and explained why it was so unlikely that the Nixon administration would reinstate or replace these subsidies in the near future. The moratorium might end but the federal government, we warned, would either permanently and substantially reduce the volume of housing subsidies or radically alter the design of the programs in a manner that would call for a greater role by state and local governments. If the federal government redesigned the programs, those states which had state housing agencies would be in the best position to assume a partnership role with the federal government and therefore to obtain the greatest amount of federal funds. If the moratorium signaled not a redesign but a federal retreat from housing assistance, then a state housing agency would be even more vital as the only means of providing decent housing to the poor.

The size and economic impact of federal housing subsidies were not generally recognized. It was important for our purposes, though, that Hauck appreciate the magnitude of these programs and be persuaded of the substantial political interests involved. The Housing and Urban Development Act of 1968 established a goal of subsidizing six million housing units within ten years and authorized vast sums of money to accomplish it. The eventual total cost of the housing subsidy program was estimated to be $85 billion, and by 1970 more than one-fourth of all the housing units started in the United States had federal subsidy commitments. The volume of subsidized housing activity, as a percentage of housing starts, declined during 1971, and in 1972 it had dropped substantially in absolute terms, from 430,000 to 340,000 units. The volume of all residential construction had climbed rapidly during 1970 and 1971 and reached a peak in early 1972, but despite the fact that 1972 was the best year the construction industry had ever had, by early 1973 there were indications of an impending decline. Not only builders, but construction trade labor unions, building supply industries such as lumber, cement, roofing, as well as mortgage lenders, were all worried about the level of home-building activity in the near future.

Minority groups and the poor had even more cause for concern. The 1960 housing census counted over 700,000 units in California which the Census Bureau classified as being in substandard physical condition. The 1970 census documented not only that one-half million households containing over three million people in the state were living in overcrowded units but that this burden fell disproportionately on minority groups and children. Over one-half of all the Spanish-American children in the State of California in 1970 lived in overcrowded housing.

It was this combination of housing concerns which resulted in the breadth and intensity of outcry against Nixon's impoundment action. And the same broad and powerful coalition of labor, industry, local government, and poverty groups could be rallied behind an effort to provide state-assisted housing. We pressed Hauck with this argument, emphasizing that our intention was not merely to do a study and submit reports. The end product was to be legislation. We intended not only to research and draft the bills necessary to create a major housing program for California but also to organize a statewide coalition of interests with sufficient political influence to get those bills enacted into law.

Although Hauck did not say much during the meeting, the few comments he did make indicated he was receptive. He could not, of course, give us a definite reply that day, but we were encouraged by his request for a more detailed cost estimate and his directions to Cartabruno to assist us.

In planning this first day in Sacramento, we had not relied entirely on our ability to persuade Bill Hauck but had also set up appointments with several legislators and staff members in the Capitol. Our purpose in doing this was less clear than it had been in approaching Hauck. We had only a vague notion that support from legislators might be helpful in our dealings with the Office of Research and that there might be other sources of funding about which we could learn.

The first stop in the Capitol was the office of George Beattie, principal staff member for the Assembly Committee on Urban Development and Housing, the Legislature's only standing committee which dealt expressly with housing. Beattie himself was looked upon as the Legislature's housing expert. Initially hired by Yvonne Braithwaite, who chaired the committee until her election to Congress in November 1972, Beattie had been retained, grudgingly, I was told, by Braithwaite's successor, Peter Chacon, a Chicano and Democrat from San Diego. Chacon had been elected in 1970 with help from Speaker Moretti, to whom Chacon also owed the chairmanship of the Housing Committee. Often, when a new committee chairman is appointed, he replaces the existing staff, but Beattie's housing expertise was respected not only generally within the capital community, but specifically by the speaker, and one of the conditions on which Chacon was offered the chairmanship was that he retain George Beattie as principal staff member. The value to staff members of maintaining good relations with legislative leadership can be considerable.

Beattie had consulted with Bob and me several times over the previous year to obtain our opinion, as private developers, on housing legislation that he had prepared for Braithwaite. We wanted to brief him on our proposal, hoping both to obtain the advice of an insider on how best to pursue the necessary funding and simultaneously to allay any fears he might have that we wished to usurp his role. After we described our intentions to him, he seemed not at all concerned that we might infringe on his territory. The field of assisted housing was expanding so rapidly, he said, that he had a difficult time staying on top of it. More staff assistance was needed, and he felt that our experience in actually developing housing could be valuable in designing housing legislation. He graciously offered to assist us in any way he could.

Our next stop was the office of Ken Maddy, assemblyman from Fresno. Over the past year we had done much of our development work in the Fresno area and in that connection had done business with some of Maddy's strong supporters. Indeed, we had met Maddy himself before and were encouraged to find, among the offices opening onto the Capitol corridors, a name we recognized on the door and a familiar face inside. Maddy was a young, boyish-looking attorney who had won an upset victory as a Republican in 1970 and during his first two-year term had served as vice-chairman of Braithwaite's housing committee. Although unsuccessful in getting that committee assignment for his second term, he had retained a strong interest in housing. We briefed him on our proposal and received his promise to help us in any way he could. Because he was a Republican we did not think he could be of any direct assistance with Hauck, but we surmised that at some point it could be useful to have a claim to bipartisan support for our project.

During the late afternoon we went to see two Democratic senators. The first was George Zenovich from Fresno with whom Bob was acquainted because his family had lived in Fresno for many years. The fact that Senator Zenovich had in the past introduced a number of bills related to housing suggested possible sympathy with our proposal. That first meeting with him was short. We did a much briefer version of the Hauck presentation—our background, political outlook, the federal housing moratorium, and so forth. He listened politely but without much apparent interest, and after giving a few obligatory words of encouragement and promising he would help us if and when we needed it, he stood up from behind his desk to indicate the interview was over.

From there we went to see Senator Nick Petris, a second-generation Greek from San Francisco and one of the most politically liberal members of the Legislature. We had arranged to see him because he was chairman of the Senate Select Committee on Housing and Urban Affairs. Select committees differ from standing committees in not being a part of the formal process through which a bill passes to become law. When a bill is introduced in the Legislature, it is immediately assigned to a standing committee. That committee hears the bill and may kill it, pass it out unchanged, or amend it. If the bill has no fiscal implications, it will usually go directly to the floor. But if it contains an appropriation or raises some other issue bearing directly on state finances, it must also pass through a finance committee. Select committees are not a part of this procedure. They have a very specific subject focus and are responsible only for undertaking research and holding investigative hearings within that purview. Because of their more limited function, membership and chairmanship of such committees carries neither the power nor prestige of the same positions in standing committees. Select committees do have professional staff, though, and can be an effective source of legislative initiative if used vigorously by their chairmen.

I recall our meeting with Petris better than any other we had that day. Part of the strength of that recollection results from the concern we had about his reaction to our background in private business. We were not made more comfortable by the presence of Bob Frank, a lawyer and the select committee's full-time consultant. A young man our age, Frank did not say a great deal during the meeting, but by his silence as much as by the few remarks he offered he did not make us feel particularly welcome. Perhaps his attitude was understandable. Bob Frank was the only other legislative consultant—besides George Beattie—who had spent considerable time on housing. We knew he had drafted legislation to create a state housing subsidy program that was to be introduced in 1973, and Frank may have felt some antagonism toward our proposal because it implied that more thought and research was required on the subject.

At first, Petris listened quietly to our presentation, which we modified to stress our interest in legal aid during law school and the nonprofit corporation which Bob and I had created and personally funded during the previous year to counsel tenants moving into subsidized housing projects. Shortly after we began explaining our intention to draft housing legislation, Petris interrupted us sharply:

"It'll never work, though. How are you going to get these people up here to vote for housing subsidies? They don't want to help the poor. Nobody's interested in helping them. My parents came from Greece, they believed this was a free country and I was raised to believe that people should be free, that America stood for freedom. But how can you be free if you're one of five kids living in a two-room tenement with a broken toilet, rats, and no heat in the winter?"

"I don't know," he replied to his own question, and began shaking his head in apparent resignation.

After a few moments' pause he continued. "I've been talking about these things for years up here. It doesn't do any good. No one gets any campaign money for helping people. You fellows have the right idea, you want to help, but nobody's going to listen. You have better things to do with your time."

He leaned back in his large high-backed swivel chair, watching us, I thought, quite carefully. He had thrown out some bait, and I had just began sniffing uneasily for the hook when Bob pounced on it:

"I disagree. I think it can be done because there is a real constituency now for this kind of legislation. We've had twenty-five percent of the housing starts in the country subsidized, did you know that?" Bob leaned forward in his chair, resting his elbows on his knees, his head close to the front of the Senator's desk. "Twenty-five percent. And Nixon has just stopped it cold, absolutely cold—it will kill the industry. It's not only the poverty and minority groups now, but also builders, developers, construction trade unions, the lumber suppliers, the League of Cities, NAHRO—even the mortgage bankers are upset.

"Do you know Galbraith's book, *The New Industrial State?* He talks about a *social*-industrial complex that will rise as the military-industrial complex declines. This is what we have to do, what we can do—build a political coalition advocating social programs that can come back to the Legislature again and again over a period of years.

"We can build an enormously powerful group to support housing assistance. Who can't we reach? With the builders, developers, suppliers, and mortgage bankers, we can even get to the most conservative Republicans.

"Mike and I aren't interested in coming up here just to do a study. We want to work with members like yourself to get housing legislation passed and we've got a chance now to create a political coalition that can do it."

Bob is a good salesman and, though we did not, I think, overcome all of Petris' misgivings, it was plain that he liked our enthusiasm and our insistent optimism that the time was right—that now, as never before, the state could be induced to provide housing assistance for the poor. We left Petris' office at about 5:30 with his commitment of support.

The encouragement we received that first day belied the amount of time it was to take us actually to obtain funding. Speaker Moretti, while generally receptive to our idea, did not find it as attractive in terms of his own gubernatorial campaign as we had expected. Housing was not an area in which he had ever taken a special interest, and he was concerned that even if major housing legislation were passed before the election, Reagan might veto it. A Reagan veto could be used against the governor if he were to run for a third term, but he was not expected to do so. Thus a veto would simply diminish the political value of whatever backing Moretti had given the legislation. Also, Moretti believed that the attractiveness of housing as a campaign issue stemmed primarily from the strong support it had from the labor unions. With limited time, resources, and attention, a candidate must focus his efforts on issues which have the greatest chance of bringing him those votes which would otherwise have gone to his opponent. Moretti already had strong labor support, and subsidized housing was not an issue that would broaden his appeal in the middle- and upper-middle-class suburbs where he would have to go to beat a strong Republican opponent.

We had, though, persuaded Senator George Zenovich. Housing was a major issue that could attract considerable attention, and it was one with which he felt comfortable, having introduced a number of bills on the subject during past sessions.

George Zenovich was born in Fresno and raised there by his Yugoslav parents. He attended Fresno State College, went on to get a law degree at Southwestern College of Law in Los Angeles, and then returned to Fresno to practice his profession. He began his political career in 1962 as an assemblyman and soon after arriving in Sacramento, became a protégé of Jesse Unruh, who was speaker for eight consecutive years (1961 to 1968), the longest tenure in the Legislature's history. Under Unruh's tutelage, Zenovich rose to be caucus leader and Unruh's probable successor as assembly speaker. The election year of 1970, though, posed a difficult strategic decision for Zenovich. The Democrats had lost their assembly majority in 1969 by losing an off-year special election. Unruh, now the minority leader, had decided to run against Governor Reagan. Nixon was in the White House and Reagan was favored for re-election. The Republicans seemed to be in the ascendancy; they were well-organized, well-funded, and seemed likely to strengthen their hold on the Assembly. If they retained a majority, that would eliminate any chance Democrat Zenovich had for the speakership. Hugh Burns, sixty-six years old and a political patriarch after serving thirty-four years in the Senate, wanted to retire. Burns' senatorial district included Zenovich's assembly district, and burns offered Zenovich endorsement for his senate seat. Choosing the more certain prestige of the upper house and the security of having to run only every four years instead of every two, he accepted Burns' offer and moved into the Senate. This decision may have cost him the speakership. Destitute and defensive, the Democrats lost most of the statewide races in 1970, but Unruh had provided the leadership to register 400,000 voters during the summer months and this, plus effective use of the resources they did have, allowed them to pick up four assembly seats and a forty-three to thirty-seven edge.

The quality which impressed me the most about Zenovich was the casualness of his manner. He is informal, offhand, so relaxed as to be almost blasé. It is this manner of presenting himself to which I think he owes much of his success. The legislative process is one of constant negotiation and his steady affability is Zenovich's poker face—the facade behind which he conceals the many political cards he holds, sometimes bluffing, but often showing aces when called. "Zeno," as he is often called with some affection, is generally thought to be a good fellow, almost always approachable, and a man against whom it is difficult to hold a grudge because of his easy-going good nature. He is shrewd and can be tough, but these are qualities he doesn't often reveal. A successful negotiator like Zenovich always conceals his state of mind; gains are made only to the extent that an opponent's uncertainty causes him to concede more than he needs to.

Zenovich rose rapidly in the Senate. Only two years after his entry into the upper house he had become a committee vice-chairman (agriculture), had won a coveted seat on the Senate Rules Committee, and was plotting, with what was generally considered a high probability of success, to unseat James Mills from his post as president pro tempore of the Senate.

At the time Bob and I talked to Zenovich he still lacked the prestige of a committee chairmanship and was receptive to the idea of a major housing study because it was something around which he might create his own committee. He could not hope suddenly to persuade the Senate to create a new standing committee, and Petris already chaired a select committee on housing, but with

Moretti's help he might be able to establish a joint Senate-Assembly housing committee. By the end of February, Zenovich had obtained an agreement from Moretti to support a joint committee which would hire Bob and me as consultants to undertake a study of state housing assistance. Zenovich would be committee chairman.

The creation and funding of a joint committee requires that a concurrent resolution be passed by the rules committee of each house and by a majority vote on the floor of both houses. When we were informed of Zenovich's intentions, Bob and I, with the help of Bill Hauck's staff and Zenovich's administrative assistant, Casey Young, drafted a resolution and began contacting lobbyists and legislators to generate support for it.

During that spring of 1973, Bob and I met with representatives of construction trade unions, home builders, real estate brokers, savings and loan associations, the state bar association, commercial banks, investment bankers, local governments, and poverty and minority groups. Some of those we saw, such as the realtors and savings and loans, we found adamantly opposed to all previous proposals for state assistance for low-income housing and unsympathetic to creating a joint committee on housing. We emphasized to them, though, that we had no preconceived ideas as to the way California ought to go about subsidizing housing, that we intended to research thoroughly the various ways in which housing assistance might be provided, and that we would be most interested in listening to their particular concerns. By promising an objective approach, we were able to obtain assurances of support for the resolution from almost every interested group with whom we spoke.

We also directly contacted a number of legislators, one of them Assemblyman John Burton (who later became a U.S. congressman), representing San Francisco and Marin County. Burton was then chairman of the Assembly Rules Committee and the Joint Rules Committee. Our resolution would be reported to the Rules Committee of each house as soon as it was introduced, and his support was necessary to ensure that it passed out of these committees for a vote on the floor of each house. He agreed to support our resolution, but only on condition that Frank Holoman, a black assemblyman from Los Angeles, be included in the project in some way that would permit Holoman to do a study of community development.

In April, Senate Concurrent Resolution No. 45 was introduced in the Senate under the co-sponsorship of Zenovich and Moretti. It proposed creation of the Joint Committee on Community Development and Housing Needs. By September it had passed both legislative houses and a budget had been approved by the Joint Rules Committee to hire Bob and me as well as to fund a subcommittee on community development. Zenovich was appointed committee chairman. Holoman was appointed chairman of the subcommittee. There were two other members from the Senate, Nick Petris and Milton Marks, both from San Francisco. Completing the committee were two assemblymen besides Holoman: Peter Chacon from San Diego and William Bagley from Marin County.

Bob and I lived on the San Francisco peninsula, so we requested that our offices be located in San Francisco instead of Sacramento. In addition to convenience, we felt that being at some distance from the capital might insulate us to some extent from political pressure. Our interest was in housing. We were aware that political pressures would heavily influence any of our legislative proposals if they were to be passed and, though we would have to deal with these pressures, we wanted to avoid being immersed in them.

The Legislature provided office space in the State Building, which flanks the San Francisco Civic Center and is just across the street from City Hall. There were two drab rooms on the first floor, which we never took pains to brighten, but which in the excitement of the following months came to seem very friendly. Here, on September 1, 1973, we began.

3

The Substance of Subsidies

THE IDEA OF STATE HOUSING SUBSIDIES FOR LOW-INCOME AND moderate-income families did not originate with Bob and me. More than ten years before, New York had begun the first such program by creating the New York State Housing Finance Agency, which was authorized to provide construction loans and long-term mortgage loans to finance new apartments. The agency raised the money to make such loans by selling bonds to private investors. This is the way states and cities have traditionally financed public works projects, servicing the bonds they issue by making principal and interest payments either from general tax revenues or from income generated by whatever project was financed by the bond proceeds. The New York Housing Finance Agency had no taxing power but made its mortgage loans at a rate just above its bond rate, which permitted it both to service the bonds and to pay administrative expenses.

The guts of the New York program was the housing agency's ability, as a part of state government, to issue bonds on which interest payments were tax-exempt. Under our federal system of government the states are sovereign and thus they and their political subdivisions (cities, counties) are not subject to the taxing power of the national government. An investor, comparing the after-tax return on taxable and tax-exempt bonds, will accept a lower interest rate on the tax-exempt securities. Thus the effect of issuing tax-exempt securities is that the issuer by being able to pay a lower interest rate, garners an indirect federal subsidy equal to the amount of federal tax revenue which would have been collect-

22

ed had the interest payments been taxable. The New York State Housing Finance Agency captured this subsidy by issuing tax-exempt bonds and passed it on to private owners of apartment housing in the form of low financing costs. In exchange for this advantage owners were required to pass on the subsidy benefits to their tenants by charging rents lower than market values, and the units were permitted to be occupied only by households whose incomes were below specified levels.

The success of such a program depends entirely on the ability of the housing agency to market its bonds. The willingness of investors to purchase any particular tax-exempt issue depends upon its attractiveness compared with other tax-exempt bonds being offered at the same time. An investor has two main concerns: the interest rate and the degree of risk that the issuer will be unable to make principal and interest payments when due. If the risk is relatively higher on one issue than another, the one with the greater risk will sell only if it offers a higher interest rate to compensate for such risk.

Usually the most secure bonds, and those which therefore can be sold at the lowest interest rates, are bonds that are backed by the general tax revenues of the city, county, or state issuing them. These are "general obligations" of the issuer and have a lien on whatever tax revenue is received by that issuer. The amount of taxes which the issuer has the power to collect each year is normally far greater than the amount necessary to service outstanding bond obligations; and barring some economic disaster which seriously erodes the issuer's tax base, the investor has considerable assurance that he will be paid as promised.

Besides general obligation bonds, there are revenue bonds which are secured not by general tax revenues, but by some specific, narrower stream of expected revenue—usually that projected to flow from the investment made with proceeds of the bond sale. For example, bonds may be issued to construct a toll bridge, water works, or sewage system. The revenue pledged as security will be that expected to result from the toll charges, sale of the water, or sewer user fees. The risk incurred by the bond holder depends on the certainty of future income. Because these revenues are almost never as certain as tax revenues, investors usually demand a higher yield on revenue bonds than on general obligation bonds. Differences in risk and return also exist among revenue bonds issues.

Other things being equal, general obligation bonds are the more attractive to a public issuer because they can be marketed at a lower interest rate than revenue bonds. Most states, though, including New York and California, have provisions within their constitutions requiring electoral approval of any general obligation bond issue. Subsidized housing is not an issue which generally creates wild popular enthusiasm. The Rockefeller administration, which originally developed the idea for a New York State housing agency, doubted that it could get electoral approval to issue general obligation bonds for subsidized housing. Investors, however, were not interested in buying revenue bonds for which the only security would be rents paid by families which could not afford market-rate housing. They had invested in toll bridges and sewage treatment plants, but housing for poor people was something else. Some additional security was needed to entice bond buyers to venture into the murky financial waters of low- and moderate-income housing.

John Mitchell, years before his appointment as attorney general, was a partner in Caldwell, Trimble & Mitchell. Mitchell was an extremely able bond counsel and demonstrated remarkable creativity in solving New York State's housing bond problem with what became known as a "moral obligation" clause. A provision drafted by Mitchell was inserted in the legislation creating the New York State Housing Finance Agency. It stated that if revenues from the housing projects financed by the housing agency were ever insufficient to service bonds issued by the agency, then the governor of New York was required to include within the budget for the succeeding fiscal year whatever amount was necessary to make up such deficit. There was no requirement that the legislature approve that budget item. If there had been, it would have created a general obligation and required voter approval. While deftly avoiding the necessity of a referendum on the one hand,

Mitchell's clause provided a specific mechanism by which the state could support the bonds and created a sufficient guarantee that they would be backed by the state's financial resources to make them saleable. In 1962 the New York State Housing Finance Agency began selling moral obligation bonds and by 1973 more than twenty states had created housing finance agencies, almost all of which used a moral obligation on the part of the state to enable sale of their bonds.

State housing agencies have two, and in some cases three, sources of subsidy immediately available to them, by which they can reduce the cost of housing. The most obvious is their ability to borrow money by issuing bonds at tax-exempt rates and passing this advantage along to developers of low-income housing in the form of interest rates significantly lower than those available from private mortgage lenders. The second subsidy results from provisions in the federal income tax law that provide a tax shelter for individuals and corporations who invest in low- or moderate-income housing. In addition to the mortgage loan from the housing agency, which supplies usually 90 percent of the money needed to build a project, there must be a private owner/investor who is willing to put up the remaining 10 percent of the money as equity or risk capital. Housing for families having low or moderate incomes is perceived as a riskier investment than conventional market-rate apartments. The most direct way of attracting equity capital would be to increase the cash flow to investors in order to compensate for the greater risk. This, however, would require higher rents that would place these units beyond the reach of those whom they are supposed to serve. Real estate tax shelters are often criticized as "loopholes" and were narrowed by the income tax reform acts of 1969 and 1976. They have not been entirely eliminated, though, and continue to supply the incentive necessary to attract equity capital to publicly financed housing while permitting state agencies to restrict investor cash return to modest levels and thereby hold down rents.

A third source of subsidy, available only in some states, is the forgiveness of all or a portion of local property tax payments.

California, for example, has in its constitution a provision which exempts from local property taxes, rental housing that is owned by a non-profit organization and occupied by elderly persons.

These subsidies, even when combined on a single project, still result in only a moderate level of assistance. A principal weakness of such state programs is that by themselves they do not provide subsidies that are sufficiently deep to reach those who have the most difficulty affording decent housing.

Passage of the Housing and Urban Develepment Act of 1968 provided new impetus for state housing finance agencies by providing a source of deep subsidies. These new federal programs were designed to be used in conjunction with financing from private lenders such as banks, insurance companies, and savings and loan associations. Knowing that private lenders would be unwilling to risk lending money on housing for low-income families, HUD provided mortgage loan insurance. If the project for which the loan was made proved unable to meet its obligation to pay principal and interest, HUD insured that the lender would get his money back. HUD, in addition to supplying subsidies to reduce project rents, thus also bore the entire lending risk. This situation made an agreement between HUD and individual state housing finance agencies attractive to both sides. The states were already in the business of lending money to construct housing for low-income families. What they needed were subsidies to reach needier families, and if HUD supplied them with subsidy funds under one of the new programs, they were willing to continue to bear the risks of lending money to finance the projects. This arrangement was soon formalized by a procedure under which HUD annually contracted with individual state agencies to provide subsidy commitments.

This federal/state partnership worked well. Between 1969 and 1973, state housing finance agencies issued $1.8 billion in bonds to finance some 90,000 units, about two-thirds of which were subsidized with federal funds. By 1973 no agency had experienced any difficulty in servicing its bonds and no state had been called upon to honor its moral obligation.

California did not have a state housing finance agency, but it had been a pioneer in the use of tax-exempt bonds to finance housing. Just after World War I the California Veterans Home Loan program was created. Under it, the state authorized sale of general obligation bonds to provide low-cost financing for veterans wishing to purchase a home or farm. The program is still very active. Veterans generate considerably more electoral support than do poor people. Since the program's creation in 1921, every authorization for the sale of bonds to finance "Cal-Vet" housing had been approved, a total of about $3 billion. Of this, $1.2 billion was still outstanding in 1973, constituting over 20 percent of the outstanding debt of California.

The first time that housing for the poor was given serious attention occurred in 1962, when Governor Pat Brown created an ad hoc commission to study and report on the state's housing problems. After some months of research, the commission published statistics documenting the large number of households in the state living in substandard dwellings. It also offered a number of recommendations for state action, one of the major proposals advising creation of a state housing finance agency patterned after the one which had just been created by New York State.

Brown's commission was chaired by the builder Joseph Eichler and included a number of other prominent businessmen. In response to the commission's report, legislation was passed establishing a state goal of providing "a decent home and suitable living environment" for every household. To pursue that end, a Department of Housing and Community Development was created within the Business and Transportation Agency. The new department was given token powers, though, and a tiny budget; it was specifically prohibited by its enabling legislation from providing housing finance assistance. Thus, having before it a major study which documented that hundreds of thousands of households in the state lived in substandard dwellings, and having declared a goal of assuring decent housing for all Californians, the Legislature nevertheless explicitly prohibited the financial assistance which had been expressly recommended as the means of achieving that goal.

Such legislative dementia resulted, Bob and I were told, largely from opposition by the savings and loan industry which had grown large and powerful financing the explosion in home building in California that occurred during the 1950s and '60s. Savings and loan associations did not object to housing the poor, but did not like the proposed means—providing mortgage financing at a cost lower than they were able to profitably charge. The prospect of the state entering their business by creating a state housing finance agency was disturbing: such an agency would be a competitor that could afford to make loans at exceptionally low interest rates because of its ability to borrow through the sale of tax-exempt bonds.

The strategy of a cosmetic response—creation of a department of housing with essentially no powers—while initially successful, was not sufficient for long. The Watts riots broke out a short time later, in the summer of 1965, and left a memory that was slow to die as the same frustrations, the same rage, echoed not only in Detroit and Newark but also, with less publicity, in Oakland and even Fresno.

Assemblywoman Yvonne Braithwaite of Los Angeles had been a staff attorney on the McCone Commission, which investigated the Watts riot in 1965. Elected to the Assembly in 1966, she had been appointed chairman of the Committee on Urban Development and Housing in 1971 and had instructed George Beattie to draft a bill that would create a housing finance agency. There had been similar legislative initiatives by other legislators including Chacon, Zenovich and Burton, as well as Senators Petris and Moscone. The most recent of these was Chacon's bill, drafted by George Beattie, which passed the Legislature in the early fall of 1973 only to be vetoed by Governor Reagan.

Despite these recent failures, Bob and I felt that a state housing finance agency was the kind of housing assistance plan which had the greatest chance of enactment. It was attractive from a political standpoint because a substantial economic and social impact could be achieved with almost no budget expenditure. A housing finance agency could generate sufficient revenue to cover its administrative overhead by charging its mortgagors processing fees and a slightly higher rate of interest than it would pay on its bonds. All it would require in hard cash from the state would be a loan of several hundred thousand dollars to cover start-up expenses. Also, state housing finance programs were operating successfully in other states and this experience could be extremely useful in selling the idea—an advantage we would not have if we attempted to develop a totally new approach. Finally, the proliferation of state housing finance agencies led us to expect that the Nixon administration would carry out its intention of redesigning federal housing subsidies with the new state agencies in mind. If California's housing policy strayed too far from the pattern, there was a risk it would not mesh with HUD's future programs and thereby would lose federal funds.

The fact that state housing finance agency legislation had passed the Legislature before was less of an advantage than it appeared. In speaking with numerous legislators during our quest for funding, we were told that many of the votes for such legislation had been cast only because of the certainty of a Reagan veto. To the extent we were perceived as capable of overcoming the governor's opposition, we were likely to encounter increased scrutiny in the Legislature.

As we evaluated our chances of success with housing finance legislation where previous attempts had failed, the savings and loan industry seemed to us the single most important obstacle. The California Savings and Loan League enjoyed a conservative image, one toward which we believed Reagan would be naturally sympathetic. We had been told that, prior to vetoing previous housing finance agency legislation, the governor had called Dean Cannon, the league's executive director, to ask his opinion on the merits of such a program. We believed the league's opinion would be an important factor in Reagan's decision on any future housing finance bill. Also, if we did have difficulty with the Legislature it would no doubt come from the more conservative members—those most likely to be influenced by the mortgage lending industry. This is not to imply that we believed that either the governor or the Legislatures was a tool of the mortgage lenders. Rather, it is to suggest that the savings and loans held, in this instance, the critical position of being that sector of the business community at once most directly affected by the program and most substantially opposed to it. If we could turn them around without alienating other interests which had backed previous housing bills, we believed there was a fair chance of passage.

4

First Allies

IT TOOK SEVERAL WEEKS TO GET COMPLETELY SETTLED IN OUR offices, but by October 1 we were well ensconced. Gina Pennestri, administrative assistant to John Burton, whose district office was on the same corridor, was a great help in cutting through the red tape of getting furniture, telephones, stationery, and the other paraphernalia we needed. She recommended for the job of committee secretary an acquaintance of hers, Michelle Welch, who was the only person we interviewed for the job.

The smaller of the two rooms assigned to us was divided into an inner and outer office by a partition which stopped two feet short of the ten-foot ceiling. Michelle had the outer portion and I the inner. Bob was next door—the larger size of his quarters presumably compensating for his less convenient access to Michelle. The arrangement worked particularly well because Bob uses what I refer to as an "open" filing system. That part of the five hundred square feet he had which was not taken up by a drunken hat rack, a large dusty fan on casters, and assorted cardboard boxes, was quickly filled by large tables covered with sometimes more but usually less differentiable stacks of paper.

Soon after Michelle began to work for us, we had an official committee letterhead and business cards for Bob and me printed up, proclaiming our status as consultants to the Joint Committee on Community Development and Housing Needs, and had the committee's name neatly lettered in black on the frosted glass pane in the door separating Michelle's office from the high-ceilinged corridor.

31

Our first mark was the savings and loan industry. The tactical problem was how to approach it—an industry which for many years had been resolutely opposed to what we wished to sell. Access to those in the industry was not a problem. We could rely on Oschin and Glikbarg to tell us who was most influential and assist us in obtaining the necessary appointments. Our difficulty was determining what kind of arguments would most effectively refute the basis for their historical resistance to a housing finance agency.

Initially we considered a defensive approach. We could make the case that the savings and loans had no reason to fear competition from a housing agency which was created to serve only those households which had income insufficient to qualify for private mortgage loans. We would argue that it constituted neither a fair nor even a rational defense of their interests for the savings and loans, on the one hand, to refuse to make loans to low-income families and, at the same time, try to prevent the public sector from serving those people on grounds that such service encroached upon their business. The problem with such an argument, we decided, was that the savings and loans would not put any faith in the limitation on the state's activity which it implied. They would figure that regardless of what income group the agency was originally designed to serve, statutory changes or bureaucratic aggrandizement would eventually result in its eating away a part of the mortgage finance market now served by the savings and loan institutions.

What we needed was to tie the interests of savings and loans to the successful operation of the state's financing of low-income housing. We needed, that is, to devise a system of delivering low-cost mortgage capital in which the savings and loans played an integral role. If they participated in the program, not only would their fears of competition with a public agency be alleviated but they might be induced to actively support state housing assistance. Bob and I considered the creation of a state housing agency as only a first step by California in meeting what we believed was its obligation to assure that all its citizens had a decent place to live. To achieve that goal would require a far greater amount of housing assistance than we could hope to have legislated in the next year or two. It would have to be done over a period of many years and that required a vigorous, durable political coalition which would be greatly strengthened if it included the savings and loans.

The possibility of utilizing the existing private mortgage finance infrastructure for distribution of publicly assisted mortgage loans was also attractive because of our very unsatisfactory experience with the federal government's attempts to accomplish the same task using a public bureaucracy. The laws, regulations, and paperwork by means of which HUD administered its subsidy programs constituted a huge and enormously complex labyrinth. Usually years elapsed between the time an application was submitted and the day on which a housing development was ready for occupancy. When we were developing HUD projects our initial applications alone were never less than an inch thick, and I recall one developer who weighed in all the paper work required to complete a project at more than thirty pounds. The longer a program existed, the more paperwork was added. By the time of the subsidy moratorium, HUD had found reason to be involved in every detail of a subsidized project, from the shape of the roofline to the width of walkways, from the kind of doorhandles to the positioning of shrubs. How you constructed the units, how you marketed them, how you managed them: HUD was there to bicker over every detail in every phase of development, from tentative approval right through to rent-up.

HUD reminded me of a deaf, half-witted great aunt who is tolerated only because she has money. Actually, doing business with that agency's numerous divisions was like dealing with a dozen such biddies at once, each of whom had to be satisfied in turn, and none of whom cared what the other ones wanted. One division talked only about architecture, another about operating costs, another about affirmative action programs, another about rent levels, and so on. The architecture division would insist on changes which substantially increased costs, without any apparent concern for the fact that another division was demanding that costs must be decreased to allow more money for operations, and still another refused to consider rent levels which provided enough income to do what either of the others wanted. I remember months of frustration, frantically rushing from one division to the next. Each had the power to prevent a project from being built simply by refusing to approve their part of it. We had to get each of them to compromise enough to end up with a single development package that could in fact be built.

The bureaucratic structure was utterly unsuitable for developing real estate. HUD had some good architects, some good appraisers, and some people in their management division who had an excellent grasp of marketing problems and operating costs. But the organization operated like an assembly line. Each task was isolated from the others. A project application passed from station to station and at each point a process might be performed in a way that was competent as an isolated task. But developing housing is not like assembling machinery. The number of variables affecting each individual housing development make every project unique. This requires a very flexible administrative structure and one which can deal with the interrelationship among these variables by dealing with several different aspects of a development at once. For example, it is important in considering the effect of structural design on the level of noise to which units are subjected from a nearby highway intersection that there be an acute sensitivity not only to the cost differences among alternative designs but also to the fact that the design has to win approval by the local planning commission. A rigidly compartmentalized bureaucracy will completely ignore the need for such an integrated overview of a real estate development.

An equally serious problem with the public bureaucracy is that the staff is rewarded not for producing successful housing developments, but for avoiding mistakes. A bureaucrat knows that so long as he adheres to the explicit wording of regulations he cannot be blamed for anything. However, a single set of instructions issued and occasionally updated by a central office is pitifully inadequate in dealing with the limitless variety of problems and circumstances which occur in trying to build low- and moderate-income housing throughout the country or even a single state. So long as there is rigid adherence to regulations, the necessary creativity will be lacking.

Bob and I had no desire to duplicate in Sacramento the mistakes that had been made by the federal government. It was possible, of course, that HUD suffered only from the various complications of organizational obesity and merely the fact that a state housing agency was smaller would make it more efficient. Bob had obtained some evidence that this was true in the course of several trips he had taken to Boston during the preceding year. He had done some investigating of the Massachusetts Housing Finance Agency and found that Bill White, at that time its executive director, ran a very tight, highly competent, aggressive agency which had consistently provided attractive, well-located housing for low- and moderate-income families.

Some of this success apparently resulted from the small size of the agency—about fifty employees compared to HUD's approximately fifteen thousand—which permitted more flexible management and the rapid decision-making which real estate development requires. Much of it, though, seemed to emanate from Bill White himself, who expressed considerable distaste for bureaucracies. He viewed the regulatory structure upon which HUD is based—the countless numbers of forms, checklists, procedures—as so many walls which bureaucrats can hide behind to protect themselves from criticism. When, sometime later, I asked White how he made the final decision to finance a project, he thumped his stomach with a fist and said: "I make the decision here; it's got to feel right in my guts."

We decided, however, that the Massachusetts experience was of limited value to us. In designing a public program, there is no way to assure it will be aggressively managed, and to the extent that small size contributed to the success of the Massachusetts agency, we could not be sure of duplicating it in California. California had more than three times the population of Massachusetts and almost twenty times the area, as well as far more diverse geography, all of which implied the need for a larger and more complex agency. We also speculated that the Massachusetts agency, which was created in 1966, might merely be enjoying a youthful vigor which public agencies often exude for the first few months or years of their existence before their bureaucratic arteries harden and they lapse into senility.

Instead of creating a large centralized bureaucracy in Sacramento to perform all the lending functions, the possibility of utilizing the existing network of private mortgage lenders to initiate and service subsidized mortgage loans seemed particularly attractive. We knew that a similar idea had been tried in New Jersey where there existed a state agency which made wholesale loans at low rates of interest to banks and savings institutions pursuant to an agreement requiring that they relend the money at a specified below-market interest rate to moderate-income households. By using private financial intermediaries, the agency limited its own functions to selling tax-exempt bonds and then negotiating the terms at which the bond sale proceeds would be loaned to private lenders. A qualified family desiring a loan did not have to submit an application to the state agency but instead contacted one of the participating banks or savings institutions and applied there. These private lenders then performed the paperwork and other tasks incident to initiating a mortgage loan, including the screening of loan applicants within guidelines set forth in the bank/agency agreement. Qualifying families received home loans at a below-market interest rate that reflected the low interest rate paid by the lenders to the agency plus an add-on which compensated the lenders for their services.

We did not like all the aspects of this "loan-to-lenders" program in New Jersey. We thought that the agency was allowing the lenders too high an add-on and that the restrictions imposed by the agency on the lenders when making the retail loans were insufficient to assure that the program benefited those who were most in need. What intrigued us, though, was that administration of the program required a very small public bureaucracy. The state, in effect, purchased the services of private lenders to perform the actual lending services and the program operated with a minimum of red tape. Some kind of similar arrangement was, we believed, the way to solve our political problems while avoiding creation of another large state bureaucracy. Precisely what form this public/ private partnership should take we did not know, but the idea gave us the basis for a deal with the savings and loan associations.

Most communication between the Legislature and the savings and loans takes place through the California Savings and Loan League. At that time Bernie Mikell was the league's lobbyist in Sacramento and Dean Cannon, based in Pasadena, was the league's executive director. Cannon and Mikell do not make policy for the league. They are hired to carry out decisions made by the league's board of directors, which is made up of executives of various savings and loan associations throughout the state. Our objective therefore was to persuade the league's board of directors. Even within such a small group as this board, though, there were certain individuals who seemed to have an especially strong influence on particular kinds of decisions. Glikbarg, Oschin, and others familiar with the league gave us the names of those members who would be particularly influential in shaping the board's opinion on this type of legislative issue.

By November we had begun a series of meetings in which we met individually with several members of the league's board. I recall particularly well our meeting in San Francisco with George Blencowe, senior vice president of Great Western Savings and Loan. The meeting with him took place in early November, by which time Bob and I had talked to several other directors and had a well-rehearsed presentation of our ideas. One of us began by describing our backgrounds, emphasizing our experience as private developers familiar with the problems of housing finance. Bob then provided some background on state housing finance agencies in the United States and generally described our conclusion that only by utilizing the private sector to a maximum extent could the state efficiently provide subsidized mortgage credit for low- and moderate-income housing. I then summarized statistics, taken from the 1970 census, on the amount of substandard housing currently in the state to indicate the size of the market which private lenders were not servicing. As a finale, Bob went through several scenarios of how a state agency might work in tandem with private lenders, all of which were variations on the theme of restricting the power of the state agency to primarily issuing bonds and leaving to private lenders the actual underwriting and processing of the loans.

When we finished I could see that Blencowe was unable to decide whether to take us seriously. His eyes looked amused and there was a hint of condescension in the tone of his voice, but the questions he asked were good ones which indicated that he had been a close listener. Who would be eligible for the loans? How much would the lenders get for providing the lending services? When a lender received a qualified loan applicant, how and when would the state agency transfer funds to the lender? Who was going to bear the risk of default on the loans?

Bob and I did not have answers to all the questions. We had, though, given considerable thought to most of the issues Blencowe touched and were able to discuss them intelligently. By the time we finished Blencowe was not, I thought, sold on the idea of state-assisted housing but the look of amusement was gone. Some of what we said had made sense to him and as we left he encouraged us to keep in touch with him as we developed our ideas more fully.

We also met with Dick St. Lezin, an executive vice president with Bay View Federal Savings and Loan in San Francisco and chairman of the league's loan procedures committee. St. Lezin's office is in the Bay View branch located in San Francisco's Mission District, so named because in it is the site of the original Mission San Francisco de Asis, established by Father Junipero Serra in 1776, and from which the city itself also took its name. This part of the city is largely lower-middle class. It is a bit shabby-looking but includes stable neighborhoods where many families own homes whose mortgages are held by Bay View. The rise in mortgage interest rates over the previous decade had driven completely out of the home-buying market many families to whom Bay View would have made a mortgage loan five years before. During our meeting with St. Lezin, we stressed that the proposed state program, by providing mortgage money at two to three points below the market rate, would permit a lender such as Bay View to again serve the moderate-income families who just a few years before had been able to afford conventional mortgage loans. The program would also be of great benefit to inner-city lenders, we urged, because the state would encourage the lending of its funds in declining areas of the central city to arrest the spread of blight. By increasing the flow of capital to the inner city the state agency would strengthen property values there and thus help protect the investment which lenders already had in central urban areas. We left the Bay View offices with an agreement that St. Lezin would arrange for us to make a presentation before the loan procedures committee.

While working on persuading the savings and loans we tried not to forget our obligations to the joint committee and the political needs of its members. The function of a joint committee is similar to that of a select committee, the difference between the two being only that the membership of joint committees comes from both the Assembly and the Senate. Select and joint committees exist for the formal purpose of conducting research and public investigative hearings on specific topics of concern to the Legislature. Standing committees, in addition to their role of screening bills before they are sent to the floor of either house, hold investigative hearings as well; the existence of joint and select committees rests on the premise that the Legislature should do more research and investigation than the some forty standing committees can handle. So important is legislative investigation considered to be that it constitutes an important rationale for the two-year legislative session. This two-year legislative calendar includes a three and a half month interim study recess, during which the Legislature does not meet, for the express purpose of allowing committees the opportunity to hold investigative hearings around the state.

In 1973, this recess lasted from September 14 to January 7, 1974, and we planned, at Zenovich's urging, to hold at least two hearings before the first of the year. The first took place on November 14 in the San Francisco State Building where Bob's and my offices were located. Bob and I wrote press releases, and Michelle telephoned several radio and television stations the day before the hearing. The following morning my radio was tuned to KCBS as I drove into San Francisco and heard them broadcast portions of a telephone interview with me, which they had taped the day before, concerning the state's housing needs.

The hearings began with a half-hour slide show Bob had put together showing apartments financed by state housing finance agencies in New York and Massachusetts. The slides were meant to convey an impression of attractively designed, well maintained units and dispel fears that the product of state assistance would resemble the huge monolithic structures produced for the federal public housing program. Following the slides, Zenovich was scheduled to read a short speech I had written for him. But in his characteristically informal way, he put aside this formal introduction and, after introducing the several committee members who were there, called for the first witness.

Bob and I had found it difficult at the outset to decide who we would have testify because we believed the hearings could have almost no substantive usefulness. I suppose an ostensible purpose of such hearings is to serve as a forum in which citizens can directly express their opinions to the Legislature, but there is not enough time in a day or two or even three to provide any kind of reliable survey of the state's eight million voters. Hiring an opinion pollster would accomplish the purpose more efficiently and with far greater reliability. Testimony by expert witnesses might help to educate committee members in the complexities of subsidized housing finance, but a public hearing is an uncomfortable place for an elected official to learn. The public expects him to be far more knowledgeable in the topics covered by his committee than he usually is and this restrains him from asking those questions which are necessary to his understanding but which might expose his ignorance. In short, hearings serve as a cumbersome and awkward forum for exchange of information between legislators and constituents. They do have some value as a symbolic gesture indicating the desire of the Legislature to elicit opinions from the citizenry and emphasizing the importance of communication between representatives and the people they are elected to represent. More important for our purposes, though, was the public exposure which hearings would provide the committee members. We wanted the members to be publicly associated with the issue of housing, believing this would increase the amount of real support we could get from them when housing finance agency legislation was introduced.

For the morning we scheduled as witnesses an investment banker from a New York bond firm and a commercial banker from San Francisco, both of whom discussed various means by which public agencies could provide financing for housing. For the afternoon we had scheduled nine witnesses including an expert in real estate taxation, representatives of several local government agencies involved with housing, and spokesmen for both the California building industry and the construction trade unions. When the committee reconvened after a luncheon recess we found, though, that we had considerably overestimated the endurance of our committee members. A number of reporters attended in the morning, but they didn't return, their deadlines for the afternoon editions having passed. The drinks and lunch, paid for by one of several lobbyists attending the hearing, were finished, and morning attendance alone was sufficient for members to qualify for their per diem expense stipend of $28.00, which they received when traveling outside their districts on legislative business. In short, there was very little inducement to remain and by 3:30 p.m. all of the committee members had left. We still had several witnesses yet to speak. Having asked them to prepare testimony and, in some cases, travel a considerable distance to attend, it seemed intolerably rude that not one member remained to receive their presentation. I was angry, but realized too that the most important purposes of the hearing had been already fulfilled. There had in fact been a public hearing on state-assisted housing. The legislators had appeared, albeit briefly, they had listened to opinions from the citizenry, the reporters had filmed it and had written about it. There was little or nothing more to be done.

During the next four weeks we continued to push on the savings and loan industry. Bob and I held a number of meetings with executives in that industry and continued to refine our ideas on exactly how the partnership between a state housing agency and private lenders ought to work. The most useful functions the lenders could perform would be to initiate and service loans for the state housing finance agency. Within guidelines established by the state agency concerning such things as maximum income limits on occupants and maximum loan amounts, the private lenders would screen loan applicants and make the lending decision. After making the loan, an initiating lender would collect the monthly mortgage payments for the agency, see that taxes and hazard insurance premiums were paid, and do the other paperwork associated with servicing a mortgage loan. We worried, though, about who was to bear the risk of loss if the loan went into default. If the state agency bore it, the lenders would have no incentive to exercise care in making the loans. But if the lenders bore the risk, they might be too careful and refuse loans to precisely those households most in need of housing assistance.

We finally decided to divide the risk by requiring a private lender to reimburse the state agency for some percentage of any losses incurred on a state agency loan initiated by that lender. We were then concerned that the state Department of Savings and Loans would object to this plan. That department regulates state-chartered savings and loan institutions and as part of that function reviews their loan portfolios to ensure that these institutions do not jeopardize the security of their deposits by making imprudent loans. The standards imposed by the department might conflict with our intention of having the savings and loans bear a portion of the risk on loans they made with state money for low- and moderate-income housing.

We met with the assistant commissioner and general counsel of the department to discuss our concerns but found them very unresponsive. They were reluctant to express any opinion at all on the desirability of a state housing finance agency or the extent to which it could share risk with savings and loan institutions without running afoul of the state's regulatory mechanism. We were aware that this department was within the Business and Transportation Agency, the head of which is a member of the governor's cabinet, and assumed that the reluctance of the department's staff to express any opinions on the subject resulted from the administration's antipathy toward any form of state housing assistance.

In addition to the state's regulators, we also had to be careful of their federal counterparts. Early in December I met with John Buchanan, assistant to the president of the Federal Home Loan Bank (FHLB) for the Western Region, whose offices are in San Francisco. The FHLB is to the savings and loan industry what the Federal Reserve Bank is to the country's banks. The FHLB regulates the federally chartered savings and loans and serves as their central credit facility. Buchanan indicated that the bank was aware of state housing finance agencies and was in the process of developing a policy that would encourage participation by its members. His reaction to our intention to have private lenders bear a portion of the risk on these loans was disquieting, though. He explained that, besides the FHLB, savings and loans are also regulated by the Federal Savings and Loan Insurance Corporation (FSLIC), a federal agency which insures savings and loan deposits. It was contrary, he said, to FSLIC regulations for any member institution to have outstanding contingent liabilities against it such as an obligation to reimburse in case of future loss on a loan. He had no suggestions for a permissable way of solving the risk-sharing problem, but recommended we talk directly with the FSLIC.

For Thanksgiving I made a personal trip to the East Coast but left a day early in order to stop off in Washington. I needed to get a better feel for how rapidly housing legislation was moving through Congress. After the subsidy moratorium in January 1973, Congress had expressed rage, indignation, frustration, and resignation, in that order. Nixon refused to reinstate the subsidies, and all Congress could do was enact a new housing subsidy program which had his blessing. At the time of my visit, several major bills were in various stages in both houses. In the New Senate Office Building I attended a "mark-up" session on one of them by the Housing Subcommittee of the Senate Committee on Banking and Currency. In mark-up hearings a bill is reviewed by the committee line-by-line, providing an opportunity for the members to consider the most technical and detailed provisions. I was not so interested in the session itself, though, as in talking with committee staff members who I hoped would brief me on the political outlook of not just this bill, but the others as well. Bob and I were very concerned with keeping closely apprised of developments at the federal level. Any state program would depend heavily for its effectiveness on the ease with which it could work in conjunction with federal housing subsidies.

The subcommittee hearing adjourned about an hour after I arrived and I went up immediately to introduce myself to Carl Coan, the subcommittee's chief staff member and the Senate's most knowledgeable individual in the field of housing. After speaking with him for a short time, I turned to go and saw California's Senator Alan Cranston, a member of the housing subcommittee, about to leave the hearing room. I went up to him and, after shaking hands, briefly described our intention to create a state housing finance agency in California and expressed our concern that whatever federal housing legislation eventually passed include subsidies for low- and moderate-income families which could be easily used in tandem with state housing programs. Cranston said he was aware generally of state housing finance programs and was pleased to hear of efforts to create such an entity in California; he promised to keep the need for a state/federal partnership approach in mind when considering the federal housing bills.

As soon as I returned to California after the holiday, Bob and I began preparing for a second public hearing by the joint committee, which we had scheduled for December 11. A part of this preparation was a meeting with St. Lezin's loan procedures committee which took place in a stark, cramped seminar room in the San Francisco State Building. Bob and I presented our ideas for a state housing finance agency that would work in tandem with private lenders. We followed the same type of format we had used with St. Lezin and Blencowe (both of whom attended this meeting), changing it only to cover the more specific proposals we had developed since then. After our presentation we answered questions for a half hour and then left the room to allow the committee to discuss the issue among themselves.

It was difficult to tell what, if any, progress we had made in these meetings with the savings and loans toward altering their position on a state finance agency. We spoke to St. Lezin on the phone several times between our meeting with his committee and our second public hearing but he was noncommittal. Of course there was nothing very definite for him to respond to, for we had no formal proposal or draft legislation and he was playing his cards close to his chest.

Originally we had planned the second public hearing to be held in Fresno, in order to maximize Zenovich's exposure to his own constituency, but as the date approached, scheduling problems arose for several of our committee's members and the location was changed to Sacramento. We had reserved one of the small committee hearing rooms in the Capitol. These rooms hold about eighty spectators who sit in theatre seats facing a large, raised semi-circular podium behind which the committee members sit in high-backed swivel chairs.

Bob and I were asked by the committee to sit with them and I well recall the gratifying sense of control and importance which results from being physically above the witnesses who sit at a table in front of and below the podium. Bob and I had invited St. Lezin to testify, and he provided the first evidence of a crack in the savings and loans' consistently adamant stand against state housing assistance. Carefully prefacing his remarks by saying that he did not represent the official position of the California Savings and Loan League, he said that he was pleased with the direction which the development of the agency seemed to be taking and that there was a real opportunity for a partnership arrangement between the state and private lenders in providing housing for low- and moderate-income households. He then went on to talk of the need to involve private lenders rather than create an agency that would lend directly and to stress the need, under such arrangement, for lenders to receive fair compensation for the services they provided.

St. Lezin also brought up the subject of risk. He acknowledged the interest of a state agency in having some risk imposed on the lenders:

"The housing finance agency wants to be sure that the original lending institution uses due caution in underwriting the loan and does not develop a careless practice simply because they know the housing finance agency is the ultimate owner of the mortgage."

But he tried to get them out from under that burden.

"I believe it would be quite improper to require the private lenders to share in the losses of these loans. In fact, this one point more than anything else . . . would be enough to remove the partnership that I believe the agency is looking for in private lending institutions."

This was the first of only two instances in which testimony given at the joint committee's three investigative hearings had substantive value. Although St. Lezin claimed he was not speaking officially for the league, we were sure he would not have stated such a position publicly unless the league's loan procedures committee had favorably regarded the presentation Bob and I had made before them. We were greatly encouraged by St. Lezin's testimony and confident that he would advocate among other members of the league's board that the league support the type of state housing assistance we proposed.

During the three weeks following this first public indication of possible support by the savings and loans our campaign within that industry ripened quickly and was finally brought to a climax by the chairman of the Commission of Housing and Community Development. The commission is a state public body created in 1965 to serve as the policy review board for the state Department of Housing and Community Development (HCD). It has nine members appointed by the governor to four-year terms. The department itself lies within the Business and Transportation Agency and the department director, a gubernatorial appointee, is in the peculiar position of being responsible both to the commission on matters of general policy, and to the secretary of business and transportation for day-to-day departmental affairs.

On one of our first trips to Sacramento in early 1973, Bob and I had met Donald Pinkerton, former mayor of Fairfield, California, whom Governor Reagan had appointed director of

HCD in September 1970. When we met him he had already announced his resignation from the $25,000-per-year job. We were told that he had collided with administration policy in attempting to manage HCD aggressively at a time when Frank Walton, the agency secretary, was planning to emasculate HCD through an administrative reorganization.

HCD had two divisions. One was Codes and Standards, which received 80 percent of the department's $3.3-million budget, largely for the purpose of hiring inspectors to enforce the state's mobile home building codes. The second division, Research and Assistance, was responsible for programs related to housing lower-income families. The most significant task engaging it was preparation of the Statewide Housing Element, a study mandated by the Legislature in 1970 which would provide an analysis of housing needs throughout the state and establish housing development goals. Phase II of the housing element appeared in November 1973 and presented data from the 1970 Census on the structural condition of housing in the state. It was something of an embarrassment to the Reagan administration and, specifically, to Frank Walton, who had discounted the need for housing assistance in California. The report revealed the existence of approximately one million housing units in the state requiring major rehabilitation or replacement; one million renter households unable to afford decent housing without spending a disproportionate amount of their income on rent; and one-half million households living in overcrowded conditions. It also documented the considerable extent to which the burden of poor-quality housing was being borne disproportionately by ethnic minorities and children.

Even more distressing to Walton was that the Legislature required a second document from HCD exploring the feasibility of state housing subsidies. The writing of it caused considerable agony within HCD, revealing conflicts between the civil service staff and the administration's appointees who managed the department. It was in an attempt to bring the department under closer political control that Pinkerton was ousted and Robert De-Monte, who had been with the Reagan administration for several years, was appointed acting director. In July 1973, Walton signed

interagency agreements prepared by the administration which effectively abolished HCD, transferring the Codes and Standards
personnel to the Department of General Services and placing the
troublesome Research and Assistance staff into the Office of Planning and Research which operated directly under the governor.

Unfortunately for Walton, reorganization required legislative approval to make it legally valid. Unable to get a validating
bill out of committee, he was forced to use other means of smothering any HCD staff support for state housing assistance.

This second document was due on June 30, 1973. Ed Tworuk,
one of HCD's staff civil servants, wrote a draft and asked that it be
released to the public for comment before the final report was
prepared. DeMonte decided the draft looked upon state housing
assistance too favorably and had one of his aides rewrite the
conclusions before it was released. Another indication of administrative displeasure with the department's research and assistance
staff was that their offices were almost impossible to find. I recall
the first time Bob and I had an appointment with Tworuk. We
found him in cramped quarters in the back of one of the old
administration buildings that surround the Capitol Park. To reach
them one entered a back door and threaded a labyrinth of stair-
ways and hallways. We would never have found Tworuk's office
without the several hand-lettered cardboard signs the staff had
pasted to the walls at strategic points in the maze.

The chairman of the Commission of Housing and Community
Development, which set policy for this troubled department, was
Elwood (Woody) Teague, chairman of the board of United Financial Corporation, which owns a number of savings and loan bran-
ches throughout the state. Shortly after the first public hearing in
San Francisco, Bob and I set up an appointment with Teague for
the morning of December 10, the day before the Sacramento
hearing. The offices of United Financial's chairman are located on
the top floor of a high-rise building not far from the Los Angeles
airport. We waited in a large outer reception room amid pastel
prints and dark finished woods until a secretary showed us into
Woody Teague's office. It continued in color and texture the same

attempt at hushed elegance. The room was large, serving as both a board room and the chairman's office. To the left as we entered was a long table of dark, highly polished wood surrounded by heavy swivel chairs. To the right, angled across the room's far corner, was a large desk from which Teague rose to meet us.

We chatted for a few minutes in the office to get acquainted and then walked to a restaurant a block away for lunch. Bob and I dispensed with our usual introductory routine, as we found that Teague was quite familiar with our ideas. Bob had written a rather lengthy critique of the HCD study by Tworuk, and we had sent a copy of the critique to Teague rather as a matter of courtesy. It was immediately apparent, though, that he had read it with some care. By the time we were seated for lunch, he began asking difficult questions. Many were those which had been asked so many times before: Who bears the risk of default? How are participating lenders compensated? What type of loan documentation will be used? Some questions were new; he pressed for details: At what point in the underwriting process would the state make a binding commitment to a lender on a specific loan? Should the lender/state relationship be different during construction than it is after the construction loan is refinanced with a permanent loan?

As he was a Reagan appointee to the HCD commission and one of the old guard of the savings and loan industry, Bob and I had no reason to be optimistic about selling Teague on our ideas for state housing assistance. We had found no one, though, who had been confident they knew his personal views on state housing assistance. We tried hard to gauge his reaction to our replies to his questions, but I found him difficult to read, for his face and tone of voice were almost expressionless. At one point in the conversation, though, I began to be encouraged. We were discussing recent activity of HCD and I detected in Teague's remarks some irritation with the way in which Reagan had set about to emasculate the department. It occurred to me that the chairman of United Financial might very well be miffed at the governor, who, after appointing him to a commission chairmanship, set about trying to destroy or at least badly cripple the department which was the commission's sole responsibility. My optimism grew when he responded to our quoting of several statistics which indicated the extent of substandard and overcrowded housing in the state.

"Yes, I know," he said. "When we hold our board meetings [of the commission] up there, those poor people come to them every time. Every time we meet, there are more of them. They aren't being served; they're left out. I know that."

Most encouraging of all was that Teague not only knew about our proposal but had clearly spent time thinking about it. He was interested. He liked the idea of a partnership arrangement between the state and private lenders, recognizing as he did a need that could not—would not—be filled by private lenders without some form of state assistance.

The lunch with Teague was prelude to the third and last hearing of the joint committee, held a week later—December 17 —in San Francisco. Bob and I decided to change the format of this hearing in an attempt to make it something more than just an exhibition for the press. Instead of having the members sit on a podium with witnesses giving formal testimony, we decided to arrange all the participants, legislators and witnesses alike, around a large table. We invited a number of people, each of whom was knowledgeable in some area of housing or public finance: the assistant state treasurer, a mortgage company president, several municipal bond underwriters, a representative of a private mortgage insurance company. The savings and loans were represented by George Blencowe and Bernie Mikell. There were representatives of local housing agencies, private housing consultants, and several lawyers. We also invited Woody Teague.

To get maximum attendance by legislators, we arranged with Assemblyman Chacon and George Beattie to make the hearing a joint one between the joint committee and the Assembly Committee on Urban Development and Housing. This worked quite well, and we ended up having to push six large tables together, around which we managed to seat everyone in a rather cozy group.

We hoped for honest exchanges—a "dialogue," in modern parlance—a forum in which real concerns about state involvement in housing could be expressed and some of the main technical points involved in creating a partnership with the private lenders explained. The experiment was moderately successful. We did succeed in raising the sophistication of the discussion considerably above the level of exchanges which had occurred in our previous hearings. Unfortunately, in doing so we almost eliminated active participation by the legislators.

Chacon made a few welcoming comments and actively chaired the hearing but not another legislator spoke until half-way through the hearing. Their silence did not inhibit anyone else and there was a lively interchange among the other participants. Finally Assemblyman Holoman, chairman of the Community Development Subcommittee, replied to a comment by Bernie Mikell that the private mortgage lenders had to think of profits in considering their involvement in financing low- and moderate-income housing.

"My thinking is," Holoman said, "that you're [the lenders] going to have to become more socially aware because you are in business at the will of the people. I think the bigger companies are going to have to become more socially aware. So it is my feeling that you are going to have to be in the position to accept this concept [assisted housing] and become more socially conscious and aware of the low- and moderate-income housing issues throughout this state."

Fifteen minutes later, Assemblyman Larry Kapiloff courageously apologized for his ignorance of housing finance and asked several questions about the mechanics of mortgage lending. Emboldened by such frankness, Assemblyman Don MacGillivray then questioned a municipal bond consultant about the ability of local governments to finance low-income housing. Over the course of the three-hour discussion, this was the extent of participation by committee members.

The most significant occurrence at the hearing was the result of our preparation for Woody Teague's attendance. Not only had we invited Teague to the hearing informally at the conclusion of our meeting with him in Los Angeles, but we also had followed our informal invitation with a letter that formally requested his participation. This letter had spelled out specifically those opinions he had expressed to us privately which we wished him to state in this public forum.

In consenting to attend he had said it was possible for him to stay for only an hour, so, very soon after the hearing began, I fed him several questions. Was it not true, I asked, that his commission's staff (HCD) had reported on the retreat of the federal government from the housing field and indicated that if there were to be housing assistance in California it would have to come from the state or local governments? Did he and the commission accept this as correct?

"I believe so," Teague replied. "I can only speak for myself, because some of the members of the commission felt differently, but during the six years that I have been a member of the commission and the two years that I have been chairman of it, I have felt I did not wish to see the State of California in either the building business, or the housing business, or the construction business, or the financing business. However, the studies you mentioned indicate that 37 percent of all households in the state now qualify for some type of federal or state or county aid. This being true, I believe that I have become converted to the position that the state should enter into some sort of limited program by which the state provides financing for as many of these underprivileged people as we possibly can."

"Let me ask you also," I said, "as chairman of one of the larger financial institutions in the state whether you believe that a partnership between the state and private industry might be designed to provide below-market-interest-rate capital to finance low- and moderate-income housing?"

"I feel there is no doubt of it. Those of us in private industry would be very pleased to work with the state."

That was the break needed. Woody Teague did not represent the California Savings and Loan League but his influence within the industry was substantial. As Governor Reagan's appointee to chair the Housing and Community Development Commission, he was the official guardian against any public encroachment on the private mortgage lending business. He was converted, and the loan procedures committee, we knew from St. Lezin's testimony in the previous hearing, was softening. In January the board of directors of the California Savings and Loan League passed a resolution supporting the concept of a state housing finance agency for California.

From Doubting to Drafting

BY CHRISTMAS, THE WEEK AFTER WOODY TEAGUE'S APPEARANCE at the hearing in San Francisco, Bob and I had been working for the joint committee almost four months. It takes a bit of time to mentally adjust from being a private developer to thinking about problems as a public policy adviser, and it was not until December that I began to have second thoughts about the wisdom of creating a housing finance agency to assist low- and moderate-income households.

Because we had been developers of subsidized housing, we unconsciously assumed that subsidizing housing was a good way of assisting low-income families. We had decided that the failings of federal housing programs were largely administrative and had gone on to design a state housing subsidy program which would avoid such problems by making maximum use of private mortgage lenders.

We were no longer developers, though, and I began to speculate on more than just how a subsidized housing development program might be made to work better. My internal questions probed the reason for trying to subsidize housing at all. Bob and I had become acquainted with a number of the families who moved into the housing we had built, and we knew that, while they had needed better shelter, they also had a number of other needs at least as, if not more, pressing. The children's teeth often needed attention, one or more of the family required medical care, and frequently it was difficult for the parents to find work because they could not afford a car. As we rented up developments for the

54

elderly, dog food sales frequently rose at the local grocery—it was the only meat they could afford to buy for themselves.

Given the range of needs which every poor family has, why subsidize housing in particular? The question was especially difficult because the housing which the federal government subsidized under the programs we had used was expensive. We had not built ugly barracks-type structures; as a developer I took considerable satisfaction in providing attractive, well-located apartments and single-family homes for poor families. But as a legislative staff-member I began to question whether this was good public policy and whether we should create a housing finance agency which would continue doing the same thing. There is some irony in providing people with new subsidized housing when all they can afford to eat is dog food. Surely, if given the choice themselves, they might rather trade some of the large housing subsidy they receive for better food, or medical care, or whatever other needs they have.

So, again, why were we trying to get the state government involved in housing rather than concentrating on some more general strategy of aiding the poor? I speculated that possibly housing was of particular concern to government because the private housing market was defective in some way. I accepted that the pricing system works pretty well in most private markets, determining the amount of goods and services which the society wants. An increase in demand for a product, whether it be tennis shoes or electrical transformers or ball-point pens, enables sellers to raise prices and still dispose of all their inventory. Higher prices, though, encourage manufacturers to increase production and permit them to pay higher wages and higher material costs in order to draw resources away from other parts of the economy. If the original increase in demand and attendant price rises are great enough, they will even encourage new manufacturers to enter the field. As production increases, inventories become more nearly equal to demand and competition among sellers to move their goods forces them to lower prices, which eventually stabilize at some level which just clears the market.

Of course the markets for some things do not work very well: for one reason or another they do not result in a nice comfortable balance of supply and demand. One example of this, which resulted several years ago in so much political pressure for governmental intervention, was clean air. We don't usually think of clean air as a product to be bought and sold, but that is only because a market for it does not exist. Like most other resources, air has competing uses and to the extent air is used for waste disposal its value for breathing is reduced. Such competition for use is not troublesome in the case of most resources because a market allocates them among users by means of price. The difficulty with air is that it can't be divided up into discrete amounts which can be bought and sold. Those who use it, therefore, do not have to pay for it, even though their use may be costly to others. So long as a factory does not have to pay for the clean air it uses as a means of waste disposal, it will have no incentive to dispose of the waste in other ways even though the cost imposed on surrounding residents in the form of polluted air is far greater than what it would cost the owner to install pollution control equipment. This poses a legitimate case for government action which can, presumably, determine the fairest and most efficient allocation of clean air between residents and the factory, and also enforce a level of pollution that represents the appropriate compromise between these two users of this resource.

Government intervention may also be necessary where monopolies exist or where there are especially severe impediments to the flow of labor and capital in response to shifting priorities for goods and services within the economy. But I was not aware that any of these ills affected the housing market. There is nothing about the intrinsic nature of housing, as there is with air, which prevents it from being bought and sold. The building industry is not monopolistic, but highly competitive, and I could not identify any severe inhibitions on the flow of construction labor and building materials which a housing agency might alleviate.

Not content with what I knew from experience about housing markets, I did some library research and found that the federal government's first major intervention in housing resulted from what it perceived as imperfections in the financial markets through which people financed purchase of their homes. Prior to 1934, a homebuyer was fortunate to obtain a loan covering any more than 50 percent of the cost of the house. Rarely was the loan term longer than ten years, and repayment was made in a lump sum at maturity. The National Housing Act of 1934 created the Federal Housing Administration (FHA), which was authorized to insure lenders against the risk of defaulting homeowners. If a borrower failed to repay a home loan insured by FHA, the lender could simply assign the mortgage to FHA, which reimbursed him for the amount of any outstanding principal and interest. Because this placed all of the risk on FHA, lenders were willing to make loans under whatever conditions the agency would insure, and these conditions were very liberal, including high loan-to-value ratios, longer terms, and amortized principal paid in monthly install- ments. The borrower was charged .5 percent per year on outstand- ing principal as an insurance premium which was supposed to cover the costs of FHA losses. Many predicted financial disaster for the insuring agency but in fact there were relatively few defaults, losses were small, and the agency began to build large reserves. Most interesting was the effect of FHA's success on the mortgage-lending industry. As the FHA portfolio grew, it became evident that private lenders had been wrong in believing that in- creased liberality of lending conditions would lead to greatly in- creased defaults. This mistake had constituted a severe imperfec- tion in the mortgage finance market which government interven- tion removed by providing more accurate information regarding the risk of loss on high-ratio, long-term loans. The industry respon- ded and the conditions of noninsured home loans rose as high as 90 percent of value with terms of up to thirty years.

I began looking for other imperfections in the mortgage fi- nance market which a state housing finance agency might cure. One major problem was that market's sensitivity to monetary con- ditions in the economy. When interest rates rose and credit tight- ened, the mortagage market suffered grievously. At the time of my research, mortgage loan volume was being squeezed to a trickle as it had been before in 1966 and 1967. When there was little mortgage credit, construction volume fell commensurately and a chart of annual housing starts for the previous twenty years was a graphic roller coaster on which the housing industry had been alternately subjected to exhilarating climbs and nauseating descents. I was sure that the volatility of the mortgage loan market was expensive. It increased the risks of doing business, and to attract producers, profit returns had to be high enough to compensate for those risks. The frequent expansion and contraction of the labor force and the building supplies industry also must have imposed heavy costs as men and capital were continually being ingested and then withdrawn. These costs were certainly being passed on in the form of higher prices to the consumer. A moderation of these credit cycles in California might be accomplished by a housing agency which would provide a large volume of low-interest mortgage loans in the state when private mortgage money was tight and then decrease its activity during periods in which private lenders had ample funds to lend at reasonable rates.

A state agency might also alleviate private market restrictions on minorities. To the extent that other means of stopping discrimination in housing fail, state-financed housing could be useful in expanding the range of housing choice for racial minorities. As lender, a state housing finance agency could insist on nondiscriminatory marketing policies by borrowers.

Also, by carefully selecting the location of housing it financed, the state might generate significant external benefits. Just as noxious emissions from a factory impose social costs reflected in the lower value of adjacent land, the presence of poorly maintained housing lowers the value of property in the surrounding neighborhood. When one individual owns all of the buildings on a block, his decision as to how well he is going to maintain each property takes into account the effect that decision will have on the value of the other buildings in the neighborhood. Usually, though, properties in a single neighborhood are owned by a number of different people, and none of the owners, in determining the most profitable manner of maintaining their property, has any incentive to consider the effects of that decision on the value of adjacent parcels.

The economics of owning land in the inner city are frequently such that each owner finds it most profitable to spend little or no money on upkeep. Each declines to make repairs but continues collecting rent until the building deteriorates to a condition which will no longer generate sufficient income to pay even minimal operating costs. Because the building is usually not saleable at this point, the owner simply abandons it. The scenario occurs when an owner does not believe he will be able to continue marketing apartments at a rent which will provide him with an adequate return on the money he spends for upkeep and repairs. The ability to demand rents adequate to support proper maintenance depends heavily on whether surrounding property owners continue to maintain their property. No individual owner has incentive to be the first to invest capital for rehabilitation, though, since he does not know the intention of surrounding landlords. Each owner waits for others to be first and the result is that nothing is ever done and property value declines. It is this phenomenon which contributes to the growth of slums as blight "creeps" through a city the way rot spreads through fruit, its presence corrupting adjacent areas, lowering the expectations of owners—destroying both their willingness to invest and that of the lenders to lend.

A state housing finance agency might be able to arrest the spread of blight by providing the incentives necessary to obtain co-operation from all the owners in a selected neighborhood. It could offer owners a carrot in the form of low-interest, long-term loans for property improvement and simultaneously exercise the political clout necessary to get the city to provide public improvements in that neighborhood—new sidewalks, improved street lighting, a small park. These inducements would be offered on condition that all owners agree contractually to undertake some minimum level of property improvement. If the area were well-chosen, it would be one in which the combination of low-interest state agency loans, public improvements, and assurance of simultaneous improvement in all properties would make participation advantageous for every owner.

While recognizing the ability of a state housing agency to correct some market deficiencies, I was still uneasy. A deliberate, rational conception of role had never directed the activity of any state housing agency of which I was aware. Some did a little rehabilitation in the inner city, but that comprised only a small fraction of the volume they had financed, and few agencies of which I was aware consciously adjusted the amount of financing they provided over time to be an effective counter cyclical force in their state's economy. Even if the legitimate roles to be performed by a housing agency were recognized by its management, there would be so many pressures to spend subsidy money in other ways that I was not sure a state agency which acted on that knowledge could survive. Home builders, housing developers, the construction trade unions are enthusiastic for new suburban construction, not inner city rehabilitation. Erecting new single-family homes and garden apartments is what they know best and what they would try to pressure a state agency into helping them do. The reason they know that type of housing best, though, is because the private markets which produce new suburban housing work rather well, which, of course, is precisely the reason it would be the wrong place for a housing agency to be active.

I became discouraged with my efforts to make a persuasive case for a state housing finance agency on the basis of its potential for correcting private market deficiencies and began to wonder if maybe I had missed the real point of subsidized housing. I returned to thinking about the families who would benefit from being able to live in decent housing at a price they could afford and this took me back to my original concern about people living in new expensive housing and still having to eat dog food.

If a poor family were offered a choice between an apartment worth $100 more per month than the one in which they were living at no increase in rent or $100 per month in cash, certainly they would take the cash. If they wanted to spend it all on better housing they could, but more likely they would spend only a portion on housing and at least some on better food or other needs. Even if the cash alternative were slightly less than $100 it probably would still be preferred to the housing. How small the cash payment would have to be before the family no longer preferred it to housing would vary, but if the need for food, clothing, dental work, or other things were great, I expect some families would take as little as $70 or $60 cash instead of the housing. If a family would as soon have $70 cash as $100 of housing, then why not just give them cash? Government-subsidized housing then is worth substantially less in value to the recipient than it costs to provide. Added to that are all the administrative costs of running a housing agency, which certainly are greater than those involved in distributing cash.

Since cash would be invariably preferred by the poor over its cost equivalent in the form of housing, the only way of justifying housing subsidies was to consider not just the preferences of those receiving them but also the desires of those providing them. Presumably those who favor providing assistance to the poor do so because they derive more satisfaction from giving some portion of their income to others than they do from using it in any other way. The implicit ethical premise is that we are, at least to some (quantifiable) degree, our brother's keepers. But if the choice between housing subsidies and cash payments is examined, it becomes evident that this desire to help others comes in at least two forms. One of these is the impulse to provide others with the means to lead what they consider to be a more satisfying life and assumes implicitly that each individual is, if not the only, then at least the best, judge of how he ought to conduct his existence. If the motive behind such giving is termed *altruism,* it can be distinguished from what might be called *paternalistic altruism,* which considers, in addition to the satisfaction of the recipient, the preference of the giver that the income he gives away be spent in a particular manner by the recipient. To the extent that the preferences of those receiving a subsidy do not correspond with the way in which the givers would prefer to see additional income spent, the givers may wish to provide and "in-kind" subsidy—such as housing, or food, or medical care—which restricts the recipients' options. If, for example, we were quite sure that low-income families receiving cash would allocate it among better housing, better dental care for their children, transportation to a job, and medical services, a cash subsidy might be perfectly acceptable. But if we believe they would spend all or a large part of it on luxury clothing, a larger automobile, entertainment, or liquor, we might prefer in-kind subsidies that do not permit such discretion but require recipients to spend the additional income in a manner we, the givers, think is appropriate.

Whether it is right to decrease the value of subsidy dollars redistributed to the poor in order to give more satisfaction to those providing the subsidy depends upon basic philosophical premises. The utilitarian ethic of John Stuart Mill, which seeks the greatest good for the greatest number, would have us add up the amount of additional satisfaction derived by the receivers if they have discretion of expenditure and then the additional amount of satisfaction derived by givers if they can specify how subsidies are spent. The policy decision will favor whichever group—the givers or the receivers—is determined to derive the greatest aggregate amount of satisfaction from having the subsidies provided in the manner they prefer. I don't think Immanuel Kant and his followers would agree. They would argue that to seek the greatest good for the greatest number is wrong if doing so results in treating individuals as means rather than ends. Those of us who provide a subsidy in a manner which decreases its value to the poor by limiting its use in order to increase our own satisfaction in knowing it will be used in a way we prefer, treat poor individuals not as ends but rather as means to our own satisfaction.

The more I thought about it, the more I became convinced that if our desire really was to help the poor, a housing subsidy program was the wrong way to go about it. A society, it seemed to me, had an obligation to assure all of its members some minimum share of goods and services, some minimum level of material satisfaction. But I was uncomfortable with the notion that societal control should accompany it. When I give a panhandler money, I am never inclined to urge that he spend it on food instead of drink. The fact that I have money and he does not in no way indicates to me that I possess any clearer insight than he into how his life should be lived.

I became sufficiently concerned with the direction we were taking that I raised with Bob the possibility of our being wrong in attempting to create a state housing assistance program. He took a rather more practical view than my theoretical wanderings. His principal argument in favor of housing subsidies was that they were a means of income redistribution that we could actually get through the Legislature and cash payments to the poor were not. A state housing finance agency was politically attractive. With only a small budgetary expenditure for a start-up loan, the agency, by issuing tax-exempt bonds, would have a relatively large economic impact, pumping hundreds of millions of dollars into residential construction throughout the state. From a political viewpoint, the fact that the agency would assist low-income families was wholly secondary to the benefit that would flow to the several industries and labor unions associated with housing.

Cash subsidies paid by the state to the poor, Bob insisted, were politically preposterous. A program of that sort would be enormously expensive, and require huge annual budgetary expenditures. Our whole strategy of obtaining support from a broad coalition of interest groups in order to achieve bipartisan backing would collapse. The only proponents of cash assistance would be a tiny assortment of poverty groups. "And," he added, "if by some miracle such a program ever did get through the Legislature, you can just imagine the chances of Reagan signing it. You're assuming that we have a choice between housing subsidies and cash assistance. That isn't so. The alternatives are dictated by political realities—housing subsidies or nothing at all."

Bob's arguments were particularly persuasive in light of Congress's failure to pass a cash subsidy program two years before we began our efforts in Sacramento. This program was the Family Assistance Plan (FAP) introduced by the Nixon administration in the summer of 1969. It would have supplemented the incomes of the working poor at a cost of about four billion dollars annually. Although Nixon guarded his conservative image by declaring it was not a guaranteed income (although in fact it was) and calling it "workfare," *Newsweek* saw it as "a humanitarian achievement unrivaled since the New Deal." The legislation which would have implemented it died in the last moments of the 91st Congress, which ended January 2, 1971. Daniel Moynihan, in his book, *The Politics of a Guaranteed Income,* gives an interesting account of why it failed. Although Moynihan shows that the obstacles to its passage were many and came from the right as well as the left, the opposition of one group he mentions is worth mentioning here because it illustrates the difficulty of enacting subsidies that are provided to the poor without certain strings attached.

Moynihan was a principal architect of FAP in his capacity as undersecretary of labor. A principal reason he desired to largely replace the current welfare system was his dislike of the paternalism inherent in present welfare programs which are administered by professional welfare workers. He quotes Samuel Gompers, who, as early as 1916, expressed distaste with social workers, whose profession at that time was nascent, but has since grown to number some 150,000. Gompers was bitter toward those who made it their business to decide how the poor should live:

> Some of these understudies to Providence are actuated by generous and sympathetic emotions. They want to do good in the world—the majority, in truth, that they may feel that glow of gratification that comes from doing *for* others. They have a vision of a new world with themselves as creators. The work of these creators and renovators has become commercialized and dignified by the title of profession—they are experts—experts in social welfare, experts on home life, domestic relations, child life, and the thousand and one problems that arise out of the lives of the poor. They are willing and feverishly anxious to be appointed upon commissions or as government agents to help the wage earners to save their money; to secure minimum wages by law; to secure legislative provisions protecting their well being. All these solutions are formulated along lines that necessitate governmental machinery and the employment of experts—the 'intellectuals'. The conclusion is inevitable that there is a very close connection between *employment* as experts and the enthusiasm for human welfare.

From the first announcement of FAP, through its triumphal passage in the House, death in the Senate Finance Committee, and resurrection as H.R. 1 in the following Congress, Moynihan asserts that the "*de facto* strategy of social welfare groups was to seek to kill the program, first by insisting on benefit levels that no Congress would pass and no president would approve, and, second, by raising issues about details of the legislation which allowed the entire initiative to be labeled oppressive, repressive, regressive, and worse." He says that the social workers would probably deny any intention actually to kill the legislation but insists that they feared it would replace welfare and the consistent thrust of everything they did in regard to FAP was to assure it did not pass.

The vigor with which groups represent their own interests in an attempt to affect public policy does not vary with the type of activity they wish to protect or expand, whether it be the manufacture of air purification equipment, military hardware, housing, or, as in this case, providing the poor with social services. I know little about the political history of FAP other than what I read in Moynihan's book, but the pattern which Moynihan describes became so familiar to me in Sacramento that I am inclined to believe his analysis is correct. There is money in poverty, so long as it is not given directly to the poor but rather indirectly through someone else who is paid to either supervise the poor in their expenditure or provide them with a specific good or service to ensure that there is no possibility of their spending subsidy income on anything of which the non-poor disapprove.

I had concluded that housing subsidies were an enormously inefficient and even inequitable way of helping the poor. At the same time I recognized that the way in which I believed an assistance program ought to be designed—payment of direct cash subsidies—could not be gotten through the Legislature. Politics being the art of the possible, I had to settle for a housing finance agency and I advocated it as vigorously as I knew how, believing that it was not the best solution but that it was better than nothing at all.

By the start of the new year, Bob and I were pleased with our progress. We were now confident of being able to obtain sup-

port of the Savings and Loan League when we introduced legislation and felt this was a major step in overcoming opposition by
the governor. We were conscious, however, that this was only a
start. Persuading the Legislature of the merits of our plan would
be no cinch.

We had two tasks immediately before us. One was to draft the
legislation which would create a state housing agency. The second
was to expand considerably the breadth of our contact with interest groups and knit together a coalition broad enough and powerful enough to overcome the resistance which state housing finance
legislation would certainly encounter in the Legislature. Bob and I
decided to approach the two tasks sequentially. We first would
draft a bill and then, before Zenovich introduced it, we would
meet with each of the interest groups whose support we wanted
and try to sell them on it. This would also provide the opportunity
of making changes in the bill to accommodate the various groups
even before it was introduced. George Beattie, with whom we discussed this simple strategy, objected to it. By drafting a bill before
we met with interest groups, he said, we would place ourselves in
an advocate posture vis-a-vis the lobbyists. He strongly urged meeting with the lobbyists first and then drafting the bill, making as
much display as possible of eliciting the ideas of those groups
whose support we needed. This should assure, from the start, that
psychologically they looked upon the bill as their own product
and would make them far stronger advocates than if they felt they
were being asked to support someone else's ideas.

We recognized the tactical wisdom of Beattie's advice but were
nonetheless uncomfortable with the passive role in which it placed
us. We had very definite ideas about the structure and powers that
the agency should possess. We believed our design would result in
the most cost-effective housing finance agency and saw ourselves
as representing the "public interest" which in some ways would be
opposed to the interests of specific groups. As legislative staff
members we saw our institutional role as advocates for a more objective, more dispassionate view of public policy than could be represented by any specific interest or even by the summed views of

all interested groups. I must say, too, that an advocate role accorded more closely with the style in which Bob and I tended to work. We had spent much time during the previous two years selling housing development concepts to government officials and local community groups, and both of us enjoyed negotiating. We had acceded to political necessity in limiting our consideration of subsidy devices to a housing finance agency but in designing such an agency we could not be persuaded that our function was limited to that of lubricating a process of accommodation among various private interests.

I also wanted to draft a bill immediately because of the discipline it would impose on our own ideas. I was sure that the drafting process would flush a number of issues that we had not yet considered but which we would want to have thought about before beginning active discussions with lobbyists on the details of housing finance legislation. Seeing how adamant we were about starting with our own draft, Beattie proposed that at least we not expose it until after we held initial discussions with the several lobbyists who would be most important to us and had requested that they submit in detail their ideas on the structure of a housing finance bill.

We finally agreed to this because including the lobbyists early in the game was good salesmanship and also because it permitted—required in fact—that we delay exposure of our legislative draft. We had begun to worry about releasing such a document, since rumors had begun to circulate that the California Builders Council (CBC) was preparing competing legislation. Ward Connerly resigned in 1973 as deputy director of HCD and, at the same time, Pinkerton left and thereafter had been retained as a consultant by the Builders Council. We learned that under the direction of Paul McCarron, the council's chief lobbyist, Connerly was drafting a housing finance agency bill to be introduced by Assemblyman Bagley.

Much of the legislation introduced originates with interest groups who not only propose ideas to friendly legislators but actually draft legislation. Such lobbyist activity is particularly important in many state legislatures where there is little or no staff assistance, for the legislators do not have time to do the drafting themselves. The disadvantages of relying so heavily on private interests are obvious, and the California Legislature does provide an alternative. The Office of Legislative Counsel now employs over fifty attorneys whose principal job is to draft legislation upon the request of individual legislators. Quite often such requests consist simply of a short paragraph describing in very general terms the type of bill desired and legislative counsel is responsible for fleshing out the concept in the form of a bill. The availability of such professional staff assistance greatly decreases reliance on drafting by lobbyists, but does not eliminate it. Although all bills must be cleared by legislative counsel before being introduced, that review may be limited to assuring proper form; and lobbyists, by doing the drafting themselves, can assure that a bill in which they are interested will include exactly the provisions they want.

McCarron's reason for wanting his own bill were, I think, mixed. He had been one of the first individuals we contacted in early 1973 in trying to obtain support for our resolution creating the joint committee. We had called on him as we had other lobbyists at least twice since then to bring him up to date on what we were doing so he would be assured of our continued interest in the homebuilders' ideas. Despite this, however, we never felt he was particularly comfortable with us. He had, I think, little confidence in his ability to influence us, and we surmised that in hiring Connerly to draft an industry bill he was attempting to demonstrate that he could work without us.

Lobbyists of course must find a cooperative legislator to introduce their bills for them. Bagley was a Republican and philosophically close to the vaguely conservative tilt of the homebuilders. Also, we believed that Bagley's willingness was related to his rumored aspiration to run for state controller in 1974. It would be helpful in such a race to have support of the builders, and the potential publicity associated with a major housing bill might be attractive as well. Shortly after the first of the year, Bagley gutted a bill he had already introduced which would have reorganized the function of HCD and substituted by amendment entirely new legislation written by Connerly.

What irritated Bob and me particularly about the bill that Bagley introduced was that Connerly had included in it several ideas which we were sure he had gotten from us. In the process of selling the savings and loans on the concept of a housing finance agency we had divulged some of our specific ideas such as the partnership arrangement between the state agency and private lenders. Several of these appeared in the Bagley bill. We decided we would not provide further opportunity for what we considered unsportsmanlike pirating by keeping the legislative draft we were about to begin under wraps until just before it was introduced.

Because Bagley's bill competed with the housing finance agency legislation which Peter Chacon intended to introduce, it was doomed to an early death. A major criticism of many state legislatures is that the volume of bills passing through the legislative process is not evenly distributed throughout the session. Typically there is a frenzy of activity in the last few days of every session to push through hundreds of bills which are acted upon with little or no consideration of their merits either in committee or on the floor. This is frequently taken advantage of by authors who feel that scrutiny would be a disadvantage, and the California Legislature has tried to make it more difficult by setting dates during the session by which bills are required to have moved past a specified point in the legislative process. Any bill introduced during the first half of the 1973-1974 session had to have passed out of the policy committee in the originating house by the end of January 1974. The Bagley bill, because of its subject matter, was inevitably assigned to Chacon's committee and because it had been introduced in its original form in 1973, it had to be out of that committee before February.

Early in January, McCarron met with Chacon hoping to smooth the way for "the builders' bill," but found the worst of his fears realized. Chacon told him that he would not even put the bill on the committee's agenda that month. In one sense this was a display of strength by Chacon—a demonstration of his ability to stifle the builders' legislation even before it got started. At the same time it also revealed Chacon's weakness as a committee chairman. If Chacon had been confident of his ability to control his committee, he could have more smoothly accomplished the same purpose by a gracious assurance to McCarron that the bill would be taken up immediately. He then might have had George Beattie go through the bill and identify its most blatant substantive problems. He could have made sure that these were raised during the hearing and combined this with adroit parliamentary handling of the committee and personal influence with other members to assure the same result. McCarron would have been just as unhappy, of course, but he would have lacked any explicit reason to blame Chacon. The way in which Chacon handled the situation was extremely honest, but in the context of legislative politics, quite clumsy. It not only injured his relationship with the California Builders Council but damaged his reputation with colleagues who heard of the incident.

I saw McCarron an hour or so after he had met with Chacon. His face was pale with anger, his outrage smothering speech. The builders, on whom we had counted as major supporters, would require very careful handling in the months to come.

We began actually drafting our legislation in January. The writing was principally my task. Bob and I never formally divided up the work we had to do, and there was considerable overlap, but most often I took on the tasks of research and writing while Bob specialized in the more purely political functions. We did, however, discuss between ourselves and at length almost all of the issues we encountered in designing a housing agency, and not infrequently our own policy disagreements were marked with sharp exchanges leading eventually to compromise. We both realized the importance of our own solidarity, though, and were by and large successful in not revealing any significant division between us.

When I sat down at my desk in San Francisco to actually begin the task of drafting, I had in front of me housing finance agency legislation from other states and many pages of notes recording the ideas which Bob and I had developed in our conversations over the previous six months. Two general concepts, around which much of our thinking revolved, guided the tedious process of structuring what I hoped was a coherent bill. One was the potential efficiency in making maximum use of the private mortgage-lending industry without jeopardizing the public purpose of providing decent housing for those who could not otherwise afford it. The second was to provide some insulation between the administrators of a housing program and elected officials. We feared elected officials might try to manipulate a housing finance agency to serve purely political ends and interrupt the flow of subsidized mortgage capital which we felt was so important to achievement of the state's housing goals.

One means of attempting to ensure that the agency vigorously pursued its public purposes was to try to anticipate the range of circumstances the agency might encounter in its dealings with lenders and to specify in the legislation what course of action the agency should follow in each eventuality. Such an approach would require the legislation, for example, to specify the fees that could be paid to private lenders for their services, or to mandate those functions to be performed by the agency and those which had to be delegated to private lenders. But it was just this kind of expectation—that statutes and regulations can be relied upon for the most detailed administrative direction—which we had experienced with HUD and to which we attributed so many intolerable delays. HUD staff members were afraid to take any action for which they did not have express statutory or regulatory authority and were constantly requesting permission from their superiors to make particular decisions. Those superiors then looked for clearance from their superiors, who wrote memoranda to their superiors on countless details which had not been and could not have been anticipated by the most meticulous draftsman. Detailed statutes are supposed to ensure the uniform implementation of public policy, but their unintended effect may be to provide administrators with a wall behind which they can hide from their own mistakes. Even worse, they may use detailed statutory provisions as a convenient excuse for refusing, in the face of any situations not covered by statute, to make any decision at all.

The alternative is to provide an agency with broad powers and carefully specified public objectives to be pursued, but little or no direction as to the means by which the goals are to be sought. The danger in such a method is, of course, that too much administrative initiative will be exercised, that public ends will be jeopardized and imprudent use made of public monies. In part because of our determination to avoid creating a mini-HUD in Sacramento, Bob and I favored the second approach to drafting. We hoped that, by emphasizing administrative initiative and providing compensation that was adequate to attract good management, we could attract the experienced executive talent necessary to establish and maintain a working relationship with the state's mortgage lenders and at the same time obtain the most public benefit from the public funds available.

We decided to structure the agency in a manner similar to a private corporation. Management responsibility would be vested in a board of directors whose members would represent a broad spectrum of both private and public interests. They would serve without pay and would hire a full-time chairman and president to administer the agency's day-to-day operations. To assure that the agency was ultimately responsible to the electorate, board members would be appointed by elected officials. We thought the board would insulate the agency from direct political influence. To prevent any one political figure from ever dominating its membership we divided the board appointments among the governor, the speaker of the Assembly, and the president pro tempore of the Senate. We also gave members seven-year staggered terms.

Composition of board membership was a particularly sensitive issue. We felt the agency should have on its board individuals with experience in housing finance and production. We also wanted to include someone who could articulate the views of tenants living in agency-financed housing, and representatives of public institutions, such as cities and housing authorities, who were familiar with the way in which local communities approached the problem of housing the poor. In addition to sound policy reasons for having a diverse and experienced board of directors, though, the choice involved political considerations. There were certain interest groups—the mortgage lenders, construction unions, the cities—as well as others whose support we needed who would demand, as a condition of support, to be represented on the board. Bob and I talked over this very difficult issue at great length and finally agreed to the following board membership:

Ex-officio, nonvoting members:
  state treasurer
  secretary of the business and transportation agency
  president of the agency
Voting members appointed by the governor:
  member living in, and eligible for, federal-assisted or state-assisted rental housing
  representative of local government
  member experienced in the savings and loan industry
  member experienced as a builder of residential housing
  member experienced in investment banking
Voting members appointed by the speaker of the Assembly:
  executive director of a housing authority
  member experienced in mortgage banking
  member experienced in organized labor of the residential construction industry
  member experienced in the savings and loan industry
Voting members appointed by the president pro tempore of the Senate:
  attorney practicing in the field of government-assisted housing
  member owning and living in a federal-assisted or state-assisted dwelling
  two members experienced in the savings and loan industry

In addition, the director of the Department of Finance was to serve as an ex-officio voting member and the board was to select a chairperson from outside its original membership who would then also become a voting member.

After completing a first draft of the legislation, I shipped it off to Pete Melnicoe, the lawyer in the legislative counsel's office who had been assigned to work with us. The assignments in that office are according to the various codes in the California statutes: penal, motor vehicles, civil procedure, etc. Melnicoe had been assigned to the Health and Safety Code, into which legislation of subsidized housing would be placed if and when it was passed. I spent many hours in his pleasant though windowless office on the fourth floor of an office building across the street from the Capitol, which is no longer able to accommodate the growing legislative staff. Melnicoe had a good eye for detail, and was an excellent editor. He was quite helpful during the intial drafting process and, later, through the writing of countless amendments.

Had I anticipated the mauling which a major bill normally undergoes during the legislative process, I might have been less concerned with what quickly became only the first of many amended versions of the bill. As it was, Melnicoe and I, in several sessions during February and March, went over literally every word of my draft. Sometimes Bob attended these sessions also, and occasionally George Beattie was there as well, but my principal recollection is of Melnicoe sitting across his desk from me, penciling margin notes in his copy of the draft or, with scissors and stapler, effecting the many organizational changes we agreed upon.

During this period of drafting, which took about three weeks, Bob, George Beattie and I began an intensive series of meetings with lobbyists. Ostensibly, the meetings were to obtain the ideas of the various interest groups as to what provisions ought to be included in the bill, and in fact there were some suggestions that we actually included. Our real purpose, though, was to obtain their support for what we had already decided was the proper design of a state housing agency. During the first week in March we met in Sacramento with the lobbyists for the California Real Estate Association, the California Savings and Loans League, the California Mortgage Bankers Association, the Securities Industry Association, the California Builders Council, the League of California Cities, the California Housing Coalition, and the Western

Center on Law and Poverty. Except for the last two groups, who were both advocates for the people to be assisted by the agency, we met with each group separately, most of them in their respective offices, which are located in office buildings surrounding the Capitol.

We grouped these meetings on a Monday and Tuesday and, for the first time, Bob and I, instead of driving back to San Francisco, spent the night in Sacramento. There are two hotels adjacent to the Capitol Park, the Senator and the Cosmopolitan. We chose the Cosmopolitan on advice that it was not quite so musty as the Senator and had our introduction to those tiny single rooms whose bile green walls, thin grey carpeting, and rubberized drapes were to become all too familiar during the months that followed.

We left Sacramento on Tuesday evening, spent Wednesday in San Francisco, and on Thursday and Friday we were down in Los Angeles, meeting Friday morning with Dean Cannon, executive director of the California Savings and Loan League. The months of exchanging ideas with that industry had distilled the issue to a single, rather simple question: To what extent would the legislation *require* that all loans made by the agency involve participation by a private mortgage lender. The league board had voted favorably on the concept of a state housing agency. They would, though, certainly require, as the price of actively supporting a particular bill, that it include quite precise language ensuring their participation in loans made by the agency.

Because we had spent so much time with the savings and loans already, the league was the first group with which we arrived at the point of discussing precise legislative language. That Friday morning was the first of endless negotiating sessions with Dean Cannon and Bernie Mikell as well as a dozen groups who had enough interest in housing to approach us and enough of a constituency to command our attention. The trade-off was the same in every case. The interest group had a given amount of political strength which they offered to give in support of the bill in exchange for inclusion or deletion of certain provisions in the bill. To be weighed against such promised support was both the political strength of any groups who we believed might oppose the desired change and the extent to which it conflicted with our own idea of how the agency should be designed.

Bob and I liked the initial selling phase of the job, but that enjoyment was tepid compared to the relish with which we negotiated the conflicts among interest groups and the conflicts between what one or another of the groups wanted and what we thought was appropriate. We usually prepared for these negotiations by discussing in detail the strengths and weaknesses of the other side, as well as our own tactics, which often involved roughing out a script for the two of us. For example, we had what I called the "Mutt and Jeff" routine, which was particularly useful in a situation where we needed a concession from someone but had very little to offer in return. Bob, for example, in the course of discussion would play "easy" by offering what little we had to give. Immediately, I would play "hard" by objecting strongly that the offer was far too generous and displaying considerable irritation indiscriminately at both Bob and our opponent, as if they were in league. Bob would then try to smooth things a bit while strengthening the impression that he was on the opponent's side and helping the both of them to persuade me, the recalcitrant partner. Ideally, Bob would, by attempting to placate me, begin to speak for the other side, in which case he and I, with flourishes back and forth, would "negotiate" out the deal we wanted. Even if the opponent couldn't be drawn into letting one of us speak for him, Bob and I could inflate the modest amount we were willing to give up with feigned anger and confusingly complex arguments so that it appeared to be far more valuable than that for which we wished to exchange it.

Negotiating on behalf of what we wanted in the bill came far more easily than advocating the ideas of others, and I cannot recall a time when any interest groups attained such strength in our political calculus that we fought for what it was demanding as hard as we did for our own ideas. Occasionally I speculated that the vigor with which we pressed our own ideas was rather presumptuous. We fancied, of course, that we represented the public interest, but then, everyone else claimed the same distinction. Although the

Savings and Loan League, the Western Center on Law and Poverty, the League of California Cities, and others may have highly parochial views, their large constituencies certainly gave them a credibility as representatives of the public that we lacked.

One of the most definite opinions we held, and that for which we went down to Cannon's office to do battle, was that the agency, while working in tandem with private lenders, should not be entirely dependent on them. We were afraid that if we restricted the agency to lending exclusively through private lenders, we would place it in an intolerable negotiating posture. When the fees for lenders' services, the amount of risk they would bear, or similar issues were negotiated, the agency would have to accept whatever terms were offered by the lenders or do no business. We began our meeting with Cannon and Mikell by articulating this concern. Cannon replied that the lenders could wield such power only if they negotiated as a bloc. In fact, though, he went on, there would be competition for the agency's business not only among the different kinds of lenders—banks, savings and loans, mortgage bankers—but also among the separate institutions within each lending group. We were skeptical, because we believed that the savings and loans would predominate and that the agency would, for practical purposes, have to come to terms with the industry as a whole in order to conduct a uniform lending program throughout the state. We mentioned to Cannon that in our discussions with Woody Teague we had raised this same issue and Teague had advised that we provide for some alternative lending route for the agency. Cannon continued to insist that the agency lend only through private lenders. We were equally adamant that the agency have some alternative. Cannon threatened opposition to the bill.

We argued that this bill represented the last chance they would ever have to participate in drafting a housing finance agency bill. The only insulation until now had been Reagan, who had already announced he would not run again in 1976. Jerry Brown was even then considered by far the strongest candidate and considered to be a liberal like his father, former governor Pat Brown. The savings and loans might have smothered the possibility of state housing assistance ten years ago, but they could not do it again. A state housing finance agency was an idea whose time had come.

Cannon parried. State housing agency legislation had passed the Legislature before, but only because a Reagan veto had been so certain that the Legislature had not taken the previous bills seriously If a liberal did become governor, housing assistance legislation might encounter considerably more resistance in the Legislature. And who was to say that Democrats were going to win? Brown, Moretti, and Alioto were all strong and the Democrats would probably exhaust themselves in the primary and leave an easy Republican victory in November.

Each side having shown its determination, we were at something of a standoff. Bob then ventured, as we had decided he would before the meeting, that our insistence on the agency having some flexibility did not mean that there could be no restriction at all on whether or not to use private lenders.

"Well," said Cannon, "we're not trying to put the agency in a straight-jacket. But we've seen the bureaucratic monstrosities that government housing programs create and don't think they're the solution for California. We are just very sure that the most efficient way for the state to make this low-interest money available is to utilize the expertise that's already out there. Why, our members as well as the banks and mortgage bankers have been making loans for years. They have to do it efficiently or they can't exist."

"Maybe we're not that far apart," Bob offered. "We've told Bernie we're not interested in creating a mini-HUD in Sacramento. Mike and I took on this project because we believed there was a better way to do it. The thing *will* work more efficiently if it uses the lenders who are already out there. We want that kind of arrangement and we'll provide for it in the legislation, but we cannot lock the agency in so completely that they *have* to do business with you or none at all."

"As I've said, though," Cannon replied, "you're mistaken in lumping all the lenders together and acting as if they're one entity. The competition is real," he insisted. "Anyway, I don't see how you can draft language that will give them that kind of flexibility and also ensure that the bureaucrats won't take over the whole thing themselves. I've been around a while, I've seen those guys work. They're empire builders and they'll take over more and more until they've got it all."

"Look," I said, "your concern is that the agency might encroach on the s & l's territory by lending to middle-income families. That's your main concern. Let's separate policy from the drafting issue. If we can come up with language that protects you against unfair competition by a state agency, then you shouldn't have a problem. Let's see if we can do that before assuming it can't be done."

"Why don't you try drafting something yourselves?" Bob injected, "and send it to us over the next week or two."

Cannon paused momentarily to determine if he was coming out where he wanted to. "Well, maybe Bernie could work something out . . ."

"You know I think it would be better if it came from our direction," I said. "I'm happy to send it down to you, and we can work on it together, but I think we would all be more comfortable if it came from us first."

"Okay, you're probably right," Cannon nodded, "that would be better. See what you can do."

The meeting ended cordially and I think with mutual respect. Neither side had directly stated the real issue, which was how large a piece of the action the savings and loans would get in exchange for their support. We talked around it instead and by doing so each had a better intuitive feel for how far the other was willing to go. In short, from our side, we had confirmed that Cannon would compromise. He was insisting on tight language that would assure his people of a continuing participation, preferably on the "better" loans, those to persons who were closest in income to the ones they were servicing now. But they wouldn't insist on being involved with everything the agency did. It was a useful meeting.

The political reasons for our overtures to the savings and loans were based almost entirely on the extent which we believed their support would influence the governor. They would certainly be useful during passage through the more conservative Senate and especially before the Senate Finance Committee, where they had probably their strongest support, but it was with Reagan that lender opposition would mean certain death.

There were, though, ways of approaching Reagan other than through the financial community, and as early as January 1973, when we first came to Sacramento, we had considered going at him directly. By October our acquaintances included all of the political appointees in the Department of Housing and Community Development, including Bob DeMonte, who served as director until the summer of 1973, as well as his successor Jim Burge, both of whom were Reagan men. In December we had decided it was time to escalate our campaign with the administration and, though unsuccessful in attempting to see Frank Walton, we did get an appointment to see the assistant secretary of the Business and Transportation Agency, Terry Chambers. In that meeting we stressed the independent structure we intended for the agency, which would have a corporate-type board and utilize the private mortgage and lending industry in making its loans. The day following the meeting, George Beattie informed us we had made an excellent impression. A friend of his at Business and Transportation said that immediately after we left Chambers' office Chambers came out and said to one of his staff: "What they're talking about is some kind of an independent corporation that uses private lenders to make loans. We can live with that."

We made our next step toward the administration in March, when we met with Don Livingston, the governor's legislative liaison. His office was in the governor's suite on the ground floor of the Capitol.When we entered Livingston's office for the first time I recall being struck by the prominence of a television which sat a little to one side but right on the front of his desk: a tribute to the medium through which his boss had secured and retained the state's first office for eight years. We waited several minutes before Livingston came in and after he greeted Beattie, whom he knew, and met Bob and me, we started selling. Speaking in turn, Bob and I went through our background, described the concept of a housing agency that utilized private mortgage lenders, and summarized the breadth of political support behind this design of a state housing agency, emphasizing the backing of the savings and loans. Livingston listened, nodded occasionally, asked several questions, and remained totally noncommittal. While refusing to speculate in any way as to the governor's general reaction to our ideas, however, he did refer to two specific items we had mentioned which he was sure the governor would not like. One was that the board of director appointments were divided between the governor and Legislature instead of being made entirely by the governor. Livingston stated the other concern categorically: the governor would never sign a housing bill that authorized issuance of revenue bonds. If he did sign a housing bill—and Livingston emphasized that he had no idea whether Reagan would—it would have to rely wholly on electoral authorization of general obligation bonds.

We had expected some comment on the issue of bond financing, as Reagan's previous vetoes of housing finance legislation had been accompanied by veto messages asserting that issuance of the necessary bonds would damage the state's credit rating. A state has a limit to the debt it can service with any given level of tax revenues. As the level of debt approaches the capacity of the state to service it, the risk increases that the bondholder will not be paid principal or interest when they come due. California has an AAA bond rating—the highest there is; the rating indicates that the "cushion" between tax revenues and debt obligations is so large there is virtually no possibility of default. If the state began increasing the amount of its debt, at some point the excess of revenues over debt service requirements would fall to where investors no longer believed default to be impossible and would begin demanding higher yields on state bonds to compensate them for this higher risk. New borrowing then would become more expensive for the state and bondholders who purchased previous issues would find the value of their holdings in decline. If they wished to sell the bonds before their maturity they would have to do so at a discounted price.

The ratio between total debt obligations of the state and total revenues at which investors begin to demand higher yields is always uncertain. Reagan could easily claim that $500 million additional debt for low- and moderate-income housing would surpass that level since even bond market experts cannot predict with certainty at what point investor confidence will begin to wane.

Complicating the issue further was the fact that investor confidence may depend not only on the amount of debt compared to tax revenues but also on the portion of debt tied up in revenue bonds as opposed to general obligation bonds. Revenue bonds are backed by the revenues from the projects financed by their sale; they do not have a direct pledge of the state's full faith and credit behind them and therefore they do not require electoral authorization before being issued, as do general obligation bonds. Some contend that issuance of revenue bonds more quickly erodes investor confidence than selling the same amount of general obligation bonds. Since revenue bonding is not subject to the discipline of having to obtain prior voter approval, the willingness of a state to issue substantial amounts of revenue bonds causes investors to fear that the state may become a profligate borrower and cause the value of its outstanding bonds to fall.

From what we could determine after considerable analysis and discussions with bond experts, it was highly unlikely that issuance of $500 million or even $1 billion additional debt would have an impact on the state's credit, regardless of whether the debt was incurred in the form of revenue or general obligation bonds. Bob and I believed that the issue of the state's credit had provided a convenient rationale for the governor, who opposed state housing assistance for other, more controversial, reasons. If Reagan really was prepared to sign a housing bill which relied upon an authorization for issuance of general obligation bonds, this reflected not so much a preference for this type of financing as a belief that the necessary voter approval could not be obtained.

Without committing ourselves to general obligation bonds or gubernatorial appointment of the board of directors, we stressed to Livingston the necessity of presenting our concept of a state housing finance agency before the cabinet. We believed our idea of using private mortgage lenders would be much more palatable to the administration than prior housing legislation had been. We were worried that our bill might be dismissed as just another housing bill unless it were appreciated how it differed from what had been presented before.

Livingston seemed optimistic about a cabinet presentation and even said he would make it personally. We immediately offered to provide him with a flip-chart presentation or slides if he preferred and any other information or material he thought might be helpful. He asked for flip-charts to be ready about mid-April and, after assuring him they would be delivered before then, we left.

6

Consensus at Last

ON JANUARY 28, 1974, ZENOVICH INTRODUCED FOUR PIECES OF legislation. Three of these were bills: Senate Bills (S.B.) 1633, 1634, and 1635. The fourth was a proposed amendment to the California constitution which had to be passed first by the legislators and then by the electorate in a statewide election: Senate Constitutional Amendment (S.C.A.) 40. At that date we had not yet drafted the complete bills, but Zenovich wanted to have tangible evidence of his commitment to housing soon after the first of the year. To accomplish this he introduced what are referred to as "spot bills"—short summary statements of their intended purpose. S.B. 1633 indicated the intent to create a California Housing Finance Corporation, a public agency managed by a board of directors selected jointly by the speaker, the president pro tempore of the Senate, and the governor. S.B. 1634 authorized a statewide proposition to be placed on the November 1974 ballot for electoral approval of $500 million in California general obligation bonds for the purpose of funding the housing agency. S.B. 1635 authorized the agency to issue $200 million of its own revenue bonds. S.C.A. 40 authorized a constitutional amendment to be placed on the November 1974 ballot for electoral approval of several changes in provisions of the constitution which would allow the housing agency somewhat more flexibility in the way it was operated than was possible under the existing constitution.

On January 29, we issued a press release under the joint committee's letterhead which began: "Senator George Zenovich (D-Fresno), Chairman of the Joint Committee on Community De -

velopment and Housing Needs, has today submitted three bills and
a constitutional amendment to alleviate the severe shortage of decent housing available to moderate- and low-income sectors of the
state's population."

We used three different bills instead of just one because of our
surmise in January, long before the meeting with Don Livingston,
that revenue bonds would be viewed by the governor as the single
portion of our legislation most in conflict with his fiscal philosophy. Although we expected having to drop revenue bonds at some
point and proceed only with general obligation bond financing for
the agency, we were unwilling to give up without a fight. There
was a possibility, however slight, that Reagan could be persuaded
to approve revenue bond financing for the agency before the bills
reached his desk. Barring that, revenue bonds might be useful in
some future negotiations with the governor—it was something we
could give up in exchange for a reciprocal concession from him.

Bob and I tried never to concede any point without receiving
something in return. Even if an issue were trivial to us it might not
be so to someone else and could therefore be valuable if exchanged for something we wanted. Sometimes we would even
amend a provision into one of the bills solely because we became
aware that it would not be liked by an interest group from which
we needed some concession. We then used removal of the
"planted" section to bargain for that group's support or their
promise of no opposition to something we wanted.

By having the revenue bond authorization in a separate bill we
felt we maximized its effectiveness as a bargaining tool. We could
accelerate consideration of the issue, delay it, or drop it altogether
without either affecting the speed with which we moved the rest
of the legislation or damaging the internal continuity of our program design. Also, this allowed us to use the revenue bond issue as
bargaining material right up to the governor's desk. A bill cannot
be amended once it leaves the Legislature—a governor cannot veto
some provisions of a bill and enact others. Reagan would be able
to veto the revenue bonding authority to please the conservative
Republicans while leaving the agency itself intact; he could then

sign the main bill (S.B. 1633) and put the issue of general obligation bonding before the people in November (S.B. 1634), thus
satisfying the moderates as well. It seemed worth a try.

On January 30, two days after Zenovich introduced the spot
bills in the Senate, Assemblyman Chacon introduced three bills
in the Assembly: Assembly Bills (A.B.) 2966, 2967, and 2968,
plus Assembly Constitutional Amendment (A.C.A.) No. 96.
The Assembly bills were identical to their Senate counterparts.
We had known for some months that Chacon wanted to introduce
his own housing agency legislation in 1974 and had been concerned that this would spread too thinly the support available for
a state housing finance agency. We discussed the problem at length
with George Beattie during November and December of 1973 and
persuaded him that there was no significant chance of enacting
housing finance agency legislation unless we concentrated all of
the available support on a single concept. As neither Zenovich nor
Chacon was willing to stand aside, Bob, George Beattie, and I proposed to Zenovich and Chacon that they each introduce the same
legislation in their respective houses.

In addition to solving the authorship problem we hoped to derive certain tactical advantages from having what was actually a
single legislative package originate in both houses at once. Assuming each of the two sets of bills passed out of its house of origin at
approximately the same time and was sent to the other house,
each would have been considered in substance already and should
find passage through the second house relatively easy. Instead of
the legislation being considered by the two houses sequentially,
the consideration would be simultaneous and this, we hoped,
would accelerate the legislative process. Also, two sets of bills
should give us two shots at the governor. While holding one of
them in the Legislature, we could send the other to the governor's
desk. The first time we could afford to be tough, making few concessions to whatever requests he might make for change in the
bills. If we misjudged and he vetoed, we would still have our reserve package on which to make the necessary compromises.

Having eight pieces of legislation to accomplish what could
have been done with two (one bill and one constitutional amend-

ment) had some disadvantages. It multiplied the number of committee hearings and floor votes, increasing the time we had to spend preparing for them and testifying. It also created confusion at times, not only in the press, but also among legislators and their staff. Fortunately the two sets of bills often moved together. For simplicity, I will, throughout, refer only to S.B. 1633 and A. B. 2966, the main bills, except where the others were dealt with in a manner significantly different.

When introduced in January, the spot bills were announced perfunctorily on the floor of their respective houses and referred to a "policy" committee. The distinction between standing, select, and joint committees has been described. Only standing committees are a part of the formal legislative process through which a bill must pass on its way to becoming law. There is one standing committee in each house which serves as the finance committee: Assembly Ways and Means and Senate Finance. All other standing committees are policy committees and each is responsible for legislation dealing with specific subject matter. The Senate did not have a committee expressly for housing matters so our bills were assigned to Government Organization, since their effect would be to create a new agency of state government. In the Assembly the bills went to the Committee on Urban Development and Housing.

S.B. 1633 and A.B. 2966 remained in their respective policy committees without being heard until the first week in April. By that time we had completed our full legislative draft and were ready to amend it into the spot bills. Before a bill can be introduced or amended by its author the bill or amendment must be approved by legislative counsel, who ensures that it is reasonably coherent, not unconstitutional, and in proper legal form. When Pete Melnicoe, after our many weeks of working together, finally delivered identical approved amendments to Zenovich's and Chacon's offices, we immediately put them across the clerk's desk in both houses.

We now had both sets of full bills in print and requested the policy committee in each house to hear each of them as soon as possible. Chacon set A.B. 2966 for the next meeting of his committee, Wednesday, April 17, and Bob and I set aside the entire week of April 8 to prepare for this hearing. We wanted to make a particularly strong showing in this first committee to begin immediately building momentum for the bill. Politicians like "winners" and an aura of success and enthusiasm around a bill can itself attract support. Few legislators actually read the bills on which they vote in committee, especially one as long and complex as this one (S.B. 1633 and A.B. 2966 were both forty pages). They rely heavily on the opinions of their staff, lobbyists whom they trust, and contacts by their constituency. They are also much affected by a feel of consensus from their fellow members, especially those of the same party. If a bill seems to be generally approved, then a member will be inclined to vote for it unless he has a specific reason for not doing so. There is in legislators, as in most of us, a bias of conservatism—maybe it's common sense—which requires some justification for change. In presenting a bill, then, one initially has the burden of showing its usefulness. But once the proponents of a measure gain a certain level of support, the burden of proof seems to shift, and instead of the proponents having to make an affirmative case, it is the opponents who must make a substantial showing why the bill should not be passed. There is, then, a subtle but important shift from defense to offense which we wished to make as quickly as possible.

In preparing for the hearing by Chacon's committee we were concerned with the kind of testimony the various interest groups would provide. In all of our discussions with them until now we had discussed only the general outlines of a housing agency design. The full amended version of S.B. 1633 and A.B. 2966 became available on Tuesday, April 9. We immediately mailed, and in some cases hand delivered, copies to all lobbyists with whom we had talked. We were worried that there might be numerous questions or concerns on specific provisions of the bill and were anxious to resolve them before the hearing.

We expected one provision in particular to draw criticism from the savings and loans: the provision Bob and I had discussed with Dean Cannon and Bernie Mikell in their Pasadena offices in early March. The issue we negotiated there was the extent to which the agency would be required to lend its funds through private mortgage lenders. We had reached a tentative compromise which I had promised to put into statutory language and send to them. Around the first of April, I dictated that language over the phone to Cannon's secretary, but we had not yet received any reaction. The language contained a general prohibition against the agency making loans without utilizing the services of a private lending intermediary, which in the bill we termed a "qualified mortgage lender." Cannon and Mikell would like that. But we also included two provisions which they would not like. First we expanded the definition of "qualified mortgage lender" to include not only private lenders, but also local public entities such as cities, redevelopment agencies, and local housing authorities. Second, we provided for two exceptions where the agency could loan directly. One was in the case of a housing development that was to be subsidized by other sources besides the low-interest loan from the state agency— such as federal rent subsidies. The second was where the agency's board made a finding that there was no qualified mortgage lender willing and able to participate in the making of a particular loan.

We knew the savings and loans would be particularly disturbed about the last exception because the agency's board could avoid using intermediary lenders whenever it wished simply by setting the price it was willing to pay for the lender's services at a level so low that no lender could profitably participate. It could then find that none were willing to participate and permit the agency to loan directly. Bob and I had already decided we could give in some on this second exception. Our strategy at this point was to make a gesture toward including the private lenders in order to indicate our willingness to work with them, but not immediately to give them all that we thought we reasonably could. We had not yet started serious negotiations with the Western Center on Law and Poverty, the League of California Cities, the League of Women Voters, and other groups whose interests might be opposed to that of the mortgage lenders. We had to have room in which to bargain—we needed to retain something to give to the lenders later on in order to get additional concessions from them.

Much to our discomfort, a week after the bills were in print we still did not have any clear feedback from the various interest groups. We had called a number of them to elicit reactions but most were noncommittal, saying they had not yet had time to study the bills thoroughly or that they had sent copies of the bill to other parts of their organization for comments which had not yet been received.

Neither Zenovich nor Chacon had yet made a play for publicity as the authors of major housing finance agency legislation. Frequently an author will hold a press conference when he introduces a bill, but the timing for a press conference had been wrong for one or the other of them both in January, when the spot bills were introduced, and also in early April, when the full legislation was amended into them. The two men finally agreed that the first hearing was an appropriate occasion. They called a joint press conference for the morning of Wednesday, April 17.

The Friday before the 17th, I drafted one press release for immediate distribution in San Francisco and Sacramento and a second one for release in Sacramento on Tuesday to ensure that the Capitol press corps attended on Wednesday. We had learned from our press efforts on behalf of the joint committee hearings that editors liked to print statements from specific legislators, so I wrote these releases in the form of a dialogue between Zenovich and Chacon, including statistics on state housing need and the potentially beneficial economic impact which a state housing finance agency could produce by its investment in the state's housing stock. That same Friday afternoon Michelle and I called a number of lobbyists from whom we were expecting support on the bill to ask that they attend the press conference. Following the press conference the reporters would have an opportunity to interview the lobbyists to get their reactions, and we hoped this would result in publication of positive quotes from the lenders, labor, and homebuilders. I made a special point of calling Paul McCarron's office; he was not in but I gave his secretary the times of the press conference and the Assembly committee hearing, saying that we hoped he could attend both. We were still concerned about his run-in with Chacon and wanted to mend fences by keeping him well-informed of our activity and making him feel included in development of the bill.

The press conference was scheduled for 10:00 Wednesday morning and actually began about 10:30. It was held in the Capitol press room and featured Zenovich and Chacon seated behind a table on the low, brightly lit stage. I took a seat in the audience near the door, as I had a speaking engagement at a luncheon in San Francisco and could only stay a few minutes. To the intermittent clicks and soft whirring sound of two cameras from local television stations, Zenovich and Chacon each made a very brief introductory statement, and then invited questions. It is my experience that often the most difficult questions—certainly the most unexpected—come from those who know the least about a given subject. The reporters knew little about the bill and the two legislative authors very quickly began to have difficulty fielding their questions. As they stumbled along, I noticed that they kept looking toward the back of the room and, turning, I saw Bob standing behind the audience gesticulating with hand signals, noddings, and waggings of his head, and making silent, exaggerated lip movements in an attempt to be helpful. This seemed to confuse the two men even more, however, and just before I left Bob went on to the stage and sat behind them where he could assist in answering questions.

I stayed too long watching the rather uncomfortable public performance and then fled to the state garage for a car in which I would have to make the hour and a half trip to San Francisco in less than an hour and a quarter. The drive was rapid but thoughtful. The press conference was the first time I had seen Zenovich or Chacon present legislation to the public. I was simultaneously embarrassed for them because they obviously knew so little about the substance of the bills and disturbed that they felt it necessary to appear knowledgeable to their constituents. I had begun to appreciate the difficulty any legislator would have in being at all expert even in the two or three dozen bills he might introduce each year, let alone the many more he would vote on in committee and the hundreds on which he would yea or nay on the floor each session. Bob and I had devoted all of our time to subsidized housing for over two years and often the two of us would have difficulty in coming up with quick, coherent answers to questions asked in public hearings.

We members of the voting public like the appearance of competence. Most legislators quickly learn that they are not re-elected on what they actually do, but rather on what they appear to have accomplished. The kinds of activity required to present effectively an appearance of accomplishment are usually very different from those required actually to perform substantive legislative work. Constituents may prefer attributing this discrepancy between appearance and reality to deliberate deception but I think it is more accurately viewed as the product of the voters' own lack of attention.

The scope and complexity of public issues have expanded greatly over the past three decades. So many decisions that once were made privately are now made collectively. Whether as a result of wisdom or carelessness, we have in fact entrusted enormous amounts of power to our public officials. The scope of a legislator's responsibility has expanded commensurately, but what constituents look for in a representative has not kept pace. We demand individuals who project themselves as slayers of the many but usually vague dragons which beset this modern world. What we ought to demand are individuals who can manage a professional staff that has sufficient skill to assemble for them the complex information necessary for intelligent decisions.

The luncheon at which I was to speak in San Francisco was sponsored by a local chapter of the National Association of Housing and Redevelopment Officials (NAHRO). My speech described our concept of a housing finance agency, including the use of private lenders as intermediaries. The members of NAHRO are employees of local public and citizen groups involved with housing and urban development, and, though my talk went fairly well, I was confronted during the question period with a considerable distrust of private financial institutions. Many of the questioners were aghast at the prospect of involving mortgage lenders in any way with low-income housing, insisting that these private lenders were the very ones responsible for the poor quality of housing in the state and that using them to underwrite state loans was like having the fox watch the chickens. I replied that the state would retain control over how the money was used and that use of private lenders was merely a means of accomplishing the considerable paperwork and administrative tasks of initiating and servicing loans without creating a cumbersome and expensive statewide network of agency loan offices. Because most of those present were employees of public agencies, I tried to present our case without any implication that private institutions were more efficient than public bureaucracies.

I drove back to Sacramento as furiously as I had left in order to make the Urban Development and Housing Committee hearing, which began at 3:30. After opening the hearing Chacon turned over the gavel to the vice chairman, Republican Don MacGillivray from Santa Barbara, and then came around from behind the podium to join Bob and me at the witness table. Chacon gave a brief introductory statement about the need for a housing finance agency and then Bob and I described the bill's principal provisions. There were some questions from committee members, after which the acting chairman asked for testimony from interested parties in the audience. One by one all of those whom we had been courting over the past several months came forward to give a statement. Bill Keiser, League of California Cities; Bernie Mikell, California Savings and Loan League; Paul McCarron, California Builders Council; Brian Paddock, Western Center on Law and Poverty; and others. As we expected, none said they were completely satisfied, but, as hoped, none of them opposed the bill either. All had virtually an identical line—that they liked the bill in concept; that there were several provisions which troubled them, but that they were working with the staff to iron these out and did not feel these differences justified delaying the bill.. All recommended that the committee pass the bill—all, that is, except two.

One of them was Emma Gunterman, a lobbyist for the National Senior Citizens Law Center. The other was Sharon English of the California Housing Coalition, whose purpose is to represent the interests of low-income tenants throughout the state. They both complained that the bill had not been in print long enough. They had mailed copies to members of their organizations in various parts of the state but there had not been enough time for replies. The two of them were quite insistent that the bill be put over until the next committee hearing, and the members, who had seemed ready to pass it until now, began to look troubled and turned toward one another to see how their colleagues were reacting. Chacon began remonstrating with the committee, stating that the bill had been out for a week, which was ample time for analysis. It was an important piece of legislation, he argued, that shouldn't be delayed; there were many more committees it had to pass where amendments could be requested.

Chacon pushed hard and I assumed the bill would be voted out. He was the chairman after all, and though Gunterman and English are reasonably effective advocates, they do not represent particularly powerful organizations. To my surprise, however, I noticed that Chacon was having very little effect. The members listened to him with a too patient look, and when he finished, MacGillivray gently but firmly began to argue with him that the courtesy of additional time should be extended. Chacon would not give up at first. MacGillivray tried to get him to back down to prevent an embarrassing rebuke to the chairman, but finally had to tell Chacon flat out that the committee was not going to vote out the bill. Only then did Chacon finally realize he had lost and agree that the bill be "put over" to be heard at the committee's next hearing on May 1.

Bob and I spent the folowing week almost entirely in Los Angeles. Oschin and Glikbarg were supporters of Jerry Brown's gubernatorial ambitions and through them we arranged to meet with one of Brown's campaign advisers. We kept the appointment in some beat-up offices which Brown's campaign staff had rented above a music store on North Vine in Hollywood. We wanted to make housing a major issue in the gubernatorial campaign. If we were successful in getting legislation passed, it would be important to have the new governor publicly committed to housing so that he would be inclined to provide the new agency with strong political backing for its activities. On the other hand, if we failed to get the legislation passed this session, we wanted to ensure that creation of a state housing finance agency was a high priority of the administration that was to take over next January.

With this objective, in December 1973, just after the joint committee hearings in San Francisco, we had talked to one of Mayor Alioto's people. The mayor had tried for the state's first office in 1970 but withdrew from the Democratic primary won by the former speaker of the Assembly, Jess Unruh. He was trying again in 1974 for probably the last time. We had tried to impress the Alioto campaign staff with the importance of housing as an issue which could draw support from labor as well as industry. In January we spent a couple of hours with a member of Assembly Speaker Bob Moretti's staff, which was also gearing up for the Democratic gubernatorial primary in June. Moretti had not been particularly excited by housing the year before when we approached him but we thought it was worth another try.

We had difficulty in selling any of the candidates on housing as a campaign issue. Low- and moderate-income households may have increasing difficulty finding decent affordable shelter, but campaigners worried that the issue would raise fears of public housing projects being forced on suburban neighborhoods. Bob and I argued that rapidly rising building costs and higher interest rates were making it difficult for even the middle class to afford single-family homes. The issue would appeal to a large section of the population which found itself priced out of the kind of home in which they had always expected to raise their families. We emphasized that no major interest group was opposed to a state housing finance agency: the liberals and poverty groups liked it, as did the builders, labor, and now even the lenders.

That housing assistance was supported by a broad range of interest groups did not, we found, necessarily make it good campaign material. Candidates are looking for controversial issues which generate press coverage and serve to differentiate them from their opponents. Differentiation was especially important in this Democratic primary, which contained a large field of candidates. Of course the controversy must be of the right kind—those opposed cannot have many votes. Candidates, like crusading knights, search for heathen to slay, and among the campaign staff of the Democratic candidates with whom we spoke there always seemed to be a reduction of interest when we told them that the savings and loans were now in favor of a state housing finance agency.

After a rather disappointing session with Jerry Brown's staff, we remained in Los Angeles for a two-day series of meetings arranged by Les Birdsall of the Los Angeles Urban Coalition. We had first met Birdsall more than a year before when we were drumming up political support to have the joint committee created. He served as coordinator for a number of public and private organizations in southern California which have an interest in urban affairs, and he was anxious to expose Bob and me to the ideas on state-assisted housing which these groups had. We started on Thursday morning in a classroom at the U.C.L.A. School of Architecture and ended Friday afternoon in a community meeting hall on a desolate-looking street corner in the central city.

We met with representatives of local housing authorities, redevelopment agencies, regional governments, and assorted municipal agencies as well as non-profit housing development groups, tenants' rights organizations, and some representatives of specific Chicano and black communities in Los Angeles. Following the brief introduction which Birdsall gave us at the start of each meeting, Bob and I described the legislation, making slight adjustments in each of the meetings to emphasize those parts of the bill with which we thought our listeners would be most concerned. After that we threw the meeting open to questions and comments. Everyone, it seemed, had problems of some kind with the bill. The board of directors was weighted too heavily toward industry; there was not enough assurance that low-income families would be represented; private lenders shouldn't be used because they had no sympathy for low-income families; private lenders who were used should be subjected to special regulations covering all of their lending activities; regional government should be given a more substantive role; more assurances were required that black and Chicano contractors would be used to build the housing; the tenant hearing procedure we had included did not provide enough due process safeguards; and so on. Some suggestions were good and eventually resulted in amendments to the bill. Many of the comments, though, concerned issues we had previously considered and ideas we had already rejected. We explained our reasoning as best we could.

The most difficult faction to please were the representatives of tenants' rights groups. They wanted stronger language to ensure that at least 20 percent of the units financed by the agency be made available to very low-income families and more specific provisions spelling out the legal procedures that would be required before any tenant could be evicted from housing financed by the agency. They also objected to the amount of control which the bill accorded to local governments over state-assisted housing located in their respective jurisdictions.

Through their lobbyist, Bill Keiser, the League of California Cities had complained to us that cities were constantly criticized for not exercising sufficient care in planning their communities but that there was little incentive for them to plan because the increasingly large amounts of housing and community development actively undertaken by the federal and state governments ignored local planning attempts. Bob and I were sympathetic with the need for cities to have some control over the number and location of subsidized units but we shared the concerns of tenant representatives that local planning endeavors are not always carried out in good faith. During the time Bob and I were developing housing with Oschin and Glikbarg, they had sued the California city of Torrance after that city rezoned a building site they controlled, solely to prevent construction of federally subsidized apartments on it.

During the many hours I spent in February working on the drafts of our bills with Pete Melnicoe, Bob had negotiated a compromise on this issue with Bill Keiser. The language they finally agreed on created a procedure by which a city could block the agency from financing any particular development within its jurisdiction. This could be done, though, only after the city found that the development did not conform to an official housing plan which provided for "a full range of housing opportunities within the jurisdiction" of the city.

During the Los Angeles meetings several groups asserted that the compromise language was inadequate, that cities could and would use the discretion it gave them to block development of low-income housing. After considerable discussion we agreed to several changes in the bill's language which would make it more difficult for a city to veto a development but left local governments what we hoped was still enough discretion to be acceptable to Bill Keiser.

In accordance with other suggestions during these meetings we tightened the language defining board members' conflict of interest, required that good cause for eviction be established by a landlord evicting tenants from an agency-financed project, and added language which explicitly directed more of the agency's activities toward low-income, as opposed to moderate- and middle-income, families.

By this time we had acceded to demands that the savings and loans have only one board member, but to mollify them we eliminated a provision they did not like—that permitting the agency to avoid using a qualified mortgage lender when it found that no private lender was willing and able to serve as an intermediary. The only remaining circumstance, then, under which the agency could lend directly, without going through a private lender, was when the housing to be financed was to receive federal subsidy assistance. This is where we had expected to end up, having included the "willing and able" language originally in order to have something to give back to the savings and loans when, as we had anticipated, we were persuaded to omit a provision favorable to them. To mollify Bill Keiser for our dilution of local government control over assisted housing developments we made municipalities eligible along with private sponsors, to develop and own projects financed by the agency.

We got these several changes to Pete Melnicoe in time for him to work on them over the weekend and on Monday they went across the Assembly desk. By Tuesday a newly amended version of the bill was in print, with added language in italics and deleted language shown with a line through each letter.

Wednesday, May 1, we were back in Chacon's committee for the scheduled rehearing. Bob wasn't in Sacramento that day, so, after a brief introduction by Chacon, I took up defense of the amended bill. I had more presence of mind at this second hearing than at the first and consciously attempted to project a specific attitude. I had, as an undergraduate, spent the spring of 1965 in Washington, D.C., writing a lengthy paper on lobbying activity in the U.S. Congress and during that time attended a hearing of the Senate Armed Forces Committee at which Robert McNamara was testifying. I recalled his air of absolute confidence and the crisp answers he gave which frequently included citation of statistics from memory. His presentation contrasted sharply with the Senators' questions, which were often hesitant and rambling. It was McNamara's competent self-possession that I had promised myself I would attempt to project if ever I were before a legislative committee.

After Chacon's introduction I began by asking the acting chairman whether the committee wished me to repeat a description of the entire bill which Bob and I had given at the previous hearing or just describe the amendments that had been made since then. The chairman indicated the latter and, following my brief descriptions of the significant changes, the committee members began asking questions. Shortly after the questioning began, Bill Greene, a black committee member from Los Angeles, entered through the door behind the podium and took his seat. After listening for several minutes he asked the chairman to be recognized and then looked down at me:

"You talk in this bill about low-income housing. Can this agency or corporation or whatever it is help low-income people?"

"The agency, by itself, can't reach truly low-income households. The only state subsidy it has is the ability to sell tax-exempt bonds by means of which it can provide financing for residential units at interest rates lower than those available from private lenders. The interest rate at which bonds can be sold, though, isn't low enough to lower the cost of housing far enough to be affordable by very low-income families. However, the agency will have access to federal housing subsidies which it can piggy-back on its low-cost financing and provide units for the really poor."

"What's all this in here about low-income housing, then? You're trying to put something over on the people. It's not going to help poor people, so let's call it a bill for middle-income housing. There's nothing in here for the poor."

"That's incorrect, assemblyman. If you'll turn to page thirty, line thirty-three, of the bill before you, you will see that it requires 20 percent of the units financed to be given to people of low income."

"Why haven't we heard an explanation of this bill?"

"Before you came in it was decided that only the amendments would be gone over, since last week. . . ."

"How can I consider a bill if you come in here and don't even explain it."

"I offered to do just that at . . . ."

"You can't come in here and try to suede shoe a bill through here. I'm not going to stand for it."

"I am not trying to suede shoe anything. This program *will* assist low-income. . . . "

"You just told me that the agency doesn't have enough subsidy to reach poor people and what I'm saying is that you should stop trying to pretend it does."

I could feel rather than hear the edge in my voice as I spoke. I could fathom no reason for this harangue and several times glanced at other committee members to see how they were reacting. I recall best the expression on the face of Assemblyman Kapiloff, who was staring intently at me showing a mixture of surprise and indignation as if I were doing something wrong.

Greene finally stopped and, after hearing from several groups that the amendments made were acceptable, the committee voted the bill out. Although still puzzled about Bill Greene I was nonetheless pleased at having got the bill out and felt good about not having backed down at all in the face of his attack. As I walked from the hearing room back to Zenovich's office, I met Greene in the hallway, standing with several cronies. I stopped to assure him again that no "suede shoe job" had been intended and that with expected access to federal housing subsidies the agency would be able to reach low-income families. He seemed somewhat less antagonistic and, after rumbling some about my not having gone through an explanation of the entire bill to begin with, walked on down the hall.

The following morning we were before the Senate Government Organization Committee to present S.B. 1633, which had been amended to make it identical with A.B. 2966. As Bob and I sat in the audience waiting for our bill to be called, Zenovich walked up and said he preferred to have just Bob at the witness table with him. The preference stung me and I sat, hardly listening to Zenovich's presentation and then Klein's answers to committee questions, trying to figure out what I had done wrong. Suddenly I saw Bob motioning me to come up to the podium, while frantically thumbing through the bill to find an answer to one of the committee's questions. As I approached the podium a voice hissed at me from behind.

"What are you doing? You don't belong up there!"

I turned to see Paul McCarron standing right behind me with his face flushed and ugly. "You, you sit down," he gasped.

After helping Bob find the relevant provision in the bill I went back to my seat in the audience, shaken for the third time in two days. First Greene, then Zenovich, now McCarron, and having not even a guess as to why, I felt there must be subterranean currents flowing beneath the Capitol corridors of which I was unaware. I felt worst about Zenovich. I was quite sure I had done nothing which would have directly given him cause to doubt my integrity or effectiveness. Most troubling was not that someone had approached him, because I knew that we had not pleased everyone in our round of negotiations, but rather that he would accede to someone else's request that I not be used without consulting or forewarning me in any way. When Zenovich left the podium he walked immediately out of the room and I had to walk quickly to catch him before he got to the elevator.

"Senator, I wondered whether Paul McCarron has said anything to you about me."

"No, he hasn't." He looked impatiently at the open elevator and then turned to me. "You're very bright," he said, "and you know this housing thing pretty well, but after yesterday's hearing some of the guys around here think you come on a little strong, so I just had Bob up today." Without waiting for a reply he walked into the elevator. The doors closed.

So, it wasn't McCarron and it didn't seem likely to me that Greene would have complained. One or more of the members must have been quite upset, however, because they had also complained to Chacon. Later that day he asked me into his office and told me that I was "being too hard on" some of the members. I remembered then Kapiloff's expression of angry disbelief. I still did not understand, though, why my testimony had been objectionable. My answers had been honest, responsive to the questions, and while I had not been deferential, I hadn't been either rude or caustic. It was then that I recalled Strom Thurmond's reaction to my model, McNamara. During the congressional hearing I had witnessed, Senator Thurmond's face had changed slowly from pink to scarlet, reacting, it seemed, not to any inaccuracy in McNamara's testimony, but rather to the defense secretary's unshakeable self-possession. By the end of that hearing, Thurmond was shouting his questions at McNamara and sputtering accusations which had no relationship to the topic of the hearing. His outbursts made no visible impact on the witness, who answered, "Yes, sir," or "No, sir," or "I don't believe that's accurate, sir," which seemed not to appease Thurmond but to feed his anger.

Zenovich never kept me from the witness table again, but it took another half dozen hearings before I began to realize that I had failed to see committee hearings from a member's point of view. Bob has a more acute political sense than I and intuited from the outset that legislators in a committee hearing are on stage. They have before them an audience of colleagues, lobbyists, constituents, and press. They want very much to appear competent and knowledgeable. The way in which I answered questions— quickly, directly, even curtly—made it too obvious that I knew more than they did about the bill. Bob, in contrast, always bore a somewhat concerned, almost worried expression when testifying. Although he knew the issues as well as I, he would take enough time in answering to invest even irrelevant or trivial questions with some weight. He began or ended most of his answers with "sir" and liberally sprinkled about short complimentary phrases like "That is a very good question, sir," or "You've hit on a critical point, sir."

To be effective, a witness must realize, as I did not, the extent to which legislative hearings are theatre. My college textbooks had emphasized that a legislature's real work is not accomplished on the floor, but in committee. But I observed very few instances where thoughtful substantive change occurred either on the floor or in committee. Rather the formal hearings merely reflected the gritty negotiations that actually took place beforehand, and that reflection, if not distortive, was extremely selective and revealed only a small part of the conflicts and compromises which are part of any major legislative effort. Theatre is an apt analogy to legislative hearings because in both, success is judged according to the way in which an audience perceives the action. Legislators are not very subtle actors and the roles they play often have the exaggerated style of actors in a melodrama. Each participant has a role to play: the black legislator, the Chicano legislator, the liberal legislator, the conservative legislator. Similarly, the lobbyists, like characters in a morality play, represent free enterprise, tenants' rights, local government autonomy. These roles are not prevarications, merely simplifications, the necessary predigestive process for a public who cannot or will not grapple with the complexity of what is actually occurring and who would become impatient if presented with the complications of reaching the compromises necessary to achieve passage of a major bill.

There is a common, if unspoken, understanding among experienced legislators and lobbyists about the function of legislative hearings and this understanding is the foundation for an etiquette which I ignorantly breached in Chacon's committee. Bill Greene was wholly within his prerogative as a black legislator to rant about the necessity to include low-income families, whether or not his remarks were actually justified by the bill's content. It was wholly unwarranted that I, a legislative staff member, forcefully object to the lack of accuracy in his generalizations.

The hearing in State Government Organization, from which I had been excluded, had gone smoothly and S.B. 1633 had been voted out. This contrast to the problems we had encountered in Chacon's committee was the more remarkable since the Senate Government Organization Committee was by reputation much more conservative than the Assembly Committee on Housing and Urban Development. It was only the first of many times when Bob and I had a reason to appreciate the strength which Zenovich had in the Senate and how fortunate we were to have him as an author.

Although absorbed that week of April 29 in legislative hearings, we had not neglected the administration. On Tuesday, the day before the Chacon committee hearing, we delivered a set of flip-charts to Don Livingston, who was to present our design of a state housing agency to the governor's cabinet. He and Bob De-Monte made a presentation the following week, and on Tuesday, May 14, we met with these two men to discuss the outcome. We were fairly confident that the presentation they made had been reasonably objective. We surmised that Livingston, as a moderate in the administration, believed the governor had to begin projecting a less conservative image. Reagan's decision not to run for re-election signaled the start of his 1976 presidential campaign and we believed that some of his advisers, including Livingston, saw the need for him to move more toward the center of the political spectrum in order to build a national coalition. At the same time, Livingston had to be careful not to move too far too soon; with two and a half years still remaining before the election, he could not yet expose himself to the criticism from Reagan's more conservative supporters which might be roused by any strong advocacy of state housing assistance.

We met with DeMonte and Livingston in the latter's office, where they described to us the presentation they had made. They told us they had had to rush it a bit because it had come at the end of the cabinet meeting and time was limited. They had talked for about twenty minutes using the charts we had supplied, which they had reproduced on 8½″ x 11″ paper for distribution to each of the cabinet officers. Livingston had urged the cabinet to study the charts at their leisure and they agreed that the issue would be discussed again after everyone had had an opportunity to consider the matter more thoroughly. No vote or other formal action had been taken. Both men emphasized that the cabinet as a whole would not take an official position, for although Reagan always discussed major bills with his cabinet, he did not ask them for a formal consensus, reserving the ultimate decision-making entirely to himself.

A.B. 2966 was scheduled to be heard in the Assembly Ways and Means Committee on Wednesday, May 8. While the amendments made prior to the second hearing before Chacon's committee had eliminated some of the reservations expressed at the first hearing, both the industry groups and the consumer/tenant representatives had combined their recommendation of a favorable committee vote with stated reservations about specific provisions on which they expected to continue discussions with the staff. The fact that no one was entirely satisfied with the bill indicated to Bob and me that we had done a fair job of negotiation; we were therefore reluctant to make additional concessions to anyone lest they upset the rather delicate compromises we had achieved. Rather, we hoped that we could persuade everyone to give the same supportive statements before Ways and Means that they had given before the Housing and Urban Development Committee. It was all right if they qualified their statements of support, so long as they concluded by recommending passage.

We did consider additional amendments on two issues in order to appease Emma Gunterman. A day or so after the first committee hearing at which she and Sharon English had successfully objected to passage, Chacon had invited them and us to his office. Their principal argument before the committee—that they had not had sufficient time to analyze the bill—masked what in fact were substantive objections. After the five of us were seated in the assemblyman's office, Gunterman quickly focused on the absence in the bill of any provision regulating late charges and prepayment penalties. She insisted that such penalties should not be imposed by a state agency lending public funds to assist low- and moderate-income families. Financial penalties would be inconsistent with the purpose of assisting the poor.

Bob and I objected. Late charges, we argued, were necessary to provide incentive to borrowers to pay on time. The agency had to receive payment from its borrowers in order to pay off the bonds it issued to raise money to make those loans. If the agency were not paid on time it would have to incur the cost of borrowing from a bank to bridge the gap between the time it paid its bondholders and the time it received the delinquent payments. The cost of such bridge loans would have to be covered somehow by the agency—either by imposing higher borrowing costs on everyone or by placing a late charge on those whose delinquency resulted in such cost. The latter choice seemed fairer to us. Our argument for permitting prepayment penalties was similar. If borrowers prepaid their loans more rapidly than anticipated, the agency would have to prepay its bondholders. Bond investors do not like to be prepaid and would demand for it a financial penalty from the agency. The most just solution, we felt, was to pass that penalty on to those borrowers whose early payment was its cause.

Gunterman finally agreed to compromise on a provision which permitted the imposition of late charges and prepayment penalties but limited them to an amount no greater than the costs which delinquent payments and prepaid loans imposed on the agency. It took several days to work out language that was acceptable to both Gunterman and ourselves. There had not been time to get the amendment in print before the second Chacon committee hearing, but we agreed to put it in the bill before it went to Ways and Means.

At the time we reached this compromise with Gunterman it seemed quite reasonable and not likely to be cause for objection from anyone else. Several days before the Ways and Means hearing I had the amendment ready to put across the desk. Bernie Mikell had called me on an unrelated matter but before hanging up I mentioned that the bill would be amended again before going to Ways and Means. I briefly described what Bob and I thought was very uncontroversial language and was taken aback when Bernie immediately objected to it.

"We can't accept that language, Mike. That's a battle we've been fighting for years now. Every session those people come up with legislation to regulate late charges and prepayment penalties. There's a bill in right now that does it which we finally got hung up in committee."

"Yes," I replied, "but this wouldn't apply generally, only where the agency's money is being used, and all it does is limit them to cost. That's reasonable."

"Hell, how are you going to determine costs? You can't break out what the costs are for something like that and you know it."

"Come on, Bernie, it can't be *that* difficult. Your members must do it all the time for their internal accounting to figure out where they're fat and where they're lean. It's no special trick to allocate fixed costs. And besides this isn't for *your* loans, it only applies to those made with state money. Why should you care?"

"Don't you see what they're doing, though? If we let this get through, they'll come back at us next year and say that the level of charges imposed by the state agency work, and that private lenders should use the same ones in all their loans. They're not so interested in the amendment for its effect on the state agency as they are for its value in the bigger fight to control all mortgage-lending fees in the state."

I told Bernie that we had not known the issue was so controversial and that I would talk it over with Bob and be back in touch with him. I then called Bob in Los Angeles and, after some discussion, we decided to back off from the amendment. We did not think that limiting late charges and prepayment penalties was much of a substantive improvement in the bill. It assumed the agency would be so badly managed that, without legislative limitation, it was likely to impose unreasonable fees and penalties on its borrowers. If that was a reasonable assumption, there was little sense in creating the agency at all. Unreasonably high penalty charges was only one of a multitude of ways in which a poorly managed agency could bungle a housing assistance program. To attempt to anticipate them all, or even most of them, was impossible. And even if that could be done, to prescribe all the agency's policies in the legislation at a level of detail commensurate with the proposed amendment would require a bill several volumes in length and filled with so many proscriptions that the agency could never respond creatively to the constantly shifting conditions in housing and mortgage-finance markets.

We had agreed to the amendment because it calmed Gunterman, for we did not wish to have her opposing us before Ways and Means. Worse, though, would be to involve the bill in a broad, intense struggle between the private lenders and consumer groups on an issue that was irrelevant to our basic program. The following day we met with Chacon to explain the dangers in carrying through with the amendment and he agreed to drop it. We also called both Mikell and Gunterman to tell them of the decision. Emma, of course, was not pleased.

The following morning, before Ways and Means convened, Bob and I were seated in the office of Willie Brown, the committee chairman. We hoped to persuade him that inclusion of an amendment on late charges and prepayment penalties would jeopardize passage of the entire bill.

Brown is a charismatic black legislator who, in the memory of staff members I knew, had chaired the Ways and Means Committee more ably than had anyone else. As we entered his large suite of rooms on the third floor of the Capitol, Brown took a phone call and then two more in succession, stabbing with his index finger the blinking buttons on his telephone console. Even over the phone he had a great range of expression. He would start a conversation talking hard and loud; then suddenly his voice was low and quick with dispassionate orders; occasionally, interspersed, there were slower, measured, thoughtful sounds. But always about him there was an electric alertness. He had been laughing with a wide full grin as he finished with the last caller, but in turning toward us his expression changed instantly to complete deadpan.

"Yes?"

"We're consultants for the joint housing committee," Bob began, "and A.B. 2966, the housing finance agency legislation, is before Ways and Means this morning. Emma Gunterman had requested an amendment that limits the late charges and prepayment penalties the housing agency could charge on its loans. The lenders are very afraid of anything like that and we're worried that the issue could jeopardize the entire legislation. It's really tangential to the bill and we don't think this is the place to fight that battle."

"I don't understand why you're talking to me."

Bob had swallowed a couple of times while talking, his throat drying up under Brown's intense, implacable, absolutely unmoving expression. Bob is not a timid man and it was the only time I ever saw him so uncomfortable. He couldn't get the juices going again.

"We think she'll raise the issue in Ways and Means," I said. "It could be disastrous for the bill if the committee accepts her amendment and we wanted to brief you beforehand."

"I still don't understand why you're talking to me. This is a finance committee and that issue doesn't concern finance. That sort of thing's for policy committee. It's irrelevant here and I wouldn't permit it to be brought up. Is that all?"

The meeting was over. We left and went up the back stairs to the committee hearing room. When we were halfway up, Willie Brown passed us taking the stairs two at a time.

The bill failed to get out of Ways and Means that day, the result not so much of adverse testimony from other witnesses as from Bob's and my own failure to have clear in our minds the role we were to play in testifying. We were, on the one hand, dedicated advocates. At the same time we were staff consultants to a joint committee of the Legislature and, as such, we felt an obligation in testifying to do more than provide an advocate case for passage. In trying to do more we often created problems for the bill in committees by saying too much about it. The best way to present legislation if you wish it to pass is to avoid making it seem complicated—even if it is. This does not necessarily mean obscuring controversy. It can even be advantageous to mention issues on which there are differences of opinion in order to convey an impression of objectivity. But to describe a bill in such a way as to make it seem complex, or in any way to imply that there are uncertainties about its effect, can seriously jeopardize passage. Legislators are accustomed to controversy; what bothers them far more is the possibility of getting a pig in a poke and being subsequently embarrassed because they didn't understand what they were voting for. A good advocate presents legislation to a committee so that the members see a round, smooth, polished surface of public policy—no corners to collect dust, no confusing textures, no more than two primary colors. Zenovich urged us after several hearings to make our explanations simpler. Bob and I felt derelict in being so superficial, though, and our testimony throughout the hearings was too complete for good advocacy, often raising issues which only prompted more questions in the members' minds instead of providing the unambiguous clarity with which they are most comfortable.

Toward the end of the Ways and Means hearing, after all the interested groups had testified, Bob and I were at the witness table fielding miscellaneous questions from the committee members. I referred, in answering one question, to "bond anticipation notes."

These are short-term obligations which we had given the agency authority to issue for the purpose of financing housing construction. They are sold to investors with the anticipation of being refunded by sale of long-term (usually forty-year) bonds, which provide "permanent" financing for a housing project. My use of the term, which I could have avoided if I had been more careful, alarmed one committee member, who remembered that years ago the state had encountered a crisis with bond anticipation notes when market interest rates had risen above the level permitted on state bonds by the state constitution. The danger of being unable to sell bonds and refund the notes when due was averted in that case only by a statewide referendum to amend the constitution by raising the maximum interest rate. I immediately began explaining that bond anticipation notes are a widely accepted means of short-term financing and are used constantly by the state and its agencies. Willie Brown cut me off, though, and passed the issue to Assemblyman Ken Cory, who had recently opened his campaign to run for state controller.

"Well, now," Brown cried, "this is an interesting issue and one which our aspirant for the controller's office will certainly have some thoughts on."

Cory had been caught unaware and was embarrassed. He covered by being absolutely adamant. He declared that the bill should not go out until this issue had been thoroughly investigated. Nothing we could say from the witness table would make him change his mind; he was suddenly cast as protector of the state's fiscal integrity, and, in that role, he wished to appear absolutely uncompromising.

Our too-detailed presentation of the bill created an uneasiness among the committee members which Willie Brown quickly sensed. It was an uneasiness I think he shared. Though he favored the bill, the reservations expressed by the several interest group representatives who had testified, including Emma Gunterman, made him believe that possibly the bill needed more work before going to the floor. When one of the members began worrying out loud about bond anticipation notes, Brown decided that the bill must be untidy and sensed that the other committee members felt the same way. Not wishing to kill it, Brown proposed an ad hoc subcommittee be established to hear the bill and work out the several problems that it seemed to have. He asked John Knox to chair the subcommittee, and he included on it Frank Lanterman, the ranking Republican, himself, and several other members of the full committee.

We left the hearing room disappointed at not getting the bill through, angry at ourselves for failing to be persuasive enough, and chagrined at the several interest groups who persisted in qualifying their support with complaints about specific provisions. As we talked, though, Bob, George Beattie, and I began to view the subcommittee with increasing optimism. The bill represented as tight a compromise among the various groups as we could manage. Our difficulty was that none of them were convinced they couldn't get more of what they wanted if they pushed on us hard enough. A subcommittee hearing would be less formal, less structured, than a full committee hearing and it might give everyone a chance to "have it out." Bob and I could step back from the mediating position we had taken thus far and let everyone beat directly on each other. Maybe then they would realize that the deals which the bill represented were tight and that they were not going to get any more than they already had. In a public forum before a legislative committee there would be pressure on the various groups to reach some kind of compromise. The subcommittee might be just what we needed to finally nail down a firm agreement on this legislation which everyone would then be pledged to support without "buts."

Before A.B. 2966 was to be heard by the Ways and Means ad hoc subcommittee, S.B. 1633 was scheduled in the Senate Finance Committee. We were particularly concerned with Senate Finance because it was considered one of the most conservative committees in the Legislature and was not given to looking kindly on social welfare programs. Also, the fact that the identical bill the Assembly side had run into difficulties in Ways and Means would indicate some weakness in support and tend to inhibit what little enthusiasm the Senate committee members might have. On the day of the hearing, though, we got lucky. Randy Collier, the chairman of Senate Finance, was out of the capital. A senator from the northern counties since 1938, he is very conservative despite being a Democrat. His absence meant that Donald Grunsky, the vice chairman and ranking Republican, would preside. Grunsky is also on the Government Organization Committee and had not only voted for the bill there but participated actively in questioning witnesses and even requested an amendment which was now in the bill. He was, therefore, solidly on record as having considered S.B. 1633 and approved it.

Zenovich began the presentation to Senate Finance standing casually at a small podium next to the witness table where Bob and I sat.

"Well," Zenovich started out, "this is the housing bill I'm carrying this year. Some of you guys are familiar with it, like Senator Grunsky, who heard it in G.O. last week. It's not much different from the housing bills that Senator Moscone and Assemblyman Chacon have had in front of this committee before. You passed those and we think this one is pretty good too. We've talked to a lot of people about it. You know you can't please everyone one hundred percent on something like this, and there may be some people in the audience that want to testify. We have talked to everyone, though, and we are continuing to work to clear up any differences on details.

"The thing we've tried to do all along is work with private enterprise so we don't create some big bureaucracy up here in Sacramento. We don't want to compete with private enterprise. They do their job, we'll do ours. But we think by working together with the lenders, we can do it cheaper and give better service."

"What does the governor think about this?" one member asked.

"I don't know what he's thinking. We've talked to some of his people about the bill and I guess his cabinet's looking at it now. But you don't know till the thing's on his desk what he'll do. *He* probably doesn't know yet how he's going to go. Let's send the thing up and see what happens; if we sent just the stuff he wanted, we'd only be here a couple of weeks a year."

Even the Republicans laughed. It was a good start. He had them relaxed. I am sure they knew Zenovich was working on them, but it was done so casually, so good-naturedly, that they liked it. Even Lou Cusanovich, an immovable conservative from Los Angeles, wore a wry smile. The audience too liked Zenovich's style and I could hear some chuckles from the gallery behind us.

Politicians usually have considerable respect for audiences, and committee members can, I think, be swayed by the mood of a large group of spectators. For example, I recall George Beattie describing committee hearings on legislation to place stringent controls over development on San Francisco Bay. There had been heavy lobbying by commercial interests to stop the bill and there was little incentive for the majority of legislators, who are from the more heavily populated southern part of the state, to respond to the pleas of Bay Area citizens to "Save Our Bay." Conservation groups from the Bay Area, though, organized busloads of supporters who came to Sacramento and crammed the committee hearing rooms. Whenever proponents of control—the "good guys" —went forward to testify, they were loudly cheered, while the opponents made their way to the witness table amid catcalls and booing. George Beattie was convinced this vociferous and visible support had been a psychological edge quite critical to the bill's ultimate success.

After Zenovich's opening, committee members began asking questions and, though Zenovich remained at the podium, Bob and I replied to most of them. At one point a member pointed out the unusual provision of having the president pro tempore of the Senate appoint members to the agency's board of directors. Unlike the lower house, in which leadership is concentrated in a single individual—the speaker—the Senate is governed to a large extent by the Senate Rules Committee. Although the president pro tempore has considerable influence, it is far less than the amount which the speaker enjoys in the Assembly and senators are chary of any move which formally increases his power.

"Senator Zenovich," said one of the members, "I notice here that the Senate appointments to the agency board of directors are made by the president pro tempore. That seems a little unusual over here and I wondered if there was a particular reason for it?"

"Is it," Grunsky added smiling, "some indication of things to come, senator?"

"Doesn't make any difference to *me*," Zenovich quickly replied. "Rules Committee is fine, I'll take that as an author's amendment."

After the committee completed questioning Zenovich, they asked for remarks from interested groups in the audience. The familiar faces trooped up to the witness table and, as they had in Ways and Means, gave the same "we like it, *but*" testimony. Zenovich had prepared the committee so well, though, in his opening remarks, that the detailed objections raised by the various groups had hardly any discernible impact on the committee. The members expressed little interest in what was being said. They seemed to have made up their minds and were impatient to come to a vote, which finally was taken: 8-2, with only Cusanovich and Fred Marler, a fellow Republican, voting against the bill.

The Assembly Ways and Means subcommittee hearing took place, as scheduled, the following day. Prior to each committee hearing, the committee staff prepares a written summary analysis of each bill that is to be heard. The form of these summaries differs among committees but most of them are short—two to three pages—so that a member can read them in the several minutes between the vote on one bill and commencement of testimony on the next. These committee analyses are often the only substantive explanation of a bill to which a committee member is exposed before testimony begins, and Bob and I always met with whatever staff members were preparing the committee analysis of our bill to ensure that they understood it. We respected their need to be objective, but wanted to make certain they understood our rationale for any parts of the bill with which they seemed concerned.

Liz Kersten was the Ways and Means staff member assigned to A.B. 2966. We had met with her before the hearing in the full committee and spent another hour in her small windowless office several days before the subcommittee was to meet. Kersten was quickly able to grasp the more complicated financial aspects of the bill. She had an efficient air about her and dealt with us in a cheerful but somewhat skeptical manner—as if she thought we might try to put something over on her. Instead of the normal summary analysis, for the subcommittee hearing she photocopied each page of the bill on one side of an 8½″ x 11″ sheet of paper, and typed comments line by line on the other, blank side of each sheet. Each committee member was given a copy of the almost fifty pages that resulted, and Knox, who chaired the subcommittee, used Kersten's analysis as an agenda for the hearing, starting with page one of the bill and going through each of her comments. As the committee members completed discussion among themselves on each page, Knox would request testimony on that page from anyone in the audience. The thoroughness of the procedure resulted in by far the most impressive legislative hearing I ever attended.

Bob and I, as usual, spent considerable time at the witness table answering questions which related almost entirely to the issues Liz Kersten had raised. I recall only one issue brought up by a committee member which was not a part of her preparation. Bob Badham, a Republican from Orange County, suddenly exclaimed at one point:

"What in the hell is a 'chairperson'"? I know what a chair*man* is, but not a chair*person,* and you've got this thing all over the bill."

I started laughing and said that I guessed a chairman and a chairperson were pretty much the same thing—but that Michelle, our secretary, was really the expert on this issue.

"When we drafted the bill in longhand," I explained, "we always wrote 'chairman' but Michelle always typed 'chairperson.'"

Michelle, whenever she typed anything for us, meticulously neuterized all nouns which she felt were too masculine and often granted the reader of our letters and memoranda a cumbersome choice of gender ("he/she; his/hers") instead of using "he" if there were any question of the antecedent's sex. This was useful when, as often, we wished to convey a "liberal" impression; at other times, when we wanted to project a rather more "conservative" image, I would ask her to retype letters using the more conventional form.

Badham did not like "chairperson," and the committee agreed to have it changed. Later, though, I appealed to Liz Kersten, explaining that the word appeared over one hundred times in the bill and that not only was the change trivial but preparing and proofing the amendments would take an inordinate amount of my time and that of legislative counsel. With her agreement I never made the change.

There was no lack of participation by lobbyists throughout the hearing. Most of them saw this as their opportunity—maybe the last—to "tune" the details of the bill to their liking. All sides were a bit miffed at Bob and me. Each felt that our refusal to make all the changes they had requested resulted from our being somehow allied with other interests. We frequently reminded each of them that we were being pushed from other sides on the same issues they raised, but to most this appeared to be simply a means of covering up our favoritism. It had reached a point where Bob and I felt uncomfortable being seen talking in the halls with any of the lobbyists. Before coming into the subcommittee hearing, I was standing with Bernie Mikell outside the hearing room when Brian Paddock, who represented the Western Center on Law and Poverty, walked past us. He wagged his head with a half-smile, partly in jest, but his expression showed real concern as well. Mikell saw him and cried:

"I'm trying to straighten him out. They've let you people screw this thing up so badly."

"Hell," Paddock replied, "the whole thing's a gift to the s & l's."

Everyone had objections to the bill, but as the parade to the witness table continued, page after page, Bob and I began to exchange smiles. It became increasingly clear that we had not favored any one group and the hearing, as we had hoped, allowed each of the various lobbyists to discover the strength of opposition to certain of their pet provisions which we had refused to include. A good example was the issue of representation on the board of directors. Every group we had talked to complained they were not adequately represented. Even those who had a designated representative insisted they should have more, and ever since the savings and loans had lost one of their representatives they had been pushing to get him back. We had told Bernie Mikell and several other lobbyists before the hearing that we had negotiated as good a deal for them as possible, and that to raise the issue in committee was dangerous. But Mikell and Dick St. Lezin, who had come up from San Francisco to testify with Mikell, insisted on bringing it up. As soon as they did so, Jack Crose, lobbyist for the investment bankers, stood up in the audience and said he would be willing to see the investment bankers seat given to the savings and loans. Immediately several other lobbyists in the audience sprang to their feet, each claiming that their clients should have the seat the investment bankers were giving up. With several groups at the hearing who did not have any representation on the board the committee was not about to vote for another savings and loan representative and I shook my head disbelievingly at Bernie to say, "I told you so." He replied with a grimace.

The formality of the hearing broke down with shouts from the audience. Joe Gunterman, Emma's husband, and also a lobbyist, began arguing for a representative of non-profit housing developers. There were demands by others for another tenant representative and a second member from local government. Finally, the suggestion that there be a realtor on the board was changed to "a realtor experienced in government-assisted housing," which offered the committee members the compromise between business and consumer orientation they had begun to grope for. It was quickly accepted as the replacement for the investment banker representative.

For the first time, the boundaries of the compromise Bob and I had worked on so long began to be apparent to others. They had come to the subcommittee hearing in order to be vindicated but left realizing they had about as good a deal as they were likely to get. After several hours, having gone through the entire bill, Knox said, "Is there anyone else who wishes to comment on this bill? Are there any objections to it to come before this committee?"

The silence was golden.

7

Things Fall Apart

WHEN WE WALKED OUT OF THE SUBCOMMITTEE HEARING, BOB and I felt sure we had a lasting compromise. The lenders, the tenants' groups, the realtors, labor, the builders, and the cities were all apparently satisfied that they had as good a deal as they could get. Strange bedfellows, indeed—the California Savings and Loan League and the Western Center on Law and Poverty, who were engaged in so many battles on other fronts. But the peace was to last only a short time.

Watching a legislature from the distance of newsprint one can gain an impression that laws are moulded entirely by lobbyists, that legislation is merely the handiwork of special interest groups. Even from our much closer vantage Bob and I overestimated the role they play. A week after the subcommittee hearing, despite the absence of lobbyist opposition, S.B. 1633 was defeated on the Senate floor, a setback due to haste and an overconfidence that affected Zenovich as well as Bob and me. The senator had received a call from the governor during the week of May 20, in which Reagan urged Zenovich to vote for certain gubernatorial appointees who required confirmation by the Senate Rules Committee of which he was a member. During the conversation the senator mentioned the housing bill and the governor's political future. As Zenovich later recounted, he told Reagan that if he wanted to be president he was going to have to start thinking about all the people who want better housing. Although Zenovich had not made a deal with Reagan on the appointees, he felt he had struck a chord with his remarks on the presidency. He became excited about moving the bill immediately and scheduled it for a floor vote on Wednesday, May 29.

The least that should be done before bringing major legislation to the floor is a head count. One should make a list of those who are sure to vote "yes," those who are sure to vote "no," and those whose vote cannot be predicted. Members in the third category usually make the difference between winning and losing, so most floor strategy is aimed at persuading some portion of them to vote with you. Bob and I did almost no such preparation before the Senate floor vote. Didn't we have all the interest groups behind us? Who would vote against a bill that was supported by everyone from the lenders to the poverty representatives?

The weekend before the vote was Memorial Day and I spent the three-day holiday climbing Mount Shasta. Tuesday, Bob and I had scheduled meetings in Los Angeles and neither of us even got to Sacramento until Wednesday afternoon. Before the Senate went into session at 4:00 p.m., I wrote a floor speech for Zenovich and had about ten minutes to go over it with him in his office before we left for the senate chambers on the third floor.

From our vantage, seated on folding chairs at the back of the chamber, Bob, George Beattie, and I could see Zenovich walking around the floor before the day's session began, stopping at one desk and then another. He would lean over a seated colleague for a minute or so and then, smiling, move on. There was not much time, though, and after only a few of these exchanges, the session was called to order. After about an hour S.B. 1633 came up on the calendar, and the president pro tempore asked Senator Zenovich to present it. Standing up to the microphone beside his desk, he delivered his speech. Beattie whispered to me that it was only the second time he had ever heard Zenovich read a prepared speech and I recall being pleased that it was mine. Immediately after he finished, Senator Bradley from San Jose rose to speak in opposition. This was no surprise since Bradley was one of the most conservative members of the Senate and he invariably spoke in opposition to bills which in any way increased the role of government in social welfare.

We became very disturbed, though, when Bradley was followed by Dennis Carpenter, the Republican caucus chairman. A conservative from Orange County, Carpenter is an intelligent, thoughtful member, respected in both parties and a good friend of Zenovich's despite their differences in political philosophy. We were sure that friendship would not alter Carpenter's vote, but thought it might dissuade him from speaking in opposition. That he did speak meant that he was strongly opposed to the bill and probably had significant support among fellow Republicans. His principal argument was that $500 million in bond authorization constituted more money than the state could afford to invest in housing and that the initial $500 million was only the beginning. Once a housing finance agency was created, it would come back again and again for additional bonding authorization until it severely strained the state's financial capacity.

George Deukmejian from Long Beach, the Republican floor leader, then rose to commend Senator Carpenter for his wise remarks and add similar cautions of his own. This legislation, he asserted, would create a state agency to do what the Federal Housing Administration was doing already. Not only was the state agency therefore unnecessary but the FHA programs had been a flop and this agency would simply duplicate that record.

Zenovich, as is customary, was then asked for closing remarks, which he made very short, concluding with the familiar, "I ask you for an 'aye' vote."

Every bill which includes an appropriation of state funds requires a two-thirds majority in both houses for passage. S.B. 1633 had an appropriation of $750,000, to be used for initial operating expenses of the agency during the period before it issued its bonds and was able to generate its own revenue by investing surplus monies. The California Senate usually has forty members, reduced at this time by one as a result of a resignation which had not yet been filled by a special election; this did not, however, change the twenty-seven votes required for passage.

Rarely does the first roll call result in twenty-seven votes for a bill as a number of the members will usually be outside the chamber at any one time. The bill's author must usually request a "call" to be placed on the Senate, in which case the president requests the sergeant-at-arms to bring in absent members. After the first roll call Zenovich asked that a "call" be placed on the house and within an hour asked that the roll be called again and the vote announced. Though only ten members voted against, only eighteen voted "aye," nine votes short.

We had made two mistakes. One was the failure to recognize that aside from the consensus we had gained from lobbyists, the members themselves would have objections to the bill reflecting their personal views and possibly their perception of the unarticulated viewpoint of their constituents. Second was the embarrassingly simple one of not finding out beforehand who was going to be absent. When the Senate is in session, all members are required to be in attendance—if not actually on the floor, then in the adjacent lounge or foyer, ready to come to the floor if a "call" is placed on the house. Absence is permitted only upon express leave by the president pro tempore. It is a simple matter before taking up a bill to call the clerk's office for a list of members who have requested a leave for the day. Had we done so, we would have discovered that attendance was to be low that day, with most absentees being obvious supporters of our bill. Even in our euphoric state we would have realized the necessity of waiting for another day.

All was not lost though. Immediately upon announcement of the vote Zenovich asked for "reconsideration" and received the normal courtesy of unanimous consent to reconsider the vote—to have the bill voted on again at some future date. Bob and I left the chambers about 6:15, disappointed but determined that we would not be foiled a second time.

We began Thursday morning to do the kind of preparatory work that should have been done before the first vote. Bob and I took notes on the senators who voted against us or who were absent, indicating how each might be lobbied most effectively; these tactical notes included entries such as:

Berryhill—Bernie Mikell may well be able to persuade him. John Witzel [lobbyist for the city of San Diego] is an old Republican PR man who may have helped Berryhill in the past.

Carpenter belongs to a Beverly Hills law firm. One of his partners lobbied

him for the bill. Find out who it was. The League of Cities should find
someone in the Orange area to lobby him and Klein, Sr. [Bob's father]
should be contacted as to Orange County realtors who might approach him.
Stull is from San Diego but is not friendly to Mayor Wilson; they are two
different kinds of Republicans. Witzel should approach him.
Wedworth's district includes Inglewood; Steve Morris of the Inglewood
Housing Authority should be contacted to organize some influence.

We called our supporting lobbyists and requested that they
contact specific members. The industry lobbyists—savings and
loans, mortgage bankers, realtors, and builders—talked with several
of the conservative senators who had voted nay. Bob and I spoke
directly to several members who had been absent to confirm our
belief that they were for us. We also asked several lobbyists to
phone some of the Republican senators who had voted for the bill
to provide supportive reassurance for those who might be pres-
sured by party colleagues to change their minds.

Bob and I ourselves took on the task of talking to Carpenter
and Deukmejian. The week following the floor vote I approached
Deukmejian as he emerged from a committee hearing.

"Senator, I am a consultant on the Joint Housing Committee
responsible for drafting the state housing finance legislation that
was on the floor last week. Several months of staff time have gone
into drafting the bill. We have consulted a number of experts in
the field as well and believe that it is excellent legislation. I wondered if I could sit down with you for a few minutes and discuss
your objections to it."

"I'm really not interested."

"Are there particular parts of the bill you have problems
with?"

"Look, I've already made up my mind and I'm not interested
in discussing it further."

We had been walking rapidly down the hall while this discussion
was taking place and were now about to enter his office. As a last
try I blurted, "Is there anything I could tell you about this bill
that would make you change your mind?"

"No, nothing. It's just another FHA."

"But, you see, it's not," I cried, "it's based on a very different concept; it is not another FHA and it doesn't duplicate FHA's functions in any way."

His reply was a very tired, exasperated look.

"There's nothing I can say?"

"No, nothing," he said, and turning, disappeared into his office.

Senator Carpenter had been equally abrupt with Bob. We had done some business with the law firm to which Carpenter was "of counsel" and we found out that the partner who had urged Carpenter to vote for S.B. 1633 was someone we knew well. I called him.

"Carpenter's killing us up here," I told him. "It's not just that he votes against us, but he's *leading* the opposition. Will you talk to him? Do something to convince him it's a good bill."

Carpenter's partner replied that he had told him the bill was technically sound and that the state needed a housing agency, but that Carpenter was a very conscientious guy and insisted it would be bad for the state.

We tried to get to Deukmejian by asking someone we knew who was a friend of a large financial supporter of Deukmejian to do what he could to get us at least a meeting with the senator. We didn't ask that anyone say the bill was good, but just that it would be worth his hearing our arguments for it. Within a day Deukmejian's office called Zenovich's and set an appointment for us to see the senator on the morning of Tuesday, June 18, the day Zenovich had scheduled the bill for reconsideration. I went to Deukmejian's office at the appointed time with some confidence that I would be able to persuade him. He received me with a politely impersonal attitude and listened quite intently while I described the bill, explaining how it differed from FHA and the advantages it had over the structure of federal housing assistance. He then responded with a number of detailed and rather thoughtful questions.

"Is the agency always required to use private lenders when making loans?"

"No," I replied, "in cases where the units are to receive federal subsidies it can make the loans directly."

"What would be the legal status of this agency? Is it a regular department of state government or a non-profit corporation under contract to the state?"

"We've designed it to fall somewhere in between those two. Legally it is a state agency and as a public entity is subject to the same disclosure and regulatory procedures as any part of the executive branch is. However, we have not made it subject to jurisdiction of any of the cabinet secretaries, believing that, as a purely financial entity, raising money for privately owned real estate, it should have more independence than a normal branch of the government."

"Several days ago I was handed this list made up by you people showing the groups which support the bill. I understand that some of them have not, in fact, taken a position on this legislation."

"We compiled that for Don Livingston to use in his presentation before the cabinet. We explained to him that not all of those listed had yet taken an official position on the bill. Rather, it is a list of organizations employing staff we have worked with on the bill and to our knowledge all of them are satisfied with it as it now stands."

I was greatly encouraged by these and the number of other queries he had, though he made no definite commitment. "We'll see" was all he would say regarding a change in his position, but that seemed a vast improvement over the conclusion to our previous conversation.

Bob and I then went together to see Senator Fred Marler, Deukmejian's predecessor as Republican floor leader. He had been reapportioned out of his Senate seat, which he would lose at the end of the year. Governor Reagan had incurred the wrath of the Republican caucus in the Senate by passing over Marler and filling two vacant posts on the Court of Appeals in Sacramento with lower court judges who were Democrats. Reagan ended that tiff in May by appointing Marler to the Sacramento County Superior Court, a post he intended to assume at the end of the session. Marler had voted against us on May 29, but since he would soon be out of the political arena we thought he might be particularly open to reasoned substantive arguments in favor of the bill. We spoke to him for about a half hour and, though he promised nothing, we left feeling he had been extremely receptive.

Zenovich had selected the 18th for a floor vote because it was a day when floor attendance was mandatory and leaves of absence were not granted. From time to time, attendance is made mandatory by the president pro tempore expressly for the purpose of assuring sufficient attendance to take up bills requiring twenty-seven votes for passage.

In the speech I outlined, with which Zenovich began the floor debate, I tried to cover the issues which had seemed to be of most concern to the several senators whom we had contacted, directly and indirectly, over the previous three weeks:

This legislative package presents a single issue to the Senate: Shall the people of this state be given the opportunity to vote on whether they wish to utilize the state's credit to finance housing for moderate-income families?

The creation of a California Housing Finance Corporation is not a radical idea. It creates the same type of program for moderate-income families that Cal-Vet has operated so successfully for the benefit of the state's veterans. The financing is done by the tried and true method of issuing general obligation bonds and servicing the bonds from monthly payments made by the owners of property on which the loans are made.

This program should cost the state nothing. The Cal-Vet program has never drawn on the State Treasury. Housing finance agencies now exist in thirty other states, and over their twelve-year history, they have financed 120,000 units of housing for low- and moderate-income units without financial default. In fact, those agencies now in full operation are generating surpluses of up to several million dollars per year.

This legislation does not create an FHA-type program or in any way duplicate the housing assistance efforts now being made by the federal government. The Department of Housing and Urban Development has terminated its moderate-income housing subsidies and is concentrating its funds on low-income families. This was done with an explicit acknowledgement by the administration that the state housing finance agency vehicle which these bills create has proven itself so effective in providing moderate-income housing that the job should be left completely to the states. To encourage the creation of state housing agencies, HUD is publishing regulations which give direct and very substantial preferences in the receipt of federal housing subsidies for low-income families to those states which create such housing finance entities.

This legislation creates a public entity founded on a financial base which has proven itself sound in California and in thirty other states. It creates a low-risk housing program that does not duplicate the efforts of FHA, but complements them and gains for California a priority for federal housing subsidies worth hundreds of millions of dollars.

The concern with the state's credit rating was one addressed from the beginning of our research on this concept ten months ago. We have had intensive discussions with the treasurer's office and numerous experts in the field of public debt. We have reviewed the analysis of California's financial position done by Moody's and the Department of Housing and Community Development. The conclusion is that given the decreasing amount of anticipated state debt due to the declining capital demands of the California Water Project, the issuance of $500 million in G.O. bonds would have no adverse impact on the state's credit. This same conclusion was reached by the Department of Housing and Community Development after exhaustive analysis and, more recently, by the state controller. In fact, if we assume that *all* of the bond issues being proposed do in fact pass, the projected issuance, for example, in fiscal years 1974-1975 and 1975-1976, would represent a smaller relative amount than in fiscal year 1970-1971, immediately after which the state's credit rating was raised from "double A" to "triple A."

This program does not in any way compete with the private mortgage finance industry. Rather, it uses that industry to provide the expertise necessary to ensure the smooth operation of the program. Other than loans made on housing which are federally subsidized, the initiation and servicing of all mortgages will be done by private or public financial intermediaries. This will result in the need for only a small staff of financial professionals at the state level.

Again, the only question presented here is whether the people of the state should have the opportunity to vote on the extension of a sound and proven financial means to provide decent housing for the state's moderate-income families.

After Zenovich's introductory remarks, Bradley got up to have his say, Carpenter made his same arguments again, and then, to my dismay, Deukmejian rose. Not only did he speak against the bill, but the effectiveness of his arguments was greatly increased by the unusual grasp he had of the bill's specifics. He argued that despite Zenovich's assurance that the agency would not compete with private lenders, the bill effectively put the state into the mortgage-lending business. Not only did the state know nothing about running such a business, the agency in charge was not even designed as a part of the normal state government. The Legislature, said Deukmejian, was being asked to provide hundreds of millions of dollars to a virtually autonomous body. After disparaging several other parts of the bill which I had only a few hours before explained to him so eagerly, he held up a sheet of paper on which, he said, was a list of alleged supporters of the bill. Although the list had received considerable circulation, he continued, and the number and breadth of the interests mentioned was impressive, he had been informed that many of those included had not in fact endorsed the bill. Specifically, he mentioned the California Real Estate Association and the Urban Coalition, which were both on the list and which he said his office had confirmed were not supporters.

Several senators then stood up, in turn, to speak in favor of the bill. One of them remarked how strange it was that if the realtors did not support the bill he should have before him a letter from that association addressed to Senator Zenovich unequivocally stating the contrary. Jack Shelby of the Real Estate Association had hand delivered the letter to Zenovich that same morning, and had had copies distributed on the floor to all members. Unfortunately for Deukmejian he had not read it and the oversight, which I am sure was an honest error, supplied a far more discrediting rebuttal than any affirmative arguments our side could have made.

When the vote was taken there were twenty-nine ayes, a gain of eleven over our previous attempt. Four of those—Senators Collier, Marler, Stevens, and Stull—had voted against us last time. Collier had been turned around by Zenovich, who approached him directly. Bob and I took credit for Marler. I don't know what accounted for the change by Stevens and Stull. We had talked to them, as had several of our lobbyist supporters. Whether it was something particular that persuaded them or whether it was a combination of all our efforts is difficult to guess.

After leaving the Senate chambers I went over to Ellis' bar—right across the street from the Capitol and a favorite watering hole for legislators and lobbyists. George Beattie was already there and called me over to his table, where he had two secretaries and a lobbyist from some public water works in southern California. The lobbyist was picking up the tab—"only buying communication, only communication," he assured me—and I partook. Jack Shelby was up at the bar and soon came over to contrast the value of the Real Estate Association's support with that of the "poverty types." I thanked him for the letter, "the right thing at the right time," I said, but wondered inwardly whether the floor debate had had any impact at all on the outcome. My guess was that it had not—that most if not all of the members knew before going onto the floor the way they were going to vote and that something far stronger than Deukmejian's argument would have been required to change their minds at that point.

I was tired and soon got up to leave. As I was going out, Sharon English came in with her husband, Bob Frank. She immediately began apologizing about the Urban Coalition's failure to support the bill officially, saying that they couldn't take formal positions on legislation without losing their tax exemption as a non-profit entity. "God," she exclaimed, "I'm afraid George [Zenovich] will never trust us again."

A.B. 2966 had breezed through the full Ways and Means Committee and, on June 14, easily attracted a two-thirds vote on the Assembly floor. Each bill now had to go through the house opposite its origin. Whenever either of the bills had been amended, we placed the same amendments in the other bill so that each left its house of origin with almost identical wording and we expected the remaining committee and floor votes in both houses to be pro forma approvals. This had been the strategy from the beginning by which we hoped to gain considerable time.

The speed with which we got a bill to the governor's desk was now critical. By this time we had been forced to drop S.B. 1635 and A.B. 2968, which authorized the agency to issue revenue bonds. The administration had stated unequivocally before Assembly Ways and Means and Senate Finance that the governor would never consider revenue bond financing and, given the certainty of a veto, neither committee had approved them. The sole financing authority that remained was in S.B. 1634 and A.B. 2965, both of which provided for a referendum on the November ballot for issuance of $500 million in general obligation bonds on behalf of the housing agency. The need to qualify for the November ballot imposed time constraints. The secretary of state is required by law to print a *California Voters Pamphlet* describing whatever issues are going to be on the ballot and distribute it to all registered voters several weeks before election day. Legislation placing an issue on the ballot must be passed before the pamphlet goes to press so that it is included in this official election brochure. The job of printing and distributing the pamphlet is enormous and for a November election the pamphlet must go to press by mid-August or, at the very latest, September 1. This was the time-frame we had counted on since the first of the year and, barring substantial unforeseen delays, we were confident of getting a housing bill passed in time.

But the June 1974 primary election altered that timing. The California Constitution permits the enactment of laws by popular vote. Proposition 9 on the June ballot was the most stringent and comprehensive law in the nation regulating the conduct and relationship between public officials and lobbyists. It passed overwhelmingly. Amid its many pages defining conflict of interest, detailing financial reporting requirements, were several sections that altered the procedures for preparing the *Voters Pamphlet.* Bob and I were unaware of them until after the election. To allow what they felt was sufficient time to satisfy the new requirements, the secretary of state's office had set a deadline of June 8 for submission of all measures to be included on the November ballot. After some prodding by us, however, the secretary of state's office agreed to include both our bond issue (S.B. 1634/A.B. 2967) and constitutional amendment (S.C.A. 40/A.C.A. 96) in the *Voters Pamphlet* and place them on the ballot, if they were passed before the Legislature recessed on June 28.

Even with the three additional weeks, though, the timing was extremely tight and the delay of three weeks in getting off the senate floor, as a result of our failure to prepare for the first vote, might be disastrous. It was now June 18 and we had only ten days in which to get one of the two legislative packages through two committees, a floor vote, and off the governor's desk. There was a chance of doing this only because both houses had already approved what, substantively, was the same bill. The wisdom of having moved identical bills through both houses was now a crucial advantage.

Only one of the two packages of bills had to be passed and since every day now was crucial and A.B. 2966 was slightly ahead of S.B. 1633, it seemed logical to concentrate on the former. A.B. 2966 had been read in the Senate on June 17 and referred the same day to the Government Organization Committee. We immediately began to push Chuck Baldwin, the committee's chief staff member, to recommend to Chairman Ralph Dills that the bill be heard that same week so that we could get it to Senate Finance by early the following week and off the floor by the 27th. Baldwin's response was bafflingly casual. He said that he needed to study the bill more thoroughly before it was set for hearing and that he expected to recommend some amendments to the committee. We replied that he had already had an opportunity to study the bill as S.B. 1633 and the committee had passed it. Yes, that was true, he replied, but he was reconsidering some of his thinking and did not feel that he could ask Dills to take it up that week. Whatever Baldwin's reasons, he knew that the delay of even a week eliminated the possibility of A.B. 2966 being out in time.

We had no alternative, then, but to turn to S.B. 1633. The day after it had left the Senate floor it was transmitted to the Assembly and assigned to the Urban Development and Housing Committee; Chacon arranged for it to be heard the following day, Thursday, June 20. Assuming Chacon got it out that day, the bill would be in Ways and Means by its next hearing date, Wednesday, the 26th, allowing two days for floor action—a very tight schedule but one which might possibly be made if everything went right.

Bob flew to Washington, D.C., on the 19th for a two-day conference on subsidized housing. I stayed in Sacramento to work on some technical legal provisions in the bill which needed polishing before final passage. There were a number of difficult legal questions raised by creation of this agency and, to minimize potential legal problems for the agency after its creation, we had worked closely with major law firms in both San Francisco and Los Angeles through the initial drafting process and as amendments were added to the bill by committee action. Despite our efforts and the considerable assistance we received from these law firms in drafting numerous sections of the bill, we had been unable to provide the agency with the structure and powers we wished it to have without creating several potential conflicts with the California Constitution.

Unlike the United States Constitution, but like many state constitutions, the California Constitution does not confine itself simply to delegating basic rights and governmental powers. In addition to doing this it serves as a repository for miscellaneous bits of public policy which from time to time and for one reason or another, were thought too important to be left to legislative decision. For example one section of the California Constitution prohibits the state from lending its funds to private individuals or companies. This provision had caused some difficulty fifty years before when the Cal-Vet Program was created to provide low-interest home loans to veterans. Since loans were to be made from state monies to private individuals, the program appeared to be unconstitutional. The issue was litigated and the courts ruled that the constitution did not prohibit public loans to private entities so long as the purpose for which the loans were made was a public purpose. Loans to veterans, the court held, served a public purpose by providing incentives for citizens to fight in defense of their country.

Whether providing better housing for low- and moderate-income families was a public purpose for which the state could lend monies had never been presented to the courts. Although we were quite sure that such activity would be declared to serve a public purpose, we wanted to remove any uncertainty and therefore included within our constitutional amendments (S.C.A. 40; A.C.A. 96) a provision which expressly declared that it did so.

Also in the California Constitution is a requirement that all employees of the state, except those under a few specific parts of the government (e.g., the University of California), must be under civil service. This was made a part of the constitution during the 1930's in the belief that it would replace the corruption of political patronage with the professionalism of career public servants selected and promoted on the basis of merit and dedicated to serving the public good instead of the ambitions of political incumbents. Because of our experience with HUD, though, Bob and I were skeptical of the ability of a civil service bureaucracy to run an effective housing program. Also, we had spoken with executives of other state housing agencies around the country, both those under a civil service system and those not. The unanimous opinion was that civil service regulations, which controlled the hiring, firing, promotion, salaries, and job descriptions of personnel, made it extremely difficult to attract aggressive top- and middle-level professionals with experience in the financing, production, and management of housing. We therefore included in the constitutional amendment a specific exemption from civil service for all employees of the housing agency.

A final constitutional issue involved the deposit of public funds. The housing agency, with access to hundreds of millions of dollars of state bond proceeds, would frequently be holding large amounts of cash between the time the bonds were sold and the time at which funds were paid to contractors for the construction of housing. The California Constitution specified that public monies could be deposited only in commercial banks. In September and October, when Bob and I were contacting all who might have an interest in a state housing finance agency, we had several discussions with representatives of the Bank of America and the California Bankers Association. They had both listened politely to us and then both politely declined to provide any support. The reasons they gave were various and somewhat vague. I think much of the reluctance stemmed from a generally conservative political philosophy held by the banks which made them uncomfortable with the notion of state-subsidized housing. They were of course aware that the agency would have large amounts of funds to deposit, but they were guaranteed this business by the constitution and so did not have to bargain for it.

Bob and I decided, though, that since the savings and loans probably would be more active than the banks as lending intermediaries for the agency, and since they were providing us with active support on the bill, there was reason to include a constitutional amendment giving them the right to hold agency deposits along with the banks.

On Tuesday, June 18, S.C.A. 40 was passed by the Senate along with S.B. 1633. Both were passed out of Chacon's committee on Thursday, June 20, and then parted, S.B. 1633 going to Ways and Means and S.C.A. 40 going to the Assembly Constitutional Amendment Committee. That week I got a call from Sam Farr, the Constitutional Amendment Committee's principal staff member. He confirmed that S.C.A. 40 would be heard by the committee on Monday, June 24, and then warned me that the bankers had been by his office to object to the language permitting savings and loans to hold the agency's deposits.

"It's a hell of a time for them to be coming in," I said. "We've *got* to have this through your committee on Monday and to the floor by Friday or we're dead. There is no way we can postpone the hearing while we straighten them out. Why didn't they come in before? This thing's been around now for five months."

"Yeah, I know you've got to go on Monday. They claim they didn't know about the amendment and happened to come across the thing almost by accident."

"That's hard to believe. We tried for months to get them to take an interest and all of a sudden with only a couple of days left they start squawking. Maybe they figured if they came in before this they'd have to compromise, but if they came in at the last minute there wouldn't be time and they would queer it altogether."

"I don't know. I told 'em to talk to you guys and they said they would."

"Okay, I better give them a call. Was it Ratcliff?"

"Yeah, Ratcliff, and another guy, an attorney from San Francisco who seemed pretty knowledgeable."

"I appreciate the call, Sam."

"That's all right. Hope you get it figured out."

I immediately called George Beattie and several other people whom I thought might be able to tell me more about the bankers' lobbyist organization than what I knew, which was very little. I found out that the San Francisco attorney was Fred Pownall, who served as counsel to the California Bankers Association. Dick Ratcliff, with whom Bob and I had met before, was the lobbyist in Sacramento who handled day-to-day legislative affairs for the association. Pownall came to the Capitol only when there were issues which were particularly complex or which the association thought were especially serious. I was also told that Pownall was well connected with the association membership; if you wanted to make a deal with the bankers he was the one to reach.

Instead of waiting for the bankers to call me I decided to take the offensive with an opening sortie at Dick Ratcliff. I spent a couple of minutes working up some steam and then called.

"Dick, this is Mike BeVier. I understand you were in to see Sam Farr about S.C.A. 40. What's the story?"

"Well, Mike, you know I'm glad you called because we had no idea that you had anything in the state housing finance bills that had to do with public deposits. You know we just can't live with something like that."

"What do you mean you can't live with it, Dick? I am terribly, terribly upset about this. How many times did Bob and I come in and talk to you about this legislation? Months ago, when the whole thing first started, we were in your office and told you then that this was a major piece of legislation, and that it was not only important to the state's economy, but that it would directly affect the interests of all lending institutions in the state. No, you guys didn't want any part of it, not your sort of thing. So we went ahead and slugged it through without you. Now, all of a sudden, after all our deals are made and we're pressed like hell to get this out before the recess you people decide you want to fiddle with it."

"Look, I'm sorry. I know we haven't been much help to you and I know you asked us to come in. But this thing on public deposits is a sacred cow. If we let the s & l's get by with this, the foot's in the door; they'll use it as an argument to go after all public deposits. My people are firm. There's nothing I can do. Really. I've got to fight it."

"It's not me you've got to convince, it's the committee, and, if I were you, I would be very uncomfortable about going in there on Monday and trying to explain where the hell the banks have been for the last five months. The committee passed A.C.A. 96 last month—unanimously—and it had the same provision. They're sure going to ask you where you were then."

"I can't help it, Mike. I have to fight it. Now, we're happy to sit down and talk if you want. Maybe we can work something out."

"Is Pownall up here?"

"No, but we're meeting on this with our people Friday out at the airport. We could talk out there or Fred and I can drive in afterward."

"Well, it's hard for me to see how we can change anything at this point but I'll be flying back to San Francisco on the 6:30 that night so let's talk out there."

No sooner had I finished talking with Ratcliff than George Beattie called to tell me that "CSEA" had just called him to object to the agency's civil service exemption.

"What is CSEA?" I asked.

"The California State Employees Association."

"Didn't we get a letter from them around last November saying they didn't have any problems with the exemption?"

"No. We did get one like that from the personnel board, but they represent the administration—management. CSEA is the labor union."

"Well, why haven't they talked to us before this?"

"I don't know. They said something about it slipping through a crack in the floor. Anyway, they're big, powerful, and right now very unhappy with us. One of their guys is coming over now; can you come by in a few minutes?"

"All right. I'll be there."

We met one of the CSEA's four registered lobbyists, Keith Welch, in Chacon's office. About thirty years old, Welch was affable and apologetic.

"I still don't know how it got by us," he said. "We still wouldn't know about it if it hadn't been mentioned on the Senate floor the other day. A friend of ours was in the gallery and called us afterward. I know it's late in the game but this is something we simply have to oppose."

Beattie and I argued that the agency was going to be very small and would have an insignificant effect on the size of the civil service. Also, we insisted, the civil service regulations would make it very difficult for the agency to attract from private industry the level of mortgage finance expertise they had to have. Welch replied that the size of the agency was not relevant: CSEA was adamant that all state employees be under civil service. He also insisted that we exaggerated the difficulties of working within the civil service system.

"Is your membership limited to those within the civil service system?" I then asked. "I mean are you permitted to organize public employees who aren't in the system?"

"Yes. We're not restricted to civil service."

"Why do you care, then? We set up an agency, you come in and sign up whoever wants to join. Their dues money is good, whether they're part of civil service or not. Am I right?"

"That's true," he answered slowly, "but you see . . . it's an historical thing." And having found a toe hold he went more quickly. "CSEA fought to get this provision in the constitution years ago. We believe in civil service. Without it there's too much politics and favoritism."

I grimaced and he went on. "I know, I know, you're thinking of a small agency and I'm not saying there would be anything wrong with it. But it's a precedent and if we let you do it there are going to be others. I know how you feel but I don't make the decisions. The CSEA board—I don't think they're going to back off. Vasconcellos tried to get exemptions for his education board in the primary. It was the only ballot proposition that didn't pass and he was going for less than you are. Before that we might have taken a neutral position but we are pretty sure now we can win. You know, you can try, but I think our board will vote to fight."

"I don't know about you, George," I said, "but I'm inclined to go for it as is. It's so damned late to start changing things.

"And," I said, turning to Welch, "how can your board justify killing something like this? There are other things in that amendment besides the civil service provision that are critical to selling the bonds. If the amendment doesn't pass, you could queer the whole thing. A lot of the housing that this agency will finance is going to be for your own people. They're the ones who will benefit from it. Do you know that?"

"Mike, I don't make the decisions. Our board has to vote on it but I'm telling you I think they'll oppose you and I think they'll be willing to spend money doing it."

"Well, as I said, I'm inclined to fight it, but the decision's up to Zenovich. At this point I can't believe he'll just cave in, though he might go for a limited number of exemptions. We've got a chairman and president who would have to be exempt. The department heads too. Let's see, we figured seven of those: construction, management, loan processing, bond finance, architecture, controller, and general counsel," I said, listing as many categories as I could think of. "It's essential that they not be civil service and I am certain Zeno wouldn't go below that."

"With department heads plus chairman and president, that's nine altogether!" Welch cried. "Normally, agencies get two and the most we've ever agreed to is four. I know we wouldn't go past that. That's an absolute maximum."

"You better talk to your people, Keith. You've come in at the last minute on this thing and you expect us to suddenly change months of work. As I've said I'm inclined to stick with what we've got—an exemption for all employees. I will talk to the senator about it, though, and maybe we'll have a chance to talk before the hearing."

Immediately after Keith left, I began making phone calls to find out what I could about CSEA. I was interested primarily in what size campaign they had the capacity to mount if we did go ahead with a full exemption from civil service and they decided to oppose us in November. Within the hour I knew that they had about 120,000 members and was told that they had in the past spent $400,000 to $500,000 on campaigns to promote passage of specific ballot propositions.

I concluded that it would be very dangerous for us to have CSEA opposition in November. We would experience enough difficulty trying to sell low-income housing to an electorate already burdened with recession and inflation. On top of that, the voters were so sensitized by Watergate to charges of political favoritism and potential corruption that even a modest financial outlay might effectively cast suspicion over civil service exemptions. Assemblyman Vasconcellos had tried in the June primary, just three weeks before, to get six staff members of the California Postsecondary Education Commission exempted. Even though CSEA had taken a neutral position, that proposition was the single failure out of nine ballot measures. At the same time, CSEA was somewhat on the defensive from having come to us so late and would also be a bit uncomfortable in a posture construed as opposed to low- and moderate-income housing. Besides, the campaign for both the bond issue and the amendment would probably be sizeable, and effective opposition would cost some money. We had the makings of a compromise and the only question was how many exemptions we could squeeze out of them. I decided to let CSEA stew a bit, thinking they would be most ready to strike a deal just before the hearing on Monday.

I was anxious to meet with Pownall as soon as possible. The bankers held a strong hand. The Constitutional Amendment Committee might not be sympathetic to them but I believed the governor would be, for we had been told that Reagan had called several bankers to ask their opinions before vetoing previous housing legislation. The constitutional amendment itself did not require the governor's signature. Once passed by the Legislature, it would be placed on the ballot for voter approval, but the amendment had no significance unless there was a housing finance agency, and one of the committees we passed through had added a provision to the amendment preventing its placement on the ballot unless legislation creating the agency were passed. The banks would fight to obtain a veto of the legislation in order to stop the constitutional amendment.

The necessity of making a deal with the banks was complicated by the nature of the issue they raised and the necessity of having any amendments to S.C.A. 40 ready for presentation to the Constitutional Amendment Committee on Monday. The CSEA issue involved merely inserting a number into the text of the amendment, but any compromise with the banks would probably require some careful drafting, and Pownall might need at least a day to clear the new language with key members of the bankers association. I felt I had to strike a deal at the Friday meeting. This would leave the weekend for drafting and any contacts Pownall felt he needed to make within the association.

By Thursday night I had tentatively decided on a compromise with the banks but was not entirely confident of it. I called Bill Glikbarg, who, along with Bob, was at the subsidized housing conference in Washington.

"Bill, we have a constitutional amendment as part of the housing finance agency package," I explained, "which permits s & l's to hold public deposits. The banks suddenly woke up and now tell me that it's unacceptable. We can't have them against us when this goes to Reagan, but I don't want to double-cross the s & l's. I'm meeting with the banks tomorrow evening and my notion was to let them hold all agency funds until a construction loan is recorded. At the start of the construction the total amount of funds for a specific project could be transferred to a savings and loan association and held there as draws are made over the construction period. The banks are concerned primarily with being able to hold the large blocks of money available after a bond sale and I don't think they care that much about the construction period. The savings and loans shouldn't be too unhappy with this because usually the bonds are sold shortly before construction begins so there'll be only a brief holding period by the banks before the funds are transferred."

After asking me several detailed questions, Glikbarg said it sounded to him like a reasonable compromise.

George Beattie and I arrived at the airport by taxi the following afternoon. Dick Ratcliff introduced us to Fred Pownall, and we went into one of the airport bars. The atmosphere among us was rather strained, and when the bar maid came up no one ordered anything stronger than coffee. I knew that Pownall wanted to get the deposit language out of the bill without altering the banks' posture of non-involvement, and I guessed he had not yet had time to analyze possible compromise positions. My objective was to obtain a commitment of support from the banks or, at the least, a promise of continued neutrality. To get this I was prepared to make concessions on the deposit language to the extent I had described to Glikbarg; to go beyond that would jeopardize the support of the savings and loans.

My negotiating position was weakened by the timing of the confrontation. If we amended S.C.A. 40 to satisfy the banks, within one week we would lose all of our leverage to ensure that the banks lived up to whatever promises they made in exchange. After June 27, by which time we expected S.C.A. 40 to have been passed by the Legislature, we could not remove or alter the language we included on behalf of the banks. They would have what they wanted and we would have no way of enforcing any commitment Pownall might make to me. This kind of situation is not unusual in making political deals. Rarely do both sides to an agreement perform simultaneously, and whoever acts first must trust that the other will keep his promise. This confidence is usually based on the necessity for major political interests to maintain their credibility within the legislative arena. The banks would be reluctant to renege on a commitment to Zenovich knowing that there would be times in the future when they would need his assistance. My concern was that there was not time to get a formal commitment from the banks. The authority with which Pownall spoke for the association was limited. Official policy was set only by the association's board of directors and any accommodation I reached with Pownall could always be eroded or even repudiated by the board.

With Ratcliff and Pownall seated directly opposite Beattie and me at a small glossy-topped table, I began with much the same line I had taken when talking to Ratcliff over the phone. Now, though, I directed myself at Pownall.

"As I told Dick the other day I am very upset that the banks have suddenly decided that our housing agency package is not to their liking. As you must know, we asked them many times to be a part of the group that developed this legislation. Your people said they didn't think their interests were affected and made it clear that they did not want to be associated with a subsidized housing bill. Okay. That was fine. We went our own way and worked for nine months putting this thing together without you. A lot of dif-

ferent people have put in a great deal of time and effort. Now that
we're about to wrap it up in you come at the last minute and say
you don't like it. That's no way to do business, Fred. I don't like
it. I don't know how you can expect us to have much sympathy."

Pownall was cool and professional; he knew he was in the position of selling and played his role well.

"I know that you fellows have put a great deal of work into
this legislation and I'm very sorry that we didn't see the public
deposits provision before. I appreciate your coming to us at the
start and I know you've been very straightforward and open with
us from the beginning. We are very late coming in and I apologize.
The simple fact is, though, that this issue of public deposits is central to the difference between banks and savings and loans. We are
now embroiled in this question of the differences between our two
institutions on both the state and national level. If we give in here
they can use it against us in the larger fight. I understand why
you're upset, I would be, too. Nor do I expect you to feel sorry
for us, but we just can't live with this language."

"I don't see what I can do, Fred. After working with the s&l's
on this for nine months you're asking us to go back and within
two days reopen the whole can of worms with them so that you
feel comfortable. Really, it's hard for me to understand how you
can be serious in asking me to do this."

"Mike, I've told you it was a mistake, and I apologize for it.
Mistake or not, though, what I am saying is that the banks absolutely cannot let this go through without vigorously opposing it."

"You're not hearing me, Fred. The question isn't whether or
not the banks like it. We are under enormous time pressure and I
really don't see how it's possible to start changing the legislation in
the time we have left."

Fred did not reply. We both sat silently, each absorbed in
looking down at the table top just in front of us. We were in the
ritual stand-off almost too quickly and neither of us wished to
indicate weakness in his position by proposing a compromise so
soon. The tension rose until George Beattie broke it.

"I don't think this is an all or nothing situation," Beattie
began. "The banks certainly appreciate that the s & l's have a legi-

timate interest in handling these funds to some extent. After all, they're the principal mortgage lenders in the state and will be the ones working the most with this agency. At the same time, the s & l's can't expect to completely exclude the banks from their traditional job of holding public deposits."

"Too soon, too soon!" I thought, and looked over at Beattie uncomfortably, trying to think of a way I might break in to maintain the hard line we had established. Ratcliff then jumped in.

"Maybe you both don't realize how serious we are. The banks will fight you on this. There's the governor's desk and afterward the election in November. Those aren't going to be easy and the banks can make it very difficult for you."

This was clumsy and it gave me my opening.

"That's ridiculous! We have got every other major interest group concerned with housing behind us. Are you telling me the banks would spend $100,000 this fall to publicize their opposition to low- and moderate-income housing? Run that by the public relations guys in the major banks and they'll start waking up at nights screaming."

"You know this is a funny way to do business," I continued. "You come to us at this late date and ask for changes. One minute you apologize and then you start to threaten. I'll tell you I'm not interested in your threat of opposition. I don't believe the banks would be so foolish as to run a campaign against us. That means if you don't like the legislation, the worst I'll get is your neutrality which is what we've got now. If you're willing to come on board with us, of course, some kind of compromise might be worked out. For example . . . ," and I described the arrangement under which funds could be transferred from a bank to a savings and loan association when construction began. "I know the s & l's aren't going to go for more than that and all you have to bargain with now is your support. If you aren't willing to give us that we might as well stop talking."

Pownall and Ratcliff finally agreed to do what they could to see that a resolution supporting the bill was adopted by the bankers in exchange for my promise to amend S.C.A. 40 as I had proposed. Afterward came the spontaneous handshakes and smiles that blossom at the release of tension after a deal is made, and the four of us parted. Before boarding my San Francisco flight I made a call to Dean Cannon in Pasadena. I described the deal and said I believed Pownall was both influential and honest. I also stressed the need to avoid any opposition by the banks at the governor's desk and my belief that there was a strong possibility of getting some financial support out of them in the fall for a campaign on behalf of the bond resolution and the constitutional amendment. Cannon agreed to the deal, and I ran down the concourse to catch my flight.

By Monday, Bob had returned from Washington but was down in Los Angeles meeting with Woody Teague, other savings and loans executives, and federal housing officials on the problems of financing low-income housing. George Beattie and I met with Ratcliff and Pownall in Zenovich's office to review the amendment to S.C.A. 40 that I had drafted over the weekend. Pownall suggested a couple of changes in my language which he felt clarified but did not alter the meaning of the amendment and we quickly reached agreement on the precise wording.

Early that afternoon I left Zenovich's office to go to one of the sixth floor hearing rooms where the Assembly Constitutional Amendments Committee was to hear S.C.A. 40. I purposely arrived several minutes before the hearing started as I still had the civil service issue to resolve with Keith Welch. Bob and I had discussed the issue by phone and agreed that we could live with six exemptions, but that we were unwilling to go lower than this figure. Last week Welch and I had broken off our discussion with my demanding nine, and he insisting that four was a maximum. I was determined to get at least three of that difference of five.

Welch was in the hearing room when I got there. The hearing had not yet begun and a number of lobbyists were milling about. I went up to several to exchange pleasantries while waiting for Welch to approach me. After several minutes he came up, looking a bit anxious.

"Mike, can we talk a minute? I spoke to my boss and we might be able to go as high as five exemptions, which is more than we've ever agreed to before."

"That gives us two top executives and only three division heads," I replied. "You know, Keith, I still really don't understand it. Why are you so terribly worried about a few exemptions. I don't think that asking for the division heads is unreasonable at all."

"I'm not even sure the CSEA board will go five," he said. "I can't guarantee anything. After the Vasconcellos defeat they really feel strong. I can recommend it, but even five is really pushing."

"Well, I think the chairman of the board, who is going to be full-time, is legally exempt in any case. If we have eight exemptions on top of that it will give us what we need, but I'll go to the wall for that."

"If I really pushed, Mike, maybe I could get six. Could you do it with that?"

"They're starting now, Keith. You know, I don't think I'm being unreasonable and I don't think the committee will think so either. Let's just leave it up to them."

He shrugged and went to take a seat in the audience as the committee was called to order. After some preliminary committee business, we were up. Attendance by committee members was low. Both the chairman and the vice chairman were absent and John Vasconcellos chaired the hearing. This was to our advantage as he was not especially fond of the civil service, still smarting from the defeat in June of the ballot proposition involving civil service exemptions for the Postsecondary Education Commission, which he had supported. Vasconcellos is a liberal Democrat and inclined to favor social welfare legislation. A lawyer, he was first elected in 1966 from Santa Clara County, which lies at the base of the San Francisco Peninsula. A biographical sketch of each legislator is published in the annual legislative directory which most members use to list their college degrees and service club memberships. Vasconcellos, instead, lists:

Prime concerns: cultural assumptions about human nature and potential, their impact on self-esteem and human growth and freedom and responsibility, humanizing institutions to facilitate personal liberation, holistic/affective education, educational goals, higher education, drug abuse, searching out a new politics of personal responsibility and human community.

This is a bit heavy by Sacramento standards and I have heard Vasconcellos criticized for allowing idealism to impede his ability to develop the compromises which are so essential to being effective within the Legislature.

During our introductory presentation I called the committee's attention to the provision which permitted savings and loan institutions to hold agency funds as deposits. I indicated that we had prepared an amendment altering this provision and asked that the committee accept it. Vasconcellos then called Pownall and Mikell to the witness table and both indicated the change was acceptable to them. Despite this acquiescence or, possibly, because of it, Vasconcellos seemed perturbed. He was, I think, suspicious of such an easy, and obviously prearranged, agreement between these two groups on a major, potentially divisive issue. He also may have thought we were unwilling participants in an arrangement forced upon us by two very powerful interests. He questioned Mikell and Pownall alternately and with such vigor that I began to worry that he might refuse to accept the amendment. If the amendment did fail it would take us several days to put a new deal together, and by the time we got back before the committee it would be too late to get S.C.A. 40 out before the recess. While questioning the two men, though, he kept glancing at me and may have read the growing alarm in my expression. Finally he acquiesed, saying that if both the banks and the savings and loans were satisfied on the issue, he supposed he ought to be too.

Then the issue of civil service was raised and Keith Welch came to the witness table. As expected, Vasconcellos showed little sympathy for the CSEA position, iterating the same arguments we had used—that the small size of the agency and high degree of professionalism required provided an excellent opportunity to try out a non-civil service agency. There were, he said, occasional allegations that civil service was not as efficient a personnel system as others, and it would be interesting to create a state agency that was not subject to civil service for purposes of comparison.

Welch, who had been so good-natured throughout our dealings with him, bridled at the suggestion that civil service might be the cause of inefficiency and testily pointed to the University of California as a state-wide public institution which was not civil service and provided ample opportunity for comparative analyses. He added that comparative studies of employee productivity in the university system and other state agencies had been conducted in the past and demonstrated that there were no significant differences.

Alister McAlister, a conservative Democrat from San Jose, broke in to say that he favored whatever it was CSEA wanted. This came out in a sort of mumble and McAlister seemed very uncertain as to just exactly what the CSEA position was. This gave Welch the opportunity to say they wanted the exemptions limited to four and thereby regain the ground he had lost in our negotiations. Before he could say anything, though, I quickly explained that just prior to the hearing Mr. Welch had indicated a willingness to support six exemptions. We were asking for nine, I said, but would be willing to compromise at seven which would include one full-time chairman and six exempt employees. There were several moments of silence during which neither Welch nor McAlister, who still seemed a little confused, said anything.

At that moment George Beattie, who was seated beside me at the witness table leaned over and, placing his hand on my microphone, whispered that we didn't have a quorum.

"We need one more," he said.

"Where is Montoya?" I replied. "I thought he was here today. He's got to be for us doesn't he?"

"Yeah, I'm sure he is. I'll see if I can find him," Beattie said and left. By the time he got back ten minutes later the committee had just finished deliberating the civil service exemptions and the proposed compromise of seven seemed to have satisfied everyone, including McAlister.

"He won't come up," Beattie whispered to me. "I called him first and then went down to his office. He's there now, but he refuses to come and wouldn't give me a reason."

"Tell Vasco and see if he'll call."

Beattie walked up to Vasconcellos and after a quick conversation the acting chairman came around from behind the committee's podium to use the sergeant-at-arms' telephone. After a brief conversation, he hung up and nodded at Beattie and me. Within five minutes Montoya appeared, smilingly cast an aye vote, and disappeared immediately through the members' door behind the podium. Why he was reluctant to come and how Vasconcellos persuaded him I don't know, but he cast the deciding vote and we were out.

At the same time we were negotiating with the banks and CSEA, a third crack appeared in our supporting coalition, one which widened rapidly under the strain of trying to get S.B. 1633 to the governor's desk by June 28. Other than the savings and loans, the group which had been most difficult to win over was the California Real Estate Association (CREA). The realtors have never exhibited enthusiasm for subsidized housing. They were originally strong proponents of the state constitutional provision passed in 1950 which prohibits the construction of low-rent public housing without an approving referendum by voters of the community in which such housing is to be built, and have staunchly defended this article of the constitution (XXXIV) ever since. Their membership of predominantly small businessmen is generally conservative and understandably anxious to prevent public action which would disrupt the pattern and growth of real estate values in the state. When Bob and I first approached them in the fall of 1973, their chief lobbyist, Doug Gillies, and his assistant, Jack Shelby, had seemed hostile. In lieu of a housing finance agency they proposed a state mortgage insurance scheme limited to low-income families. We believed it had no chance of passage and suspected Gillies was using it merely as an excuse for not supporting our bill, which he knew might be successful. By the time S.B. 1633 was introduced, though, we had obtained CREA support. We were aided, I think, by the growing belief that housing finance legislation might pass even without their participation, as well as by appeals made to them by the lenders and builders, who believed that only a united front by the several industry groups could prevent the legislation from including provisions that might be undesirable to each sector of the private housing industry.

Since their conversion, Gillies and Shelby had met with us numerous times to obtain changes in the bills' language. One of their principal concerns resulted from the fact that new single-family tract homes are usually marketed by a sales staff hired by the builder. The CREA membership consists largely of independent realtors whose business is predominantly the brokering of existing dwellings. The realtors wanted to ensure that they would benefit from agency financing and urged on us provisions related to the financing of housing already in existence. We accepted several of these amendments, for the rapidly rising cost of new construction made existing homes the greatest potential source of decent shelter for low- and moderate-income families.

There were two changes they had wanted, though, which we had consistently refused to make. We had included in the bill anti-discrimination language which prevented an owner of housing financed by the agency from discriminating against potential buyers or renters on the basis of "race, sex, marital status, color, religion, national origin, or ancestry." CREA objected to the inclusion of "sex" in that list on the grounds that it would prevent landlords from refusing to accommodate homosexuals. There was some debate among Bob, George Beattie, and me as to whether this was their primary reason or whether they perceived it as a more acceptable argument than their real concern of being forced to deal with single women. Whatever their motive, we had told them numerous times that we would not agree to the amendment and that if they felt we were being unreasonable, they should take the issue up directly with Chacon and Zenovich or bring it up in a committee hearing. I recall Gillies raising it briefly with Zenovich one time to feel him out on it; getting no response, he dropped it quickly.

The other point on which the realtors had gotten no satisfaction was the language relating to eviction of tenants from apartments financed by the agency. In the case of private apartments, upon expiration of a lease, state law permits a landlord to evict tenants without giving a reason for eviction. S.B. 1633, though, provided that a landlord who had received the benefit of state agency financing could evict tenants only upon a showing of "good cause." Exactly what would be considered sufficient cause for eviction was not clear. That determination was left to agency regulations and to the courts. Whatever the ultimate definition of good cause, though, this was a further restriction on the exercise of an owner's discretion in managing his apartments. CREA includes within its membership a large number of apartment owners and Gillies had argued that, despite the limitation of the good cause requirement to projects receiving agency financing, it constituted an unwarranted intrusion by the state into the management of privately owned rental housing.

On the other side of the issue were the poverty/consumer groups, most notably the Housing Coalition (Sharon English) and the Western Center on Law and Poverty (Brian Paddock). Good cause for eviction was something they very much believed should apply generally to all landlords and they had been adamant that it be applied to housing which received state financing. They argued that shelter is such a basic necessity of life that it ought not be within the power of any private individual arbitrarily to remove another from his home. Where the federal government owns the housing or is providing subsidies, loans, or even loan guarantees, the federal courts do not permit eviction without due process of law, which must include some showing of cause for eviction by the landlord. The Western Center had been involved in several federal district court cases which specifically required a showing of good cause by landlords attempting to evict tenants from housing financed with an FHA-insured loan and subsidized by HUD. In New York, the same requirements had been extended to housing assisted by state agencies and there seemed little doubt that the courts within California would do the same if presented with a case involving housing financed by a California housing finance agency.

Bob and I had included the good cause language in S.B. 1633 with some misgivings. The legal proceedings by which good cause is established in the case of federally subsidized housing are cumbersome and time-consuming. When there are substantial delays in removing undesirable tenants, an apartment project can suffer physical damage, loss of revenue, and deterioration in the general morale of the other tenants. The interest of tenants in not being arbitrarily evicted from their homes must be weighed against the possibility that the proceedings to establish cause may result in

considerably prolonging the exposure of other tenants to such undesirable activity as drug pushing, physical harrassment or pros-
titution.

Gillies and Shelby had periodically voiced their objections to
the good cause language, but had never insisted on its removal as a
condition of their support. This posture changed very suddenly
after S.B. 1633 left the Senate. They seemed to feel that the obvious assistance the CREA letter had been to Zenovich during the
Senate floor debate had strengthened their bargaining position,
and they demanded the good cause language be taken out. The
Senate floor vote was on Tuesday, June 18, and we met separately
with Gillies, Shelby, and Brian Paddock several times during the
remainder of the week and on the following Monday. I argued
with Paddock that we really didn't need the good cause language
since it was clear that the courts would impose a good cause
requirement anyway. He replied that if that were true there was
no reason for Gillies to object to its being in the bill. When I argued
with Gillies that to remove the language would not help him
because the courts would require good cause anyway, he answered
that if the courts were going to require it, then there was no
reason to put it in the bill. His chief substantive argument against
the good cause requirement was that when tenants in federally
subsidized apartments refused to pay rent the procedure for
demonstrating good cause was so time-consuming that the tenants
often got several months of rent-free shelter before being removed.
We proposed compromises; for example, that the good cause language remain but that tenants requesting a hearing on good cause
be required to continue paying rent. But nothing we suggested
pleased either Gillies or Paddock.

During the few days over which Bob and I attempted to resolve this conflict Doug Gillies met with Zenovich and told him
that if the good cause language were removed, he would attempt
to persuade Frank Walton, secretary of business and transportation, to support the bill or at least to withdraw his opposition to
it. We knew that Walton remained one of the strongest opponents
to housing assistance in the cabinet. Gillies told Zenovich that he
had done a substantial favor for Walton during the 1973 campaign

to win electoral approval of a Reagan-sponsored ballot proposition restricting future expansion of state taxes. As his part of the deal, Gillies offered to cash in this favor on our behalf.

The showdown came on Tuesday, the day after the Constitutional Amendment Committee hearing, and the day before S.B. 1633 was scheduled for Ways and Means. Bob and I, Doug Gillies and Jack Shelby, Brian Paddock and Sharon English were all standing uncomfortably in the small reception area outside Zenovich's office. Bob had come up with several more compromise proposals and was trying vigorously, but unsuccessfully, to sell them to the protagonists. The door behind me leading to the senator's office opened and Zenovich asked me to step in.

"How's it going?"

"There's no way around it, George. Neither of them will give and we're going to have to go with one or the other. Which do you want?"

"If it comes to that, we've got to go with Gillies. I have to have him when I see the old man [Reagan] downstairs."

It was then he saw that the door was open a crack and reached over to shut it. After a few minutes more discussion I went out and guessed from the look on Paddock's face that he had heard us. If he had not, then he surely guessed the outcome; he was looking very discouraged. There was little more for Bob and me to say. We had tried every compromise we could think of and neither side had been willing to move toward any of them. We all stood there uncomfortably for several more minutes until we thanked them all for coming over and they left.

We spent the remainder of the day preparing for Ways and Means, which convened at 8:00 a.m. the next day. By the following morning we had our last batch of amendments ready for introduction. Among them was an amendment removing the good cause requirement. Ways and Means had a very heavy schedule that day. A number of authors were trying to get their bills passed before the recess. We were scheduled to be heard in the afternoon, but I took the amendments into the committee room shortly after 8:00 a.m. to be sure that Liz Kersten would have a chance to look through them if she felt it necessary. As usual during the committee hearings, Kersten was seated immediately beside Willie Brown. Since the committee was alreading hearing testimony, I had the sergeant-at-arms take the sheaf of typed amendments up to her at the podium. I waited until I saw her take them in hand and show them to Willie Brown before I turned to leave. As I did so Willie Brown interrupted the hearing with a sudden announcement.

"Whoever just brought these amendments better know that this committee is not receiving any today." Looking directly at me, he continued:

"We have too many bills in here today. There is no time for us to consider new amendments."

I was sure any protestation would do nothing but harden his position and so I simply nodded and left for Zenovich's office. Bob was there and I told him what had occurred. Our position was grave. Removal of the good cause language was only one of several amendments we had to make in the bill before it went to the governor. Some involved accommodations made for political purposes, others were to correct several small but important technical defects which had been pointed out to us by the law firms which we had had review the bill. We were sure that Brown, having once announced the committee policy, would neither reverse it nor grant us an exception. Our only hope, we decided, was that he would consent to pass the bill out of committee as it was and permit us to amend the bill in a conference committee.

If S.B. 1633 were amended in any way by the Assembly so that it passed the lower house in a different form from what had come off the Senate floor, the bill would have to go back to the Senate floor for concurrence on the Assembly amendments. Zenovich could arrange for the Senate to refuse concurrence, which would throw the bill into a conference committee. A conference committee is comprised of three senators and three assemblymen selected ad hoc to resolve disagreements between the two houses on the form of a single bill. Their members are appointed by the Senate Rules Committee and the speaker. They have considerable discretion over what they do with a bill and since we were confident that Zenovich and Chacon could influence who was appointed to the conference committee for this bill, the amendments prepared for submission in Ways and Means could be adopted in conference.

We were not sure that Brown would cooperate with such a strategy. Once he passed the bill out of Ways and Means he lost control of it, and he might be reluctant to see it leave his committee without an understanding that it was in its final form. We reasoned that the only issue presented by the amendments to which Brown might be sensitive was the deletion of the good cause language. Surely we could overcome that concern by impressing on him the absolute necessity of getting the bill out before the recess in order to get the bond issue on the ballot.

Bob and I went back to the hearing room and, catching Liz Kersten's eye, motioned that we wanted to talk with her. She left the podium and we met out in the hall, where Bob and I described the problem and asked her to see if Brown would hear the bill without amendments. She said she didn't think so but went back in while we waited. Five minutes later she came back shaking her head. Had she told him that if we didn't get out by the recess the bill would be dead, we asked? Did he understand the urgency?

"Listen," she said, "he is in no mood to do anything with that bill today. I told him what you said about having to get it out. He's not interested."

We were at a loss as we walked back to the office. How could this be? After nine months of work, having won the support of so many people, it seemed impossible we would be stopped by Willie Brown, presumably one of the strongest supporters of aid for low-income families. Was it that he didn't really understand or believe that we couldn't get on the ballot if the bill wasn't out by Friday? We hadn't specifically told Liz that Prop. 9 had necessitated moving up the deadline for submission of ballot measures. Maybe Brown, recalling previous years when submissions were accepted in August, figured our alarmist view was a ruse to pressure the bill through. If this were so, it might have increased his desire to hear the bill himself, suspecting there was something in the amendments we didn't want him to see.

On the other hand, the problem might be Chacon. Over the preceding several months a quiet but ferocious battle had been waged in the Assembly. By running for the Democratic gubernatorial candidacy, Bob Moretti had forfeited his chance to run again for his Assembly seat in November and therefore had to relinquish the speakership. This he had refused to do until after the June primary. His position as Assembly speaker had given him some added prestige as a candidate and had assured his continued access to substantial staff resources. Willie Brown was the successor Moretti had chosen. At any time prior to the June election, Moretti could have secured the speakership for Brown, for even though he was a lame duck speaker he had a shot at governor and that prospect sustained the considerable power he had within the assembly. But on June 5, having come in third behind Jerry Brown and Joseph Alioto in the primary, he had nothing to offer to anyone. He would not be governor. He would not be speaker. He would soon have no elected office at all. He had lost all of his political currency and the coalition which he and Willie Brown had built had begun to dissolve.

This is not to suggest that Brown's speakership candidacy was merely a result of Moretti's paternalism. Brown had certainly accumulated a power base of his own and possessed many qualities which made him a natural candidate for speaker: intelligence, energy, political insight, confidence, and a good measure of personal charisma. In fact, I believe if any one thing kept him from being speaker it was that he had an overabundance of such qualities. The choice of leadership within the Legislature involves a tension between the members' desire to elect those who will command general respect, conveying to the public a proper sense of wisdom and dignity, and their fear of someone who might accumulate too much power, attract too much attention to himself, and thereby detract from the importance of individual assemblymen.

Brown's opponent for the speakership had been Leo McCarthy, who was similar to Brown only in that they both were from San Francisco. McCarthy's manner was quiet, almost deferential, his voice modulated, his choice of words careful. McCarthy did not excite enthusiasm, but then neither did he spawn animosity. He was someone around whom a stable coalition could be built. There had been no thought of his leaving the Assembly, while it had been rumored that Willie Brown, if he got the speakership, might try for mayor of San Francisco. The Assembly had had its fill over the last two years of a speaker preoccupied with campaigning. The prospect of shortly undergoing another period in which both the speaker and his staff resources would be diverted from legislative business was not appealing.

When the cracks in Brown's pre-primary commitments had begun to appear, the critical block of votes became that of the black and Chicano members. Despite the opportunity to elect the first black speaker in California history, almost all of the black and Chicano members had switched their allegiance in June to McCarthy. According to the Capitol scuttlebutt, two black members had been largely responsible for the drift. One was Assemblyman John Miller of Berkeley, chairman of the black caucus. He was the Democratic floor leader just before Moretti became speaker and had been a Brown rival for some time. Miller's support of McCarthy made it easier for other black members to avoid any "Uncle Tom" stigma if they voted for McCarthy.

The other key black member was Leon Ralph of Los Angeles. Ralph was originally a Brown supporter and had supposedly been offered chairmanship of the Assembly Rules Committee. But Ralph had learned that Brown had changed his mind and intended to renege on his promise. McCarthy assured Ralph that he would get the Rules chairmanship if he changed camps. Ralph switched his allegiance and brought others along with him.

The Assembly Democratic caucus voted June 18. Brown had twenty-two votes to McCarthy's twenty-six. He refused to quit, however, and in a move very unusual for the speakership fight, Brown rallied constituent supporters from San Francisco who canvassed the Capitol corridors, confronting the minority members who had turned. Chacon was among those who had switched. Perhaps our difficulty with Brown stemmed from the fact that Chacon was a co-author of S.B. 1633.

There was another possibility. Brown might be incensed at our decision to remove the good cause language. This hardly seemed sufficient grounds on which to jeopardize the bill. But it was possible that someone had persuaded him that this was a crucial issue and we decided Paddock and English would know if this were the case. After calling their offices to be told they were in the Capitol, we found them both just outside the Ways and Means hearing room. We got them into a quiet corner of the hallway and explained what had happened: the committee's refusal of amendments, Brown's refusal to pass the bill without amendments, and the absolute necessity of getting the bill out of the committee today and passed by Friday. We also reviewed the possible reasons for Brown's antipathy, including our suspicion that someone had approached him on the good cause issue. At that, Paddock raised both his hands in front of him, wagging them back and forth as he took a step backward.

"I swear I haven't said anything to Willie since we thrashed it out in Zeno's office and I didn't ask any of our people to contact him either. Really."

Sharon English stood tight-lipped, strengthening our suspicion of her. We had to get both of them to assure Brown immediately that it was all right with them if the bill went ahead today, but to get them to do this without putting the good cause language back in would take some deal-making. We got Zenovich to come up from his office and Bob developed a proposition. If Paddock would convince Willie Brown to pass the bill out today without amendments, Zenovich would commit himself to introducing legislation in the next session which would put the good cause language back in. After getting the senator to agree, Bob proposed this to Paddock, who, along with English and several other of his consumer/poverty colleagues, walked several yards down the hall to huddle.

As we stood there waiting for an answer, I turned to George Beattie and wondered aloud whether it was possible that one of the poverty advocates had actually risked queering nearly a half billion dollars of housing aid to their clients because of this detail. It seemed especially thoughtless since it would take the agency at least a year before it was sufficiently organized to begin financing any housing and by that time, with Reagan no longer governor, there would be an excellent chance of amending the bill to put the good cause language back in. Beattie replied that the poverty advocates had developed a reputation for their reluctance to compromise and that a number of times in recent past their very principled stands had resulted in their getting nothing at all.

After about ten minutes, Paddock's group broke up and we all clustered with Zenovich. Paddock consented to appeal to Brown but only if, in addition to sponsoring a bill next year to put back the good cause language, Zenovich also promised to assist the Western Center in passing two additional housing-related bills of their choosing during the next legislative session.

The senator raised his eyebrows and puckered his lips, thoughtfully. "O.K. Yeah, I'll do it. O.K."

Feeling alive again, Bob and I went into the hearing room and motioned to Kersten. She came out into the hall, obviously irritated at our persistence. Paddock, as he promised, assured her that his people were satisfied and felt the bill should go out today. Kersten took that in and we waited, nervously walking in little circles. She returned within five minutes and said Brown's only reply was, "They're even worse than I thought."

We had one last chance. That was to have Zenovich make a direct appeal to Brown. We waited until the committee was reconvening from the lunch recess. Brown had just taken his seat behind the podium when Zenovich went up to him along with Bob, George Beattie, and myself. Chuck Baldwin, the Government Organization Committee staff member, had also come along, since he was in Zenovich's office when we left for the committee room and was someone with whom Zenovich seemed to feel especially comfortable. The senator started explaining the necessity for getting the bill out that day and Brown sat there smoldering until Baldwin happened to add a supportive remark. This gave Brown an acceptable target.

"Chuck, when you keep pushing this hard on something you make people suspicious. We've got 1634 in here today too and we'll get it out. That's the only one that goes on the ballot. I'm damned if I'm going to put out 1633 today."

Zenovich saw that Brown wasn't going to budge and by pushing harder we would do nothing but antagonize him. "All right, Willie," he shrugged, "O.K." and turned away.

Because of his willingness to pass S.B. 1634, Brown was apparently sensitive to the necessity of getting the bond measure passed and to the secretary of state before the recess. Though S.B. 1633 was the main bill that created the agency and defined its powers, the bond issue was entirely within S.B. 1634, and Brown had decided it was all that had to get out that day. Technically, this was correct. The problem was that this would require S.B. 1634 to go to the governor's desk alone, which placed it in an extremely weak position. Reagan could too easily veto the bill on grounds that he could hardly be expected to approve a half billion dollar bond issue for use by an agency which hadn't been created and whose policies and authority had yet to be determined. The slight chance that he might sign it was better than nothing, of course, but so little better that before taking it we decided to try pushing back still further the deadline for submitting the ballot measures. I went back to Zenovich's office to call Bob Stern in the secretary of state's office. He wasn't in so I talked to Hal Isenberg there and asked him to describe the schedule for printing and distributing the *Voters Pamphlet.* As I understood what he told me, to print some twelve million pamphlets and get them out to the voters before November meant the presses had to roll by August 31. Proposition 9 required a twenty-day waiting period after final type was set which required everything to be finalized by August 12.

"Why," I asked, "did you set a deadline of June 8, two months before you had to have them? I talked to Stern a couple of weeks ago and he let us off that date but acted as if July 1 were absolutely the last possible day to get ballot measures to him. You're telling me that you don't really have to have them until almost the middle of August."

"Look, I didn't set the deadline and if Stern said they had to be in this month, then you better get them in."

"We can't get out before recess. We're stuck in Ways and Means. But if you don't need it until August we'll have time after the recess."

"I don't know. Bob's in charge of the ballot measures and the pamphlet. If you need more time, better talk with him."

"Where is he?"

"He's out of town this week, on vacation. I don't think he can be reached."

We now had the choice of putting S.B. 1634 on the governor's desk before the recess or waiting until the Legislature reconvened in August to send both S.B. 1634 and 1633 together. The first option increased the probability of a veto but we were assured that, if it was signed, it would be in time to get on the ballot. By waiting until after the recess, we increased the chances of Reagan's signing the bills, but risked not getting the bond issue on the ballot. Given the schedule that Isenberg had described to us there seemed to be no reason why, if we got the bills out in the first ten days of August, they could not still make the ballot. This sounded like a better chance than sending S.B. 1634 alone to Reagan.

As Willie Brown promised, S.B. 1634 was voted out of Ways and Means that day and, along with S.C.A. 40, passed the Assembly floor the following day. We had made technical amendments in both while they were in the Assembly so both were sent back to the Senate floor for concurrence. Zenovich took up S.C.A. 40 and got it passed out. Proposed constitutional amendments do not require the governor's signature in order to be placed on the ballot, so it could be immediately sent to the secretary of state. Zenovich did not ask for a vote on S.B. 1634, but left it on the floor as part of the "unfinished business" which the upper house would consider upon its return in August.

Bob and I kept track of the floor action on Thursday, moving with the two pieces of legislation between the two houses, whose chambers are on opposite sides of the Capitol. At one point, while standing in the foyer to the Assembly chamber, Willie Brown rushed past us toward the floor.

"Excuse me, assemblyman," Bob called out, "could we talk with you for just a moment."

Brown turned and walked the few steps back to us.

"We wondered," Bob continued, "whether you could hear the housing bill on August 5, the first day you get back. It is extremely important that we get it to the governor's desk that first week."

Brown had opened his mouth to answer when, through the doorway leading from the foyer to the floor, he heard his name being called from the desk. He snapped around without replying and was gone. Somewhat to my surprise, though, he returned ten minutes later and began talking immediately as if there had been no interruption to the conversation.

"I'll hear it on the 5th, but you get the word out. I want everyone who's got any interest in this bill to see those amendments you've got. That's your responsibility. We're going to have a complete, thorough hearing on that bill before it goes to the floor. Do you understand?"

We agreed and he was gone once again.

8

The Governor Decides

"ARE YOU TWO GUYS SENATORS?" THE QUESTIONER, TANNED, with sandy hair, dressed in faded Levis, an open-necked polo shirt, and sandals, looked as if he might have just stepped out of "Beach Blanket Bingo." Bob and I were in the NBC television studios in Los Angeles watching reruns of several taped news stories on housing in California. Stu Honse, the chief staff member for Frank Holoman's Community Development subcommittee, had mentioned seeing an evening news spot on the rapidly rising cost of homeownership and shortly afterward I had called NBC and arranged for us to see it. We admitted to our curious projectionist that we were not legislators, but staff members. This did not seem to disappoint him at all, though, and he not only showed us the tape we requested but enthusiastically dug out more footage on the subject of housing which the network had recently taken but never aired.

We needed a presentation for Governor Reagan, something which during the course of a half hour meeting would provide maximum impact and impress him with the need for state housing assistance. The flip-chart we had made and which Livingston had used for the cabinet meeting wasn't adequate. Something more polished, more professional, was required and a network-produced audio-visual seemed a perfect vehicle. The content of the NBC footage was also good for our purposes. We feared that a major obstacle to Reagan's acceptance of housing assistance might be his impression that it would benefit only low-income families. While the legislation mandated that at least 20 percent of the units financed by the agency be provided to low-income families, the

161

agency would be authorized to assist moderate- and middle-income households as well. It was this latter group of working, middle-class citizens, the "silent majority" of the Nixon years, which we felt would elicit most sympathy from the governor. The NBC footage emphasized that the rapidly rising cost of single-family homes was putting the "American dream of homeownership" beyond the reach even of those earning $10,000 to $15,000 per year. It included an interview with a very appealing young family in that income bracket who had dreamed for years of owning a home. They had gone to some sacrifice to accumulate several thousand dollars for a down payment but found the prices of even very modest homes beyond their reach. This was just what we wanted, and, after some discussion, an NBC executive was kind enough to provide us with the desired footage.

The day was Tuesday, July 9, in the second week of the summer recess, when legislators return to their districts for political fence-mending, and staff members can be found in their Capitol offices sipping coffee and, in comparative leisure, poring over the mounds of reading material and paperwork that accumulate during the frenzied in-session periods. I had spent the previous week in our San Francisco office answering the pile of neglected correspondence regarding the housing legislation which we had received over the previous several months. Questions on the content of the bills, statements of support or concern, requests for amendments—all had to be answered.

We walked out of the NBC building, passing huge painted sets stored outside the auditoriums and maneuvering through the groups of tourists taking guided tours. It was an unusually clear day for Los Angeles in mid-summer. We were enjoying the more comfortable pace of the recess and, in good spirits, we took a cab downtown to speak at a luncheon meeting of businessmen. Bob and I had developed a regular "dog and pony show" for such occasions, which we had been performing now and again for the past six months before a variety of civic organizations around the state. Our presentation combined statistics on housing need in California with a description of the state housing finance organization which our package of bills would create. We had retrieved for use as our major prop the flip chart used for Livingston's cabinet presentation and by this time our act was so well practiced that the greatest effort it required from us was that of sounding fresh and enthusiastic. We doubted that a bond issue for subsidized housing could pass without a fairly large statewide campaign and we considered these presentations as not only the opening salvos of that campaign but a means of generating support among those who might in the early fall be prevailed upon to contribute money for the media expenditures so essential to reaching a mass voter audience.

After the lunch, our speechifying, and about a half hour of answering questions we left for a meeting with the *Los Angeles Times* editorial board which Bob had been instrumental in setting up. We hoped to persuade the *Times* to come out in favor of the state housing agency, for we thought that their editorial support might strengthen our case with the governor as well as serve as a cornerstone for the press support we would need for the fall campaign.

We arrived at the *Times* building about a half hour before our appointment with the editorial board and spent some time in the lobby before being conducted to a softly lighted conference room and introduced to the several editors who were arranged opposite us at a circular table. As we finished the preliminary nods, smiles, and handshakes a secretary entered to say that she had a message for Bob from Dr. Franklin Murphy (Chairman of the Times-Mirror Corporation). Whether Bob had specifically arranged for that to occur or whether it was simply coincidence I am not sure, but his ability to mention or have mentioned the right name at the right time is a specialty which I could never hope to duplicate. We did not use the flip-chart here, but our presentation was similar to that given at lunch. Figuring the *Times* to be somewhat more liberal than many of our audiences, however, we placed more emphasis on potential assistance to the truly poor rather than what the agency might do for moderate- and middle-income families. After our introductory description we answered the board's numerous questions and then left for the Los Angeles airport to catch a shuttle flight back to San Francisco.

Besides such proselytizing around the state to prepare for confrontation with the governor and to lay groundwork for a campaign on the bond issue, we had one other principal task during the recess. The *Voters Pamphlet* contains an official and presumably objective description of every issue on the ballot, a legal analysis of each issue by the attorney general, as well as "pro" and "con" arguments relating to each. How extensively and intensively the *Voters Pamphlet* is read can only be guessed, but it is enclosed with a sample ballot mailed to every voter in the state and, because of this broad coverage, must be considered by both proponents and opponents of ballot issues as a very important document. The objective descriptions, prior to 1974, had been written by the legislative counsel's office, but Proposition 9 transferred that responsibility to the legislative analyst. "Pro" arguments are usually requested from some proponent of a measure which, in the case of measures placed on the ballot by legislation, is usually the principal author of the bill. Those writing "con" arguments are either legislators who were opposed to the legislation or representatives of some major public interest group known to be in opposition. Zenovich would therefore be responsible for the "pro" arguments in support of the housing bond issue (S.B. 1634) and the constitutional amendment (S.C.A. 40). Bob took responsibility for the bond issue argument and I for the constitutional amendment.

In early July I received a call from Kathy Hardin of the legislative analyst's office, who was writing an official description of both our constitutional amendment and the bond issue, anticipating that the latter would be passed in August and would be accepted by the secretary of state. She wanted to discuss S.B. 1634 and S.C.A. 40 and on Monday, July 8, the day before our Los Angeles trip, I flew up to Sacramento to meet with Hardin and her boss, Art Peckingham. It was critical that the bond issue description they were to prepare strongly imply that the housing agency would be self-supporting. Although the bonds to be authorized would be backed by the state treasury, the state housing agency was designed to generate sufficient income to service the bonds itself. The loans it made with the bond proceeds were to be at an interest rate slightly higher than that paid on the bonds, so that the repayment of those loans would be sufficient to repay the bonds and cover administrative expenses of the agency. This is the way in which the veterans loan program had worked since 1921 and not once, even during the Great Depression, was Cal-Vet unable to cover its bond payments and administrative expenses. In the June election Cal-Vet had received an additional $500 million in bond authorization from the electorate. The official description stated:

Fiscal Impact:

The Legislative Analyst and the Department of Finance advise that adoption of this measure should result in no cost or saving to the state and local governments because the bonds as well as interest and administrative costs should be supported by payments of participating veterans.

Prior experience with similar bond issues has developed a clear history of self-liquidation and payment of principal and interest by veterans without cost to the general taxpayer. Nevertheless, these are general obligation bonds to which the full faith and credit of the state is pledged, and any failure to receive sufficient funds through payments by veteran purchasers of property would obligate the general taxpayer for the difference.

I pointed out this wording to Hardin and Peckingham, arguing that it was appropriate to treat a description of our bond issue the same way. In the case of both Cal-Vet and the housing finance agency it was impossible to guarantee solvency of the program. If there were an unexpectedly large number of defaults on loan payments and large foreclosure losses, there might not be enough income to pay off the bonds and the difference would have to be made up by general tax revenues out of the state treasury. Legislative counsel had considered the probability of self-sufficiency of the Cal-Vet program to be great enough to justify asserting that there "should" be no cost to the state and I argued that it was appropriate to describe our bond issue in the same manner.

Hardin argued, though, that while the intent to be self-sufficient was present in the structure of both programs, Cal-Vet had over a half-century of self-sufficient operation while the state housing agency was a new and untried venture. It was this proven track record which made them comfortable in saying that Cal-

Vet "should" pay off their bonds, and the absence of an operating history made them uncomfortable in giving such an expression of confidence in the case of our bonds. I pointed out, though, that state housing finance agencies existed in more than twenty other states. Such an agency had never failed to make bond payments when due and surely a California housing agency, so similar in design and purpose, would also operate successfully.

They seemed to be somewhat persuaded by my arguments and asked that I provide them with documentary evidence on the experience of other state housing agencies. Meanwhile they would prepare a draft of their descriptive paragraphs. The following day Bob and I were in Los Angeles, from where I called Kathy Hardin to tell her that I had the statistics on the successful operating history of housing agencies in other states. She told me, though, that after talking with other members of their office she and Peckingham had decided that such evidence was not a relevant consideration in assessing the probable success of a California housing agency bond issue.

On Wednesday I flew to Sacramento to review the draft descriptions Hardin and Peckingham had prepared and again made my case for language stating that the agency "should" be self-supporting. Again they seemed to be somewhat persuaded but the most I could get from them was a promise that they would discuss the issue that afternoon with A. Alan Post, the legislative analyst. I gently offered to participate in such a meeting. After some hesitation they decided that would not be appropriate but they had no objection to my meeting with Post beforehand or calling him to express my views directly.

After leaving their office I raced back to San Francisco in a state car to deliver a luncheon speech and then went over to my office to call Post.

A. Alan Post had headed the legislative analyst's office since 1949 and watched it grow steadily to a size of almost fifty budget analysts. His durability and the remarkable credibility he had among legislators resulted from an apparent determination to provide them with unbiased analyses of legislative issues. Because of his reputation for objectivity, Post's recommendations were heavily relied upon by legislators of both parties. I had hoped to talk with him before he met with Hardin and Peckingham, but by the time I reached him he had already discussed the issue with them and reached his decision. He told me that personally he believed state assistance for low- and moderate-income housing was necessary, but insisted that such a loan program would encounter financial risks greater than those incurred by Cal-Vet in making home loans to middle-income veterans. The experience of housing finance agencies in other states was not sufficient to justify as strong an implication of confidence that the California agency would generate enough income to service its bonds. I could not persuade him otherwise.

During the last two weeks of July I took a vacation, but by the time I returned to the San Francisco office on Thursday, August 1, it was as if I had never left. On my desk were the *Voters Pamphlet* descriptions of both the bond issue and the constitutional amendment by Post's office as well as legal analyses from the attorney general. The several discussions with Hardin and Peckingham had focused primarily on the bond issue description and I found no surprises in it. I was very disturbed, though, with their treatment of the constitutional amendment. One provision in S.C.A. 40 exempted housing financed by the agency from article XXXIV of the state constitution that requires local electoral approval before public housing can be built in any California community. Article XXXIV was not specifically intended to apply to activities such as those in which the housing agency was to engage. Public housing is actually *owned* by a state or local public entity while the agency was empowered only to *finance* housing that was privately owned. Nonetheless the law firms we had had review the bill advised us that since a constitutional amendment was necessary to take care of other issues such as exemptions from civil service it was worth explicitly exempting the agency from article XXXIV to be absolutely safe from any constitutional challenge. The legislative analyst's description, however, placed great emphasis on the article XXXIV exemption, implying, I thought incorrectly, that it would seriously erode the requirement for local electoral approval of public housing.

I immediately made an appointment with Post for the next morning to discuss the issue with him. Shortly thereafter I got a call from Bob Stern in the secretary of state's office.

"Mike, I don't see how we can qualify your bond issue for the November ballot. We extended our deadline several weeks to June 28 already; I can't do more than that."

"Yes, but I talked with Isenberg just before the recess and he said that you didn't absolutely have to have everything in hand until type is set August 11. Then you've got the required twenty days before the presses start on the 31st."

"But that's wrong. We have to have final type set by August 8 and the twenty-day waiting period runs before that. The absolute final day passed some time in July."

"Prop. 9 doesn't stipulate that a measure has to be passed before the waiting period starts does it? The reason for the twenty days is to give someone a chance to file suit, to prevent an issue from being placed on the ballot or to object to the description or arguments in the *Voters Pamphlet*. S.B. 1634 hasn't been passed, but anyone can read it and object to it if they want. You got our 'pro' arguments and Post's description on time. There's nothing that violates either the letter or the spirit of the law."

"They could still amend 1634, though."

"We're not going to amend it, Bob. If we do then you can throw us out, but it's going to pass with the same wording it had on the 28th."

"Are you going to amend 1633?"

"Yes, but there's nothing in that that goes on the ballot. I don't see why it matters whether it's amended or not."

"The arguments submitted for the *Voters Pamphlet* on 1634 refer to it, though, don't they? It's an integral part of the concept. If 1633 doesn't pass, there's no housing agency and no reason for the bonds."

"Well, the amendments we intend to make in 1633 don't concern any of the provisions that are in any way referred to in the arguments."

"But they *might* have been referred to if the changes had been made before the arguments were written."

"Come on, Bob, you're creating a problem where there isn't one. There's nothing that requires bills merely related to ballot measures to be in final form before the *Voters Pamphlet* goes to press. If the Legislature wanted to, it could make major amendments to the bill—even those that did change provisions referred to in the pamphlet any time between now and November."

"Okay, maybe so. I'll check with the a.g.'s [attorney general's] office."

Friday morning I flew to Sacramento to meet with A. Alan Post. I explained to him why I felt the article XXXIV part of our constitutional amendment was relatively insignificant. I urged him to change his *Voters Pamphlet* description which, I said, was not only misleading but which could be crucial in terms of voter reaction. After some discussion he seemed persuaded, but said he wished to talk with legislative counsel. If they had no objection, he would request the secretary of state to remove the offending language from the description.

Leaving Post's offices, I walked to those of the attorney general. I was offended by the legal analysis of our constitutional amendment which they had submitted for the *Voters Pamphlet*: a portion of it seemed incoherent. My appointment was with George Roth, who I had been told was the author of the analysis. After some discussion he agreed that the language I objected to was ambiguous and offered to change it. Unfortunately, the letter he dictated to the secretary of state requesting the change had to be approved by his superior. Because I wanted to hand deliver it, the letter was typed immediately and then taken away for necessary approval. After a fifteen-minute wait, instead of approval on the letter, we were told that Roth's superior would meet with us. He informed me that *he* was the author of the legal analysis I had questioned and expressed complete confidence in its accuracy and coherence. After more discussion it came out that this analysis had been approved by the superior's superior, the superior's superior's superior, and the attorney general himself—four bureaucratic layers in all. To change it would require each of those who gave the approvals to admit to his boss that he signed off on a faulty or unclear legal analysis. I had not the time nor the energy to accomplish such a nearly impossible task. The change would not be that significant to voters perusing the official pamphlet. I extricated myself as quickly as possible then and made the early plane back to San Francisco. On the way I picked up a copy of the *Los Angeles Times* and turned to the editorial page. Our meeting with their editorial board had paid off with a strong position in favor of the bill, entitled "Promise in the Housing Dilemma," which urged the Legislature and the governor to take quick action to pass the Zenovich bill.

Bob and I were back in Sacramento early Monday morning, August 5, to meet with Bob Stern. He had pushed hard on the attorney general's office he said, and had gotten them to agree that the twenty-day waiting period required by Proposition 9 could run on 1634 even though it had not yet passed the Legislature, so long as it was not amended after the twenty-day period had begun. We gave him assurances that the bill would not be changed from the version existing at the end of June and he promised to get it into the *Voters Pamphlet* if, but only if, S.B. 1633 and S.B. 1634 were passed *and* signed into law no later than 5:00 p.m. on Thursday, August 8.

"By the way," Stern said as we got up to leave, "Post called me about changing his description of your constitutional amendmend. I can't do that. After the twenty-day period begins it takes a court order."

"Surely not here, Bob," I replied. "We've got both sides agreeing to the change. There's no dispute to be settled, no reason to go to court."

"Now don't try to push me on this too. Whether or not there's agreement, nothing can be changed without a court order. That is absolutely clear from Prop. 9."

We walked back to Zenovich's office trying to figure out how we were going to get 1633 out of Ways and Means, passed on the Assembly floor, concurred in by the Senate, and signed by the governor—all before Thursday evening.

Early that afternoon we went to see Dixon Arnett, a liberal Republican who had worked for Stanford University before his election to the Assembly in 1970. As the minority whip he was a valuable ally. He not only supported our legislation but had been persuaded by Bob to lead a delegation of Republican legislators to the governor's office to urge Reagan to sign the bill as soon as he received it. Our meeting with Arnett that day was merely to confirm that he had an appointment with the governor for the next day. He said that he had and listed the several Republican members who would be going with him. We also asked him to give Chacon some help when S.B. 1633 came to the Assembly floor. Chacon had had some trouble when he carried S.C.A. 40 on the Assembly floor just before the recess. During the floor debate several questions were put to him which he had answered incorrectly. Inaccurate descriptions of legislation are not uncommon during floor debate, but Chacon's answers made S.C.A. 40 sound much more controversial than it actually was and several strenuous objections were raised. Before a vote was taken, Chacon left the floor and, after consulting with Bob and George Beattie, he solicited commitments from other members to make supportive speeches and correct any misimpressions of what the amendment was supposed to accomplish. We wanted to be better prepared this time, and Arnett agreed to speak in favor of the bill and give Chacon whatever other support he could arrange on the floor.

Arnett had some bad news for us though. The issue of state assistance to housing had been raised before the State Republican Platform Convention when it met in July. The resolution had been handled by its proponents in a clumsy manner and been soundly defeated. Although this probably would not affect the position of Republican legislators, it could give Reagan the comfort of official party endorsement if he were otherwise inclined to veto the bill. There was nothing we could do about it then, however, and we left to prepare for the Ways and Means hearing.

S.B. 1633 was scheduled to be heard by the committee early that afternoon. When I arrived in the hearing room shortly after lunch I was shocked to see John Foran in the chairman's seat instead of Willie Brown. Even though I had been told of the change previously, in the few months of my Capitol experience I had come to associate that important legislative gauntlet with Brown, and the committee seemed entirely different without him. Foran, in contrast to Brown's crisp confidence, was tense and hesitant in this, his first day in the position.

Foran's presence in lieu of Willie Brown, though strange, was comforting to us. Brown's enmity toward Chacon and the difficulty we had had with him prior to the recess made us uneasy about facing him again. Leo McCarthy, the new speaker, strongly supported our legislation and we were told that Foran, his former law partner, had explicit instructions to move the bill that day. Committee debate was very short and after only a few minutes our bill was voted out. Then it was like dominoes. The Senate convened at 4:00 p.m. and passed 1634. The Assembly convened at 4:30 p.m. and passed 1633, transmitting it immediately to the Senate floor for concurrence in the amendments that had been made in the Assembly. The Senate took up the bill almost as soon as it was received and concurred.

The speed with which the bills moved that day was the result of considerable preparation. Bob had met more than once during the recess with Speaker McCarthy, making him fully aware of the necessity for getting 1633 out immediately. We had met with the staff members responsible for briefing Foran on each of the bills pending in Ways and Means and impressed them with the necessity for speed. We also alerted the chief clerks of both houses to ensure that 1633 was transmitted immediately from committee to the Assembly floor and then from the Assembly to the Senate floor. Zenovich also spoke with both McCarthy and President Pro Tempore Mills.

Suddenly, after months of work, the Legislature was behind us. We had no time to celebrate, though. The toughest hurdle was immediately ahead; we had but two days in which to get Reagan's signature and a court order that would allow alteration of Post's description of the constitutional amendment and the "con" arguments which had been submitted on both the amendment and the bond issue. These two latter paragraphs had been prepared by the staff of Senator Carpenter and contained several factual errors. Bob had spoken to Carpenter the previous week and obtained his agreement to change any statements in his submission which were untrue. The only concern Carpenter had was potential publicity of the necessary legal proceeding. We promised not to issue any press releases relating to the court action and assured him that if we were questioned about it we would refer to it as merely a legal formality, which in fact it was.

Early Tuesday morning I began drafting the pleadings necessary to get into court. It took considerable effort to sit in the legislative counsel's law library and construct the rather dull forensic arguments knowing that Bob was bringing to a climax the campaign we had been running during the previous several weeks to stimulate a flow of letters to the governor's office urging him to sign S.B. 1633 and S.B. 1634. Bob had been successful in getting Houston Flournoy, the state controller and winner of the Republican gubernatorial primary, to write Reagan a strongly worded letter urging that he sign the bills. He also persuaded a number of other prominent business and political figures in the state to communicate their support of the bills to Reagan. The only direct involvement I had in this was a phone conversation with Bill Keiser of the League of California Cities to confirm that he had arranged for the state's two most prominent Republican mayors Pete Wilson of San Diego and John Redding of Oakland—to make supportive calls to the governor's office. He had and in doing so had discovered something else.

"Mike, I thought you told me you had maneuvered the banks into a supportive or at least neutral position."

"Yes, I made the deal with Pownall."

"Well, I just talked to John Tooker [legislative assistant to the governor] and he told me the banks called him and said they were against the bill."

"I'll check it out immediately, Bill. Thanks." I called Pownall, who was at that moment meeting with Ratcliff, and told him I had heard the banks had communicated a negative position on the housing bills to the governor's office. He assured me he had done no such thing and then asked Ratcliff whether he knew of any such communication. No, he said, he had consistently given a neutral position.

Then I called Tooker directly and asked him what the banks told him.

"They're against it," he said.

"But I just called Ratcliff and Pownall and they assured me that they gave a neutral position."

Tooker replied that Ratcliff told him that the *official* position was neutral, but that off the record the banks still didn't like it. I was angry, but the damage had been done; there was no way in which I could undo it at that point.

Besides these three calls I interrupted my hours in the library for a meeting which Bob and I had with Zenovich to prepare for his presentation to the governor. Dixon Arnett and his contingent of Republican legislators were to make their plea that afternoon, and Zenovich had an appointment with Reagan shortly after that. Bob and I had looked forward for some time to this meeting with our chief protagonist and we suggested to Zenovich a specific agenda.

"We feel a two-part meeting might be most effective," Bob began. "The first part would be about fifteen or twenty minutes during which Mike and I will cover substantive issues. We have ten minutes of film from NBC that covers housing needs in California and then we could take five or ten minutes to explain the agency's financing to take care of concerns he might have that the bond issue will affect the state's credit. It might be best if Mike and I left at that point and you could then make the gut political arguments you've got."

Zenovich was silent for maybe a half minute before he replied.

"Well, I don't know about the film. I do want Mikell, Gillies, and McCarron to come, though, and maybe we'll just go in there and see what we can do."

"Do you want us there?"

"No, maybe you guys ought to wait out in the lobby and if I need you I'll ask you to come in. See if you can get those three for me and ask 'em to be over here at four."

I was shocked at first, then worried, and finally, puzzled. Zenovich's decision to exclude us from his final pitch to the governor seemed quite sudden since Bob and I had several times spoken to him about some kind of presentation to Reagan, and the discussions always assumed our participation. It angered me because I felt he was pulling rank to exclude us from what could be the single most important meeting of our entire effort. We were quite worried, too, that our expertise would be needed if Reagan's concerns were substantive; that he might, for example, really believe the creation of a housing agency would damage the state's credit.

I recalled the description by George Beattie several months before of the relationship between legislators and staff as one of "love/hate." Legislators with competent staff personnel appreciate the extent to which it increases not only the competence of their offices to deal with legislative issues but also the prestige of their legislative position. As the sphere of public influence and thus legislative decision-making becomes increasingly complex, though, the adage "knowledge is power" is even more applicable and legislators often sense a threat from staff members to their own sphere of personal influence and self-esteem.

When Zenovich met with the governor, he wanted to ensure that it would be his show. This desire was not necessarily petty. A legislator's effectiveness depends to a large extent upon the impression of influence and power he is able to convey. The regard in which the governor holds a legislator, his confidence in the legislator's ability to help or hinder legislation, will determine the amount of concessions he may be willing to offer that legislator when he wishes to affect the passage of a bill. The ability of a legislator to negotiate such concessions from other members and from the governor is probably the most accurate measure of his power. Direct contact between the governor and most legislators is infrequent, which makes it all the more important for a legislator to convey as strong an impression as possible whenever the occasion does arise.

The governor's office is located on the ground floor of the Capitol and is often referred to by legislators as "the corner office." It consists actually of an entire suite of offices for the governor and his immediate staff and is entered through a reception room which opens, by means of large wood double doors, onto the main hallway of the Capitol's ground floor. Six months later, after Jerry Brown had taken office, I found these doors frequently thrown open and clusters of visiting school children or tourists milling around exhibits of American Indian artwork. Now, though, this physical preface to Mr. Reagan's administration resembled the reception area of a large bank. There was a sort of regal hush as the doors closed behind you, and traditional arrangements of sofas and large soft chairs were grouped about coffee tables on either side of the room. Several large landscapes in oil hung on the dark walls and lent a quiet, dignified air.

Zenovich and his entourage of lobbyists gathered in this room at 4:00 p.m. and shortly thereafter were asked by a secretary to follow her into the governor's office. Bob and I remained in the reception room nervously thumbing magazines and pacing the thick carpeting. Shortly before 5:00 p.m. our party emerged and walked directly out into the hall. I saw Bob follow Zenovich going back to the office and I stopped Bernie Mikell to get his impressions.

"I don't know Mike," he said shaking his head. "You really can't tell. He very politely listened to us and then just as politely said he hadn't yet made up his mind. I think Zeno was disappointed."

This wasn't exactly encouraging. But then he hadn't said no. And how, I wondered, trying to encourage myself, could he veto the bill now? We had every major interest group behind us, two-thirds of both houses of the Legislature, including a large number of Republicans, in addition to the Republican gubernatorial candidate whom Reagan was supporting, and a number of other prominent Republicans from around the state. In addition, I knew that some members of Reagan's immediate staff had a very personal interest in seeing the bill pass. Reagan's departure from office in a few months' time would leave them without jobs and several hoped to obtain appointments to some board or commission before he left. A position on the Workman's Compensation Appeals Board, for example, is a very desirable reward for an outgoing governor to give a loyal staff member. Such an appointment, however, requires confirmation by the Senate Rules Committee on which Zenovich sat. Senate Rules has five members, and determined opposition by any one of them, especially when he belongs to the majority party and even more so when that party is not the governor's, can be an insurmountable obstacle. Zenovich would not be inclined to favor appointment of anyone whom he suspected of working in opposition to his major legislative program for that session.

Having pumped myself back to a state of cautious optimism, I responded to an invitation from Bill Keiser for a drink and dinner. I gulped a hefty gin and tonic at his bachelor apartment across from the Capitol—the same building in which Governor Brown was to locate his mattress six months later—and then walked with Keiser down to Frank Fats'. For many years Fats' has been the favored eating and drinking establishment for legislators and lobbyists. Posey's has some share in this very steady clientele and, more recently, Ellis' has become an acceptable meeting place. As the legislative staff has grown over the past decade and governmental decisions at the state level have become increasingly important to an ever widening sphere of interests requiring professional legislative advocacy, the amount of politically related drinking and dining has become more than Fats' and Posey's can handle alone.

By the time Keiser and I arrived, both the bar and tables were closely packed, the smoky air filled with a deep inarticulate roar. We walked to our reserved table toward the back of the room and wherever I looked were faces which had stared down at me from committee podiums. They were now much animated by drink and conversation, and seemed strangely out of place.

Keiser had invited Bob, who arrived later, and a man I had never met who was a member of the state Board of Equalization. The conversation turned rather quickly to housing, but it was clear almost immediately that this gentleman did not in the least care for subsidized housing and Keiser, to avoid an argument, steered us away from that topic as soon as he could. We then started talking about Reagan and given the man's views on assisted housing, which seemed rather conservative, I was surprised to find that he much preferred Pat Brown to Reagan. Brown had been accessible, he said, you could get in to talk to him, but Reagan had turned his office into a fortress.

When we got up to leave, Bob, who had finally joined us, went over to another table to talk to Assemblyman Knox, and on our way we stopped at Zenovich's table to ask whether he had heard anything more from the governor's office. Nothing.

I spent Wednesday in a little back office of Zenovich's suite completing the pleadings for our case to change language in the *Voters Pamphlet*. I finished the documents by mid-afternoon and had Casey Young, the senator's administrative assistant, take copies to Senator Carpenter, A. Alan Post, and the secretary of state. Meanwhile I took a cab over to the Sacramento County Courthouse. I filed the documents, paid the required filing fees, and succeeded in obtaining a conference with the presiding judge in his chambers. I explained to him the necessity of the *Voters Pamphlet*'s going to print that week and urged him to hear the case no later than Friday. He was extremely reluctant to proceed with only one day's notice to opposing parties but I assured him that all the parties were thoroughly aware of the case and had already agreed to the changes. We had tried to get the secretary of state's office to change the wording without court action, I explained, but they had refused and this suit was merely a formality to assure compliance with new procedures for submission and alteration of arguments established by Proposition 9. The judge consented to calendar the case for Friday morning.

On Thursday morning Bob and I were in the office by 8:30 making phone calls to double-check on commitments which had been made to us for supportive calls to Reagan's office. The tension was almost palpable. The deadline given to us by Bob Stern was 5:00 p.m. that day, which we had communicated to the governor through Don Livingston. The day wore on, though, and we could extract nothing from the governor's office but what was obvious—that he was having a difficult time making up his mind.

Over the preceding weeks there had arisen another dimension to the political calculus of Reagan's position on the housing bill. Its effect on Reagan was difficult for us to evaluate at the time, and I have often wondered since whether Reagan had equal difficulty in dealing with it. Gerald Ford was at that moment searching for a vice-president. The ambivalence with which Reagan responded to questions from the press regarding his own possible candidacy made us no less certain that he wanted the appoint-ment. We assumed that Ford's decision would be based largely on who he believed would make the strongest running mate in 1976. This, in turn, depended on how Ford thought he would be perceived after two years in office. A conservative image would dictate the need for a liberal vice-presidential candidate to attract Democratic votes in the general election, while a moderate to liberal stance, we speculated, would require alliance with a conservative who could secure the strong conservative financial backing which the Republican party had cultivated under Nixon. We saw it as a contest between Rockefeller and Reagan.

If Reagan believed that Ford was leaning toward choosing a liberal Republican he might conceivably favor the housing bill as an attempt to demonstrate his willingness to cultivate a more moderate image. But this seemed unlikely. Reagan was too strongly identified nationally as a conservative to begin changing now, and a sudden liberal gesture would not only fail to attract support from moderates but could weaken the base of support Reagan had built among conservatives over the past eight years and on which any hopes he had for a presidential bid must rest.

How, we wondered, did these national political considerations weigh against the broad, powerful array of support we had succeeded in amassing within the state? The decision to sign the bill seemed as difficult for him to make as that to veto it. Caught between a rock and a hard place, Reagan's most attractive alternative might be to neither sign nor veto in which case the bill would, in twelve days, become law without his signature. This possibility was as troublesome to us, though, as a veto because enactment would not occur until after the *Voters Pamphlet* went to print and that would prevent us from getting the bond issue on the November ballot. This made the option unattractive from Reagan's standpoint as well. If the bill became law without his signature and yet was ineffective because of the twelve-day delay, he would attract the same enmity from proponents as if he had vetoed, and, simultaneously, he would compromise himself in the eyes of conservatives for not taking a stand against subsidized housing.

If we could somehow structure an arrangement whereby the bill could be effectively enacted without Reagan's signature, it might provide him with a means of avoiding what were two very unattractive alternatives. The day before, we had discussed with Zenovich the possibility of arranging a deal between Reagan and Jerry Brown. If Reagan promised Brown that he was not going to veto during the twelve-day period, then Brown might consent to print the *Voters Pamphlet,* including the bond issue (S.B. 1634). We saw no legal problems with this. Our main concern was that Brown would refuse, fearing Reagan might trick him into printing the pamphlet with the bond issue in it and then veto the bill at the last minute. This would require Brown to scrap the first printing, take out the bond issue, and reprint the pamphlet, resulting in great waste of taxpayer money and late distribution. It could all be very embarrassing for the Democratic gubernatorial candidate so close to the election.

The three of us had agreed, though, that it was worth a try, so early Thursday morning I had called Bob Stern to ask him to try the idea out on Brown. Stern finally called me back about 2:00 p.m. to say that Brown had problems with it and, if any deal were to be made, Zenovich would have to call Brown directly. The logistics of reaching Brown were complicated because he wasn't in his office, but Stern gave me a number where he could be reached in San Francisco over the next hour or two. I immediately took the message to Zenovich, who was in a hearing, and urged him to call immediately. I then went back to the office, assuming that the senator would notify us as soon as he finished talking with Brown.

By 4:00 p.m. there was still no word from him, and I became very nervous. To the best of our knowledge, Reagan still assumed a deadline of 5:00 p.m., and if Zenovich could reach some understanding with Brown, the governor had to be contacted about it within the hour or it would do no good. As I was going out to find Zenovich, I met Bob in the hall.

"I talked to Stern," he said breathlessly. "Zenovich hasn't called Brown yet."

We rushed up to the committee hearing room where I had last seen Zenovich, but it was empty. Following one lead, then another, we rushed along the Capitol corridors, up the stairs, then down, then up again, and as the temperature rose beneath my suit coat, so did my irritation with Zenovich. He was being too casual this time. At last we found him on the sixth floor in Senator Alan Short's office. We urged him to call Brown immediately. He dialed the number Stern had given me and soon had Brown on the line.

According to Zenovich, Brown said he would risk including the bond issue in the pamphlet only if he got Reagan's promise in writing not to veto the bill. "And the governor sure isn't about to do that," said Zenovich.

Bob and I walked downstairs to the office. After eleven months' work, there was nothing to do but wait. It wasn't long. Just after 5:30 Eleanor Anderson, Zenovich's secretary, rushed into our part of the office.

"The senator has a call from the governor. Can you get him? He's on the floor."

I raced up the stairs two at a time and reached the foyer outside the senate chambers just as Zenovich emerged from the senators' lounge. He had just been informed that the call had been put through up there and, glancing at me, he walked to one of the phone booths marked "For Members Only" and closed the small folding door.

I stood there, breathing heavily, staring after him, thinking of nothing, until he reappeared.

I knew at once the answer. It is the only time I can recall being able to read his face. He could not help but betray the disappointment.

"He vetoed it."

Walking slowly, he disappeared back into the lounge.

9

Last Chance

LESS THAN AN HOUR AFTER SEEING ZENOVICH, PALE WITH DIS-
appointment, emerge from the phone booth, I returned to his
office. The door from the small reception area to the senator's
office was half open and, hearing voices, I walked in. Zenovich
lounged in his chair, feet on the desk; seated on the couch opposite the desk, and in arm chairs about the room, were the members
of his political menage: Chuck Baldwin, Mike Valles, Casey Young
and several others—young men, all of them, sharing a kind of intimacy with the senator and among themselves that grows rapidly in
the hot climate of state politics. Some were on his immediate staff
others were staff members of committees on which Zenovich served.
Most owed their present positions wholly or largely to Zenovich
and in return gave him their loyalty. They served him as political
lieutenants, campaign tacticians, fund-raisers, speech-writers, political organizers.

I felt, as I walked in, almost as if I were intruding, for Bob and
I were never really included in this inner circle. We got along well
with them all. Whenever we asked for help on the housing bills,
they always cheerfully gave it and the few slack times we spent in
the Capitol had often been filled in one of the tiny back offices
swapping political stories with these men. But Bob and I had never
been "out in the trenches" for Zenovich, we had not made the
commitment these other young men had made for Zenovich, we
did not have a stake in his political future, and we were not
bound into the intimacy that created.

From the snatches of conversation I heard as I entered the
room, it was clear they were discussing the possibility of over-

riding Reagan's veto. Bob and I had been determined that Reagan should sign the bills and only rarely over the last several months had we allowed ourselves to consciously admit the possibility of a veto. Our reluctance to consider any post-veto strategy reflected our knowledge of how small the chances of override would be. Although a veto override requires no more than the two-thirds majority of both houses which we had already mustered for initial passage, it is set in an entirely different political context. Republicans who did not feel bound or even greatly influenced by the administration's opposition to subsidized housing could find the override of a Republican governor's veto to be an intolerable embarrassment to their party. A two-thirds majority required a substantial block of Republican votes and the difficulty in obtaining those was evident from the fact that during his eight years in office Reagan had exercised his veto power unremittingly but had been overridden only once. The broad, vigorous support we had amassed would almost certainly be enough to overcome any difficulties in the more liberal Assembly, but the Senate would be very tough.

"How does it look to you George?" I asked.

"There are twenty-two Democrats. We've got to hold five 'Reeps,'" Zenovich replied.

"We'll need more than that. We lost two Demos this last time," I reminded him.

"Yeah, but on an override Stern should go with us and maybe I can get Randy [Collier]."

"Well," I said, "we've come this far."

He looked quickly at each of the faces around the room. "Okay, what the hell. Let's go for it."

The next morning, Friday, I was the first one into the still-darkened courtroom. After arranging my papers at the counsel's table, I walked through the door behind the judge's bench and presented myself to the clerk. Several minutes later Bob Stern showed up and then a young lawyer from the attorney general's office who was to represent both A. Alan Post and Senator Carpenter. We were soon shown into the judge's chambers and waited several minutes before he entered. We then explained the nature of the case, emphasizing the absence of any real dispute. He put several careful questions to each of us, and having satisfied himself that all of us were in agreement as to how the language in the *Voters Pamphlet* should be changed, he consented to the amended language. First, however, being a careful man, he insisted there be a brief appearance in the courtroom to assure an adequate public record. Five minutes later he was seated at the bench in robes and we three lawyers were at the counsel's table giving a brief formal presentation.

Our only audience was several reporters, and one of them, from the *Sacramento Bee,* stopped us as we were leaving the courtroom.

"All right," he said skeptically, "now tell us what really happened here."

"Disappointed, eh?" jibed Bob Stern.

"You heard all that there was to it," I said, as we walked down the hall. "There were some errors in arguments submitted for the *Voters Pamphlet.* Everyone agreed to the changes. We came to court only because it's required procedure under Prop. 9."

They seemed unconvinced that there wasn't more juice in the affair but they had nothing else to go on and we had neither the time nor the desire to try to persuade them.

Bob Klein arrived as we were leaving and was surprised that our appearance was over already. The four of us walked the several blocks back to the Capitol. Conversation was light and masked a concern which both Bob and I felt about the additional time which the override effort was going to take. It was Friday, August 9, already past the deadline which Stern had set and we still needed several more days. We did not discuss the problem in front of the attorney general's staff member because the printer's deadline offered Reagan a very neat way of avoiding any possibility of override. An override vote could not be taken until after the formal veto message had been received by the Legislature. The insistence by Bob Stern that he had to have a signed bill by 5:00 p.m. on the eighth had forced Reagan to take action the night before or risk being accused of cowardice in letting that deadline serve as a de facto veto. But even if we succeeded now in pushing the deadline back, it could only be for a few days and the governor could quash any attempt at an override merely by delaying transmission of the veto message until after the *Voters Pamphlet* had gone to press.

The attorney general's representative who walked beside us may have been oblivious to the relevance of an extension of the secretary of state's deadline, but we could take no chances, and it was not until after we parted with him on the street that Bob and I began pressing Bob Stern to give us a few more days. Zenovich had told us that in his phone conversation with Jerry Brown the night before Brown had said the presses did not have to start until next Wednesday, the 14th. We followed Stern back to his office using this information in our plea for more time. He replied that while the presses didn't actually start running until the 14th, the printer had to have a few days to get the type set and the layout completed. We insisted that he could set the type and do his layout as if the housing measures were going to be included. No, was the rebuttal, if the pamphlet were set up for printing and at the last minute the housing bond issue and constitutional amendment were withdrawn, it would mean several blank pages right in the middle of the pamphlet. Why couldn't they be put at the end of the pamphlet? If the override were not successful, the printer could just take them out and several blank pages at the end of the pamphlet wouldn't be noticed. Stern then tried to argue that this would result in additional cost, but given the importance of the bill he knew that was a weak reply. Besides, I think he personally favored state housing assistance and was also aware that Jerry Brown would not like to be accused of having aborted a major housing program for low- and moderate-income families because of slightly increased printing costs.

After we verbally pummeled poor Bob Stern for half an hour, he finally relented, warning us as we left that the 14th was an absolute deadline.

With hopes alive once again, we returned to the Capitol and were walking along the first floor corridor on our way to Zenovich's office when Bob abruptly turned into the treasurer's offices. I followed and heard him ask for Don Moore, with whom we had worked closely on a number of technical financial provisions while drafting the bill. We were immediately shown into Moore's office and, while I was still wondering why we were there, Bob started arguing with Moore that the treasurer had used fallacious arguments in attempting to persuade the governor to veto our bill. Immediately after the call from Reagan to Zenovich the night before we had begun trying to determine who had advised the governor to veto. The story we had pieced together by that time was incomplete and not entirely reliable but it included a concerted effort by the treasurer, Ivy Baker Priest, to get a veto. We had been told that she called the governor to insist that creation of a state housing agency with the authority to issue bonds would lead to erosion of the state's credit rating. She had used New York State as an example, pointing out that several years after creating the first state housing finance agency it had suffered a lowering of its credit rating from AA to A, and alleging that such a rating change would not have occurred but for the sale of bonds by the New York housing agency.

Moore stopped Bob almost immediately, saying we should talk instead with Alex Steinkamp, Mrs. Priest's deputy. Five minutes later we were in Steinkamp's office and Bob started over again, insisting that the New York housing agency had nothing whatever to do with the decline in New York State's credit rating. He had brought a clipping with him which documented that when New York State's credit rating was lowered to A, that of the New York State Housing Finance Agency remained at AA because its financial position was judged to be stronger than the state's. Steinkamp refused to discuss the issue in any specifics. He would neither confirm nor deny that he and the treasurer had used New York as an example in conversations with the governor. He vigorously defended the veto decision on grounds of his conclusion—based, he said, upon decades of experience with the financial markets—that a housing finance agency would jeopardize California's credit.

Even the most conservative financial analysts we had consulted did not believe a state housing finance agency would damage the state's credit. New York had been compromised not as a result of borrowing by the state housing agency but because it had exercised almost no discipline at all in creating a profusion of different state agencies which had authority to issue bonds. This resulted in a huge debt load that had come perilously close to exceeding the state's ability to service it. The following day I spoke with Merrill Ring, a vice-president of the Bank of America who is an expert on municipal bonds and has closely followed California's bonding activity for many years. When I told him of Steinkamp's arguments, he replied that given the state's present financial position, a half billion dollars in additional general obligation bonding authority to finance housing could not affect the strength of California's credit in any significant way.

Bob and I did not attribute Steinkamp's arguments to his ignorance of the bond market, but instead suspected that he used the issue of the state's credit as a stalking horse for the real objections which the administration was reluctant to state publicly. He provided some evidence of this by implying that if we had limited the eligible beneficiaries of the program to elderly persons the bill would not have been vetoed.

Whatever the reasons for the veto, however, they were now immaterial to our remaining chances for passage. If we received the veto message in time, the only relevant issue would be whether Reagan could flex enough political muscle to prevent the embarrassment of an override. If the governor could not control thirteen members of his own party in the Senate it would show a lack of political strength which at this time could cost Reagan an offer for the vice-presidency. Bob knew of course that arguing with Steinkamp could in no way help us now; even if Alex Steinkamp and Ivy Baker Priest had been instrumental in obtaining the veto, and even if we could magically reverse their opinions, nothing they said to Reagan now could have the slightest effect on the vigor with which an override attempt would be fought. Neither housing, nor the state's credit, was at issue any more; the political impact of having a veto overridden would be the administration's sole concern. Bob had led us into Steinkamp's office out of sheer tenacity: he just couldn't bear to let the veto pass without getting in a few last licks at those we believed responsible for it.

We left the treasurer's late in the morning. That afternoon, August 9, we received the veto message addressed to "The Honorable Members of the Senate."

Greetings:
I am returning without my signature Senate Bill No. 1633 entitled "An act to amend Sections 37931 [sic], 37032, and 37033 of, and to add Division 31 (commencing with Section 41000) to, the Health and Safety Code, relating to housing, and making an appropriation therefor."
S.B. 1633 would create a California Housing Finance Corporation. This quasi-public corporation would have vast powers and would be authorized to make loans for housing purposes through private lending institutions. Funds for the loans would come from the sale of State general obligation bonds.
Though I recognize the need for increased housing—especially for low- and middle-income Californians—this bill has serious defects and would substantially alter the state's fiscal policies.
California is one of only fourteen states which have the highest possible bond credit rating—AAA. One reason for this, according to Moody's Investor Service Credit Report, is that "The state does not use its credit to back agency obligations." This policy would change with the creation of this new agency and the State's credit rating would be placed in jeopardy. In fact, based on the amount of California bonds outstanding, the drop in rating could cost the taxpayers as much as $100 million in added interest.

The letter went on to mention several other alleged deficiencies in the bill, but the principal justification for veto was based on the credit rating argument. After all the explaining we had done, after all the research concerning potential effects on the state's credit, it was difficult to be presented with a veto message that was so completely inaccurate. Even the statement "S.B. 1633 would create a California Housing Finance Corporation" was not true. What the bill did was authorize inclusion on the November ballot of a measure which would create such an entity only if passed by a majority of voters. This was a critical distinction and we had frequently emphasized to the governor's staff that all we were doing was giving the people a chance to vote on the issue. The fairness of allowing the electorate to vote on major issues was a position which Reagan had used vigorously a year earlier in obtaining a special statewide election for a far-ranging tax limitation plan that was to be the capstone of his eight-year reign as the country's leading conservative governor. The plan had been sound-ly defeated at the pools. We were asking only that housing assis-tance be given the same chance at electoral approval, and it was disturbing that what S.B. 1633 actually did was so completely distorted by his veto message.

The statements regarding the state's credit rating were also in-furiatingly false. Moody's credit report was accurately quoted as stating that California "does not use its credit to back agency obligations." But it was wholly untrue that the creation of this housing agency would change that policy. The agency was not au-thorized to issue any bonds of its own, with or without the back-ing of state credit. The legislation provided only for a referendum to be placed on the November ballot which, if passed, would per-mit the state to sell an additional $500 million in bonds and make the proceeds available to the agency for the purpose of financing housing. What Moody's applauded was the fact that California, un-like other states, had not offered to provide backing for obliga-tions of state agencies which could issue bonds without any con-trol by the electorate. The legislation did precisely the opposite of what the veto message claimed. It did not change the state's bond policy but used exactly the same method of raising funds for low-income housing that the State had used to finance Cal-Vet housing since 1921.

My anger in reading the letter was considerably reduced by the relief of simply receiving it. The fear that Reagan might complete-ly forestall any attempt at a veto, by not delivering the veto mes-sage until after the printer's deadline, was gone. The veto message was all we needed to proceed with the override attempt, and I flew back to San Francisco that evening with renewed determination.

The following Monday, August 12, Bob and I were in Zeno-vich's office by 8:30 a.m. We had two days in which to orches-trate the veto override. I recall being warned at that time that the one Reagan veto that had been overridden was the first override in California since 1946! That had occurred the previous January on a bill requiring legislative approval before closure of any state hospital. The override followed a month of intensive political groundwork by Assemblyman John Burton, who was at the time chairman of the Assembly Rules Committee and Democratic state chairman. To have any chance of accomplishing the same feat— and accomplish it before the printer's deadline that Wednesday— would demand, at the very least, the full support and careful co-ordination of all our supporting interest groups.

We began that morning on the telephone, trying to arrange two meetings with all the various lobbyists, one in the late morning and a second in the early afternoon. The morning session was to include public and nonprofit groups such as the League of Women Voters (Kay Knepprath), the Western Center on Law and Poverty (Brian Paddock), and the League of California Cities (Bill Keiser). In the second we would have the savings and loans (Bernie Mikell), the builders (Paul McCarron), the realtors (Doug Gillies), and other industry representatives. The reason for dividing our supporters into two groups was the need to assure a frank discussion of tactics. We needed to know from each lobbyist which legislators he felt he could be most successful in influencing. This is rather sensitive information, to be disclosed, if at all, only among friends, and our bill was one of the few behind which the industry and nonprofit groups found themselves allied. They were frequently—almost invariably—opponents on other legislative issues and would be reluctant to disclose their strengths and weaknesses in front of each other.

Several phone calls made clear that a morning meeting was not possible. Several of those we intended to include would not be free until after lunch. This gave us the alternative of having a single meeting or holding a second meeting later in the afternoon. We decided that time was too precious and set up a meeting to be held in Zenovich's office at 1:00 p.m.

We invited every lobbyist in Sacramento who had given us support over the past six months and by 1:30 Zenovich's office was full of those faces which had become so familiar to us. The senator was en route from Fresno and due any moment, but we felt we had to get things started. Bob began by reviewing the last Senate floor vote on S.B. 1633. He emphasized the necessity of getting Stern and Collier, the only two Democrats who had voted nay, and the need to hold on to five of the seven Republicans who had been with us.

When Bob finished there was an uncomfortable pause finally broken by Bernie Mikell.

"Bob, you and Mike have got to realize that I am presently working on God knows how many other bills. Everyone else in this room is in the same position. We have worked with you guys all the way, but there are just so many times we can ask a member for his vote."

I had watched Doug Gillies walk the perimeter of the room while Bob was talking until he stood behind Zenovich's desk. He seemed perturbed and spoke with a sharp tone.

"You don't know how much you're asking. It isn't worth our while to put out for this unless there's a hell of a good chance for passage. I'm not and I don't think anyone else here is going to commit himself unless Zeno assures us that he's got at least twenty-four votes right now. If he does, we'll break our backs getting the last three, but if he needs more than that the chances are too small. It isn't worth the effort."

"Besides," added Denny Kennedy (mortgage bankers), "with due respect to the ladies" (he looked at Kay Knepprath and one of her colleagues), "I am sure as hell not going to make any specific commitments so long as they're in the room. We're on opposite sides of everything else."

It was finally agreed that the meeting should adjourn to allow each of the lobbyists to compile a list of those members with whom each thought they could be most effective. Before 4:00 p.m. they would, individually, stop by the office to see Zenovich privately. Upon his assurance that he already was certain of at least twenty-four votes, they would commit themselves to work on specific members.

When the lobbyists began to drop by the office around 4:00, Zenovich told them of his decision, which shocked even us, to bring the bill up that afternoon. The senator knew there was no real chance for passage at this time since Ralph Dills and Alan Robbins, both Democrats, and both sure votes, had submitted notices of absence for that day. Zenovich wanted to have the roll called, though, in order to find out for sure which Republicans were willing to go with us. I hastily wrote out a speech and handed it to Zenovich as he left for the floor about 4:30. He read it verbatim to begin the debate, replying point by point to the principal arguments of the veto message.

The governor states that the state should not use its credit rating to back agency obligations.

This legislation does not result in a backing of agency obligations. The revenue bond bill which provided for such a financing scheme was wisely kept in the Finance Committee. This legislation uses the same financing technique —general obligation bonds—which has resulted in this state's AAA credit rating. Controller Flournoy, who sits on every statutory bond committee in the state, has given public assurance that this legislation would result in no adverse financial impact on the state.

The governor states that this bill would not assist low-income families.

This is incorrect. HUD has informed us that a housing agency in this state would be eligible to receive a priority allocation of Section 8 subsidy funds. These subsidies, used in conjunction with state financing, provide the most substantial assistance for housing low-income families available from any source today. A state housing agency would have access to a sufficient amount of these subsidies to place low-income families and elderly in 20 percent of the units they finance. This is the maximum percentage of low-income households that can be housed in a single housing development without incurring the social and economic problems of low-income household impaction.

The governor expressed concern about the state absorbing risk for private financial institutions.

This issue was dealt with at length in the Legislature. Provision is made for the agency to loan its money to financial institutions under terms and conditions that require relending of that money only to qualified low- and moderate-income families. The financial institution holds the mortgage security on the property and bears 100 percent of the risk. In the alternative, the state agency may just use the services of a mortgage lender and hold the mortgage itself. In this case the state agency is authorized to purchase private mortgage insurance and in that way imposes the risk on the private sector. This arrangement is precisely similar to that which the Federal Home Loan Mortgage Corporation has used so successfully for years.

The governor states that the state agency might compete with private mortgage lenders.

The entire bill was structured to prevent this. Except in cases where federal subsidies are involved all loans must be made through financial intermediaries. Mortgage lenders themselves back this bill. We have worked very closely with and have the strong support of both the California Savings and Loan League as well as the mortgage bankers.

The governor expresses concern with nonprofit sponsors receiving loans covering 100 percent of costs.

This issue was dealt with very carefully in committee and received special attention from Senator Grunsky. One hundred percent loans are available only in very limited cases to finance housing for the elderly and only to non-profit sponsors who have substantial records of successful development.

The governor states that there is insufficient financial and legislative control of the agency.

This legislation requires that an annual report be made to the governor, the state treasurer, and the Legislature. In addition, it must submit a report to the Joint Legislative Audit Committee and the Joint Legislative Budget Committee who must, in turn, submit a report on the agency's activities to the Legislature. There are detailed provisions indicating what those reports must include such as the number of units assisted, the incomes of households occupying assisted units, the monthly rentals charged, the sales prices of housing financed, and numerous other data. Finally, the corporation must have a thorough audit of its books done every year by a certified public accounting firm.

The last point in the veto message is that the legislation does not have strong enough conflict of interest provisions.

The conflict of interest provisions for members of the board and employees who will manage this agency cover almost three entire pages of the bill. They are extremely specific and constitute tighter and more stringent conflict of interest safeguards than have been applied to any other state agency or commission in existence.

After this the senator extemporized, emphasizing that the effect of the veto was to deny the citizens of California an opportunity to vote their preference on this major public policy issue. If the electorate did not want the state to subsidize housing, it could simply indicate that at the polls. A vote against the bill, Zenovich argued, was a vote of no confidence in the state's electorate.

Senator Bradley from San Jose was first to speak in opposition. Deukmejian then spoke against it, as he had each time before. Zenovich had been careful to line up several speakers in favor, the most articulate of whom was George Moscone. The roll was called, the vote announced—twenty-four ayes, thirteen noes—and Zenovich immediately moved to reconsider the vote. Only a majority vote is required to obtain reconsideration on the same day the motion is made or on the succeeding legislative day. It is considered a courtesy and Cusanovich from Los Angeles cast the only no vote. S.B. 1634 was brought up immediately afterward. Zenovich briefly explained that the bill was tied directly to S.B. 1633, that it put a $500 million bond issue on the November ballot, passage of which was required before the housing agency in 1633 could be authorized. The vote was twenty-four to twelve and reconsideration was granted.

A comparison of this outcome with the Senate vote on S.B. 1633, which sent the bill to the governor on August 5, indicated where our efforts over the next twenty-four hours had the greatest chance of success. The August 5 vote had given us twenty-seven ayes—the minimum we had needed then and what we needed now. Stern had voted aye this time leaving Collier as the only Democrat in opposition. We had held on to five Republicans: Behr, Grunsky, Marks, Nejedly, and Stevens. We had lost only two: Craig Biddle and Jack Schrade. Both Dills and Robbins, who had been absent, were strong supporters, so with full attendance we had twenty-six votes—only one short. The twenty-seventh seemed most likely to come from Collier, the lone opposing Demo, Schrade, or Biddle, the only Republicans who had turned.

Leaving the floor, we met a knot of our supporting lobbyists clustered just outside the door to the Senate chamber's foyer, beyond which only members, their guests, and staff may pass. Zenovich had shown them more strength than they expected and as we all caucused there in the hall with the senator, they eagerly agreed to do whatever they could before the next day's session. In addition to Biddle, Schrade, and Collier, assignments were taken for John Stull and Howard Way. While the latter two were doubtful converts at this point, Stull had voted for 1633 the first time through on June 18 and might be brought back into the fold. Way had voted consistently against 1633 and was the least likely. If we could just get one of these two it would give us some insurance against the possibility that either Biddle or Schrade could not be brought around or one of the Republicans who voted for us today would crack under the considerable pressure the governor could be expected to exert on the five Republicans who had stayed with us.

We got back to Zenovich's office about 7:00 p.m. Earlier in the day Bob and I had made a number of calls to people we knew in various parts of the state who might give us some help with particular members. One of these, for example, was a good friend who was close to the top management of a large lumber company. Collier's senatorial district includes large tracts of commercial timber in northern California and the logging industry is a substantial part of its economy. A state housing agency would inject capital into the residential construction industry by providing low-interest mortgage financing. This would increase the demand for lumber and thus benefit Collier's constituency. It can be difficult to arrange this kind of thing in the very short time we had and I spent considerable time on the phone trying to make sure that Collier would be contacted before the next day's session.

Bob and I spent the night, as usual, at the "Cosmo" Hotel and by 8:00 a.m. were back in Zenovich's office. The tension built inexorably over the next ten hours. This was it, our last shot. Shortly after 9:00 we crossed Senator Way off our list of possible votes. We were told that a close acquaintance whose opinion Way valued had called him to urge that he change his vote to support the override. Way told him that as a Republican he could not consider overriding a Republican governor's veto under any conceivable circumstances. This was not an encouraging start for the day. What I found most difficult, though, was the waiting. Bob and I had by that time exhausted all of the means we knew of to affect the vote. There were a few phone calls to make to confirm whether or not our supporting lobbyists had been able to contact the members they had committed themselves to see, but by mid-morning I found myself nervously, purposelessly pacing. I decided at last to go up to the third floor for a shoeshine.

When I got there Paul McCarron was sitting in one of Earl Reeves' two chairs. We hadn't spoken since our run-in three months before.

"Any news, Paul?"

"Well, I talked to Whetmore, but he said his people just wouldn't stand for it."

"Did you see Biddle?"

"Yes. Or, well, that is, I talked to Gillies and he says Biddle is 'no.'"

His shoes finished, he lowered his bulk carefully off the raised chair, dipped into his pocket for Earl, and then rotated slightly toward me to nod goodbye. I had never determined how it was I had slighted him, but his parting nod told me I was forgiven.

I hurried back to the office, where Bob told me that the lobbyist contacts of Schrade and Stull had been negative. I told him what McCarron had said about Biddle and we became desperate for something more we could do. Our nervous pacing took us in short aimless excursions into the hall and on one of these Bob saw Senator Marks standing just outside his office at the end of the corridor. As he was probably the strongest Republican supporter of housing in the Legislature, we thought he might provide us with advice on how to persuade his troublesome Republican colleagues. We stopped him in the hall and, just as Bob began describing how we stood, Marks caught sight of Senator Dennis Carpenter emerging from his office, which was between Marks' and Zenovich's. Marks clearly did not want to be heard and immediately retreated into his suite, taking Bob and me with him. Then, while Marks sat at his desk, we reviewed with him the several Republicans who seemed most likely to be persuaded, assessing their probable bases of campaign support, how conservative their constituency was, their relationship with Zenovich, and how close they were to the administration.

Because of the short time remaining, we could not hope to have any impact on the vote unless we concentrated on just one member, and, as we talked to Marks, it became clear that Biddle was our man. His career had been comprised almost entirely of public office. After Occidental College, he graduated from the University of Southern California School of Law in 1956. Two years later he was in the Riverside County district attorney's office, where he was a public defender when he ran successfully for an Assembly seat in 1965. He was re-elected three times and then, following the resignation of Senator Gordon Cologne in 1972, ran for his seat in a special election. He had been chairman of the Republican Central Committee in Riverside County but was generally considered to be a moderate with no particularly strong ties to the Reagan organization. Riverside and San Bernardino counties include a substantial number of elderly and moderate-income families that would be benefited by state housing assistance, and we presumed that was why he had voted for the bill consistently until now. Also, he was facing an election that November and was expected to have a very tough fight against Bob Presley, a Democrat and undersheriff of Riverside County. Marks calculated that Biddle was in need of financial support and could ill afford to antagonize the array of interest groups backing our bill.

Also important to Biddle was Zenovich's friendship with Bob Presley. I have said that Zenovich was a major figure in the Senate and a major source of his influence results from the fact that he is very secure in his own district. The confidence that he will be a legislator for years to come makes him a formidable opponent and valuable ally. His colleagues know he will be in Sacramento long enough to ensure settlement of all his scores: to reward those who aid him and punish those who refuse. The more effective a legislator is, the more valuable he is to interest groups who are able to obtain his support for their legislative ideas, and the more willing they are to provide campaign support in order to obtain access to him. With secure districts, though, legislators like Zenovich can assure their re-election with a very modest campaign. This leaves them with time, energy, staff resources, and money which they can use to assist or oppose other candidates. Biddle had been afraid that Zenovich would help Presley in the coming election, for it was just such assistance that might easily tip the scales in a tight race. Biddle had negotiated a "non-aggression pact" with Zenovich and Zenovich's threat of withdrawing this could be used to pressure Biddle.

Bob and I were not sure Zenovich would play this card. We had urged him twice since the previous morning to call Biddle and he was clearly reluctant to do so. Maybe Zenovich had received something from Biddle—some promise of future assistance or co-operation—in exchange for the promise of non-aggression. Maybe Biddle had committed his vote to Zenovich for president pro tempore. If Zenovich threatened to call off the non-aggression pact and Biddle still voted against us, Zenovich would have to carry through on his threat. There are few things more damaging to a legislator's effectiveness than to be known as someone who does not make good on promises, for promises constitute the chief political currency within a legislature. But if Zenovich helped Presley, and Presley lost, Biddle certainly would not help Zenovich in a pro tempore fight. Bob and I believed that Zenovich was within one or two of the twenty-one votes necessary to oust President Pro Tempore James Mills and that Biddle's vote could be critical to Zenovich's chances.

If this were true, Zenovich now faced a very difficult decision. The ultimate cost of threatening Biddle would depend on the probability of Biddle's ignoring the threat and voting against the override anyway. If he did this, the non-aggression pact would be off and Biddle would almost certainly vote for Mills if Zenovich asked for his pro tempore vote. Zenovich would therefore probably have to wait until after the November election for a pro tempore bid in hopes that, with his assistance, Presley would win and that the rest of his support would not be eroded by the elections. The calculus was even more complex than this, however, because Zenovich was not simply weighing his desire to get an override against his ambition to be president pro tempore. If he played safe and didn't threaten Biddle, he didn't risk losing that important vote, but it reduced the chances for an override, which itself could greatly increase both his stature and the probability—almost to a certainty, I judged—of his becoming pro tempore.

Bob and I did not discuss with Marks these possible pro tempore calculations. What we wanted was to ease Zenovich's burden by getting Marks to call Biddle and try to persuade him. The difficulty was that Marks did not have anything to gain personally if the override were successful and he was understandably reluctant to indebt himself to Biddle by asking a favor which only helped Zenovich.

"No," Marks replied while relighting his cigar, "there's no sense in me calling Biddle. It would just get me between the two of them. Get Zeno to call him."

"We've asked him," Bob answered, "several times, but he says he's waiting for Biddle to call him."

Marks speculated that either Zenovich knew what political concession Biddle would demand in exchange for his vote and did not want to give it, or that he believed he could override without Biddle's vote. In any case he was sure that Biddle would not commit himself before the session that night. If he had not already made a deal with the governor, he would wait until Zenovich had twenty-six votes. Then, when he had maximum leverage, when he was the difference between winning or losing, then Biddle would start negotiating.

We walked back to the office discussing the possibility that Biddle had already made a deal with the governor. We had been told earlier that Gordon Luce, Republican State Chairman, was making calls to Republican legislators from his San Diego office urging party unity and stressing that an override could jeopardize Reagan's chances for a vice-presidential appointment. I was also told that Frank Walton had received two calls the night before from Republican legislators who had asked how much a no vote was worth to the administration. Reportedly, Walton refused to make any deals. Why would Walton refuse to make a deal? Had they already gotten votes that we did not know about?

If Biddle had made a deal with Reagan already, there was little we could do. If, in order to extract the maximum amount from Zenovich, he planned not to commit himself until the last minute, this presented a severe problem with Senator Dills. Robbins and Dills had been absent the day before and we needed them for the twenty-fifth and twenty-sixth votes. Robbins was back, but Dills was still in Albuquerque, New Mexico, where he was to be honored that night by the National Society of State Legislators. Zenovich had called him the night before to tell him about the results of the first vote and emphasized how crucial his presence might be. Understandably, Dills was reluctant to come unless Zenovich could assure him that he was the twenty-seventh vote, but if Biddle was playing a waiting game Zenovich would not know this until it was too late to get Dills back for the vote that night.

By the time Bob and I returned from Marks' office it was late morning and the Senate went into session at 4:00 p.m. We made reservations for Dills on a flight leaving Albuquerque at 2:20 p.m. Pacific Coast time, connecting in Los Angeles with a flight to Sacramento. The best estimate we could get of cab time from the Albuquerque Hilton, where Dills was staying, to the airport was twenty to twenty-five minutes. Allowing five minutes to put through a call to Dills and for him to catch a cab, plus five minutes as a contingency, we figured 1:40 p.m. was the last possible minute Zenovich could decide to ask him to return and still get him back by commercial airline in time to vote.

It was almost noon and the excitement of the impending vote had drawn a number of people to Zenovich's suite. The regulars were all there: George Beattie, Casey Young, Mike Valles, Stu Honse, besides several other staff members and friends who had helped us at various times. Someone said, half jokingly, that we should find some rich Democrat with a private jet and get him to fly Dills back. The suggestion was taken seriously by several, and after a few minutes discussion, Bob and someone else were on the phone to follow two possibilities. As they were calling, George Beattie began laughing and said he had just had a great idea—we should try to get the governor's jet. I grabbed a phone and made several calls trying to find the office responsible for scheduling Reagan's plane, which the state leases for his use. A secretary told me that the man in charge was out to lunch but would call me as soon as he returned. By the time I finished, the other two leads had been exhausted without result.

Bob and I went into Zenovich's office and briefed him on the means of getting Dills back. We gave him the 1:40 p.m. deadline, by then only little more than an hour away, and said there might be a chance of getting some kind of private aircraft if a decision couldn't be made by 1:40. We could do nothing more to push Zenovich. He would play Biddle however he thought best.

Shortly after 1:00 p.m. I got a call from Don Livingston.

"Hello, Don."

"You have some gall."

"About what?"

"I just got a call saying that you want the governor's jet for a trip to Albuquerque."

"I asked about it. I understood that the plane is available for lease by legislators and other state officers when Reagan isn't using it. Is he using it tonight?"

"No, damn it, he's not using it, but you've got a lot of nerve leasing it to bring back a member to vote on an override."

"I'm sorry you feel that way, Don. We may have a need for it, though, and I would appreciate knowing how to arrange that."

There was a short pause before he answered very determinedly. "All right, I'll show you how open we are. You can call . . . ," and he told me how to make the lease arrangements.

I was encouraged that Livingston was upset at the prospect of our bringing Dills back. In counting his votes Reagan may have assumed Dills would be absent and stopped short of making a deal with Biddle or any of the other Republicans who had voted with us the day before. I immediately followed Don's directions to find out what it would cost to get Dills to Sacramento and back to Albuquerque that night. I confirmed that the plane was currently in Sacramento, which would require it to travel the one thousand mile distance between Sacramento and Albuquerque four times. It would have to get down to New Mexico, fly Dills round trip, and then return to Sacramento. The estimated price was about $4,000, a sum that would be hard to raise in an afternoon.

Bob and I went back into Zenovich's inner office. It was 1:30. We told him of the almost prohibitive cost of leasing a private jet. Dills had to come by commercial airline and the absolute deadline was in less than ten minutes. The senator was undecided and very nervous; he seemed to have been waiting for something that he had expected to receive by now—maybe a call from Biddle. He said he just could not call Dills yet and with excruciating tension we watched 1:40 approach . . . and then pass.

Still we didn't give up hope. If Zenovich would only call Dills, we maintained a fanatical determination to find some means of getting him to Sacramento in time. Just twenty minutes later, shortly after 2:00, Zenovich burst out of his office with an expression of excitement and determination on his face. He would now call Dills. I grabbed for the phone and within twenty minutes we had quotes for an Albuquerque-Sacramento round trip from several aircraft leasing firms in the southwestern U.S. I had three jets on tentative stand-by in Denver, Little Rock, and Dallas. The decision involved both price and timing. Each of the planes was in a different state of readiness and, though Denver was closest to Albuquerque, the aircraft there would take the longest to get in the air. Price was still a problem. The three quotes I had were less than that for the governor's jet, but not by much. I kept calling around, though, and by 2:30 had located an aircraft lessor in Los Angeles who had a jet available immediately at Los Angeles International Airport. I yelled for someone to find the next commercial flight from Albuquerque to Los Angeles; Eleanor Anderson found one departing at 3:00 our time. Zenovich called Dills immediately and spent a few agonizing minutes being told by Dills that his wife did not like him to fly in private planes. He finally agreed to come, though, and hung up about 2:35 to make a dash for the airport.

While Zenovich was talking to Dills, Bob was on the telephone trying to raise money. Because the private jet was already in Los Angeles and the Los Angeles-Sacramento-Albuquerque run was shorter than Albuquerque-Sacramento round-trip, the cost was down to $2,500. I called the governor's office to let them know we would not be using Reagan's jet. I had realized by then that revealing that we were trying to bring Dills back had been foolish. So long as they left Dills out of their vote count they could be certain of victory on the basis of Monday's vote. If they thought Dills might get back in time, they might still have unexpended political ammunition which, even in the short time before the session began, could be used to clinch one of the marginal Republicans such as Biddle or Nejedly. I hoped to rectify my error by canceling our tentative reservation on the plane.

I called the governor's secretary to do this and found her to be uncomfortably curious.

"Have you found anything else?" she asked.

"Well, we just don't know yet. The time is almost too short and we hadn't realized that leasing a jet was so expensive. Don Livingston seemed upset at the prospect of our using the governor's plane tonight. I would certainly appreciate it if you would call him and relay our decision. I am sure he would like to know."

I hung up quickly to forestall any more questions. Bob had just gotten off another phone and walked over to me.

"We have the money," he said quietly.

I immediately called Los Angeles and confirmed our order for the plane, hesitating only a moment before putting the order under my name. Bob and I had worked together on many tight, frenzied deals; if he said we had the money, it would be there. I also arranged with the Los Angeles Airport to have a service car meet Dills as he stepped off the plane and drive him directly around the jetways from where Texas International parked to the door of our chartered jet.

I then told Donna Hanlon, Zenovich's other secretary, that if I got a call from Don Livingston she was to tell him I was in a meeting and not taking any calls. Having confirmed the plane charter, I was no longer able to say, as I had to the governor's secretary, that we still didn't know whether or not Dills was coming. If Livingston called and put the question directly to me, I would have to tell him.

Bob and I then went into Zenovich's office to explain the logistics which we calculated would put Dills on the Senate floor at about 6:30 p.m. He was not only relieved, but gleeful at the prospect of murmured approbation from his colleagues that would come when Dills, in the latter and critical moments of the override vote, stepped onto the floor to cast the decisive vote. This would be a political upset, a coup, with a dash of spectacle in which any politician would delight.

"Now, I don't want anyone to know about his coming. I want to surprise a few of those guys when he comes in."

Donna then came to the door to tell me that Livingston was on the line.

"I'm sorry, Mike," she said, looking embarrassed and worried, "he didn't tell me who he was until after he asked for you and I had already told him you were here."

If I didn't take the call, Livingston would assume something was up, and might start scurrying around for more votes. If I did talk to him he might not ask directly about Dills and remain confident that we had less than twenty-seven votes.

"Mike," he began, "the governor's secretary told me you won't be using the governor's plane after all."

"That's right. The time is too short now for us to get it down there and back and, besides, we can't afford it."

"Are you optimistic at all about the vote? I guess Dills won't be coming in, then, and without him I don't see how you could get twenty-seven."

"I don't know, Don. I don't know if you could say we were optimistic."

"Well, without Dills coming in I just don't see the votes there for you."

My conscience stirred at this point but I decided that silence was permissible; it simply permitted him to draw his own conclusions. After a brief pause, I tried to get off as quickly as possible.

"We certainly appreciate your cooperation on the jet, Don."

"You had the audacity to ask for it and we had the audacity to say 'yes.'"

"Yes, well, thanks again, Don."

After calling Albuquerque to confirm that Dills had made his plane, we again were left with the agony of waiting. So far as we knew there had been no change in the position of Biddle or anyone else. With Dills we had twenty-six votes. Biddle had not yet given Zenovich a commitment, and now he almost certainly would not do so before getting on the floor. Zenovich was apparently confident, though, that Biddle could be had at the last minute. If he knew what it was Biddle wanted, he had decided to pay the price. There was nothing further we could do.

Around 4:00 we were with Kevin Gupton, another of Zeno-vich's aides, in one of the small back offices. He said that a few minutes earlier Zenovich had seen Biddle in the hall and called out to him: "You know what I did? I just picked up $2,500 for a jet to get Dills here in time for the housing vote. That's all right, eh?"

Ironically, Casey Young took me aside a bit later and said that Zenovich was disturbed because the story of a $2,500 plane ride was spreading rapidly through the Capitol. I told him Gupton's anecdote and speculated that someone had heard Zenovich him-self, since most of the doors opening from members' suites on to the hall are left open.

Before going to the floor, Zenovich returned to his office and from there I walked up to the chamber with him.

"I'll tell you," he gloated, "a lot of guys are going to be sur-prised to see Dills walk out on that floor. This is really a class operation!"

After a few minutes on the floor I went back to the office to call the Los Angeles Airport and make sure everything was ready for Dills' arrival. I stayed by the phone until after I got a return call from the airport to confirm that Dills had just taken off from L.A. It was about 5:30 before I returned to the floor.

I was pacing the area at the back of the chamber when Casey Young rushed up to me.

"We can't find one of our votes! We've looked all over. He's not in the chamber. He's not in the members' lounge."

"Okay, I'll go back down and start calling around. Does Klein know?"

"I don't know. I'll see who I can find and cover the rest of the building. If you're down in the office we can coordinate from there."

The possibility of another absentee—one of our twenty-six votes—had seemed so improbable that we had not checked atten-dance other than to verify that only Dills had a formal leave for that day. Absence without leave is rather serious and the president pro tempore can require the state police to forcibly compel the attendance of any member absent without leave.

I knew nothing about the absent senator, other than that he was a Democrat and had consistently voted for our bill. On reaching the Zenovich suite, I had no idea where to look for him. Mike Valles came in right after I did and I told him the problem. He immediately grabbed a phone book.

"Try the 'Cosmo' bar and Posey's. I'll call Fats', Ellis', and a couple of other places."

We phoned a half dozen bars with no luck.

"He might be in any of those places," said Valles. "He would just tell the bartenders to say that he's not there. Round up anyone you can. We'll have to go to every place ourselves."

Within fifteen minutes we had someone headed for each of the several bars within walking distance of the Capitol. I dashed across the street to the Cosmo. The bar is small, dimly lighted room just off the lobby and I stood at the entrance rummaging through a legislative directory to find the senator's photograph. Peering into the gloom, I saw several men at the bar and a few seated around the cocktail tables along one wall, but no one who in any way resembled the tiny portrait in my hand. I asked the bartender and one of the waitresses. They hadn't seen him.

I ran back across the Capitol park and up to the office. Each of the others came in to report no luck: Posey's, Fats', Ellis'. We tried his home, his administrative assistant, his secretary. I stood up, almost frantic with frustration. There was nowhere else to call, no place we could think of that we hadn't tried.

It was then that George Beattie and Stu Honse walked in.

"It's all over, Mike."

"Just now?"

"Yeah," Beattie replied, "a couple of minutes ago."

"Did Dills make it?"

"He walked in at 6:30. Biddle went against us."

I was stuffing things into my briefcase when Bob came in a couple minutes later. There was nothing to say and he just picked up his things. We passed the door to Zenovich's office on our way out. Mike Valles and Casey Young were watching Zenovich, who had returned from the chamber and was already on the phone, talking with the staff in his Fresno office.

He said into the receiver, "Rick? The non-agression pact with Biddle is off. Yeah, let's get on it."

Sticking my head in, I interrupted, "Thank you, gentlemen," and the senator looked up and waved.

We walked, still without speaking, over to the Cosmo to pick up our bags. Coming out, we met George Beattie and Stu Honse heading in for a drink. Both of us declined their invitation, too sharply I realized, as they turned away.

"Thanks," I called after them, "but really we just want to get out of here now."

We loaded our bags into Bob's car and headed west on the interstate to San Francisco. The sky was exquisite pale blue above us with long thin clouds near the horizon slowly reddening with a Pacific sunset. We were too tired, too disappointed to talk. I watched the black silhouettes of the trees rushing past, an endless variety of shapes against the darkening sky.

Epilogue

ON JUNE 27, 1975, GOVERNOR EDMUND G. (JERRY) BROWN, JR., signed into law the Zenovich-Moscone-Chacon Housing and Home Finance Act creating the California Housing Finance Agency. This successfully culminated our second effort to enact such legislation. After the failure to get our housing bills past Governor Reagan, we had begun again on December 2, 1974, with the start of the new legislative session.

The November election had given us a much-altered political context in which to work. The Democrats picked up two additional seats in the Senate, raising their majority to twenty-five—only two short of the two-thirds needed to pass appropriations or override a gubernatorial veto. One of the Republican losses was especially satisfying for us. Craig Biddle was beaten by Bob Presley in the 34th Senatorial District by less than 700 out of some 150,000 votes cast. In the Assembly the Democrats returned with more members than they had had since the last century—fifty-five, one vote more than two-thirds.

The most significant change for us was the fact that on January 6, 1975, Ronald Reagan would be governor no longer. In terms of the housing legislation, it had made little difference whether Jerry Brown or his Republican opponent, Houston Flournoy, won. Both men were solidly on record as supporting creation of a housing finance agency.

On December 2, 1974, the 1975-1976 legislative session began. Shortly afterward, Zenovich made his play to unseat James Mills as president pro tempore. Despite Presley's victory, Zenovich could not muster enough votes at the last and was defeated. Bob and I were afraid that Mills, in retaliation for Zenovich's challenge, might strip him of all important committee assignments and thereby substantially reduce the influence of our principal author. Jesse Unruh once said, though: "If I had slain all my political enemies yesterday, I wouldn't have any friends today." The Senate leadership acknowledged the wisdom of that aphorism in dealing with Zenovich. He lost his vice-chairmanship of the Agriculture Committee and his seat on Rules, but he was permitted to stay in Government Organization and received his first chairmanship of a standing committee—Industrial Relations.

During December three bills were introduced, each of which would create a housing finance agency. One was S.B. 29 by Zenovich. It was almost identical to the legislation vetoed by Reagan four months before. Instead of separating the enabling legislation and bonding authorization in separate bills, we included the authority to issue both revenue bonds and general obligation bonds in the bill which created the agency. Also, while the general obligation bonds were subject to voter approval, neither creation of the agency nor its authority to issue revenue bonds required anything more than enactment of the bill. We decided against submitting another constitutional amendment, being resigned to the fact that CSEA could prevent us from exempting the agency from civil service; the few limited exemptions we might negotiate did not seem worth the effort. We were reasonably confident that issues such as Article XXXIV and public purpose would be interpreted by the courts in favor of the agency.

In addition to S.B. 29, Senator George Moscone introduced S.B. 50, a bill which had been drafted by Bob Frank, staff consultant to the Senate Select Committee on Housing and Urban Affairs, chaired by Nick Petris. A third bill, A.B. 116, was introduced by Chacon. All three bills would create a housing finance agency but they differed substantially in the administrative structure, powers, and proscriptions under which such an agency would operate.

Changes in legislative leadership affect not only the hierarchy of members themselves, but frequently the position and tenure of staff as well. Chacon had retained George Beattie as senior staff member of the Committee on Urban Development and Housing at Moretti's insistence. If Willie Brown had become speaker, many of the key personalities of the Moretti organization would have remained in power and Beattie may well have been able to retain both his line of communication with the speaker's office and his job. But McCarthy's ascendancy meant a complete shift in power and Beattie had no one in the speaker's office to stick up for him. He was fired by Chacon and replaced by Renée Franken, who had drafted an entirely new housing bill for Chacon.

There had been several indications during the previous session that Chacon felt he was being upstaged by Zenovich. He seemed disappointed with the amount of publicity he had received from the bills compared to Zenovich and believed that he had less control over the substance of the bills than did the senator. We guessed this to be the reason for his introducing a separate bill instead of approaching Zenovich on the possibility of again jointly authoring the same bill.

As early as January, however, there was already considerable pressure building for consolidation of all three housing bills. Only one bill creating a housing finance agency could be passed, and the leadership of both houses wished to avoid a time-consuming and potentially unpleasant competition among the three authors. They were reluctant, however, to favor any one of the three bills over the other two. All three authors were strong Democratic members and it could hardly benefit the leadership to do one of them a favor at the cost of angering the other two. They strongly urged Zenovich, Chacon, and Moscone to work something out quietly among themselves.

The authors had little to gain by forcing the Legislature to choose among them. So long as what was eventually passed clearly bore their names, each would secure the political benefits they sought. The result was agreement on a single piece of legislation titled the "Zenovich-Moscone-Chacon Housing and Home Finance Act." In substance, the Zenovich bill was the one used, with a chapter from the Moscone bill relating to rehabilitation of urban neighborhoods grafted on to it.

Once this agreement was reached, instead of amending one of the three bills and dropping the other two, it was decided that the leadership would request Governor Brown to proclaim an extraordinary session of the Legislature. The purpose of the extraordinary session would be to consider housing legislation, and an entirely new bill, reflecting the consolidation agreement, would be introduced.

The possible use of an extraordinary session was an idea which Bob had come up with in the fall of 1974 when he and I first began planning strategy for 1975. Under the California Constitution a bill which is passed at a regular legislative session does not take effect until the following January 1. If we succeeded in getting our bill passed in 1975, the new agency would not come into being until 1976 and thereby forfeit any allocation of federal housing subsidies made during 1975. This could substantially delay the commencement of a low-income housing program in the state.

On August 22, 1974, a week after our failure to override Reagan's veto, the Federal Housing and Community Development Act of 1974 became law. It formally ended the housing subsidy moratorium which had caused Bob and me to travel to Sacramento for the first time nineteen months before. This act, one of the few victories which the Nixon administration achieved in domestic policy, was signed, ironically, by President Ford. The new law consolidated all the previous housing subsidies under a single program of monthly rent subsidies which it amended into Section 8 of the United States Housing Act. A crucial difference between the new program and those it replaced was the absence of federal financing for construction of low-income housing to which the Section 8 subsidies would apply. There were, however, special provisions in the act to permit use of Section 8 subsidies in tandem with state housing finance agency financing, and special allocations of these subsidies were expected to be made annually to housing finance agencies capable of financing the construction of apartments which could be subsidized under Section 8.

Exactly when a state agency would have to apply in order to receive a subsidy allocation for 1975 was not clear, for by January 1975, HUD still had not published regulations implementing the new law. In any case we were quite sure that unless a California housing agency were in existence during at least some part of the

1975 calendar year, it would have no chance at all for a 1975 allocation. The only way of creating the agency before 1976 was to enact the legislation at an extraordinary session of the Legislature, as statutes passed during a special session take effect on the ninety-first day after the special session adjourns.

At the request of Speaker McCarthy, Governor Brown proclaimed on February 17, 1975, the First Extraordinary Session of the Legislature, for the purpose of considering legislation relating to housing for low- and moderate-income families. Since the Legislature was already meeting in regular session, the proclamation had almost no noticeable effect on legislative procedure. Before hearing bills which were introduced pursuant to the special session, committees simply announced the special status of the legislation and, prior to floor consideration, there would be a declaration from the presiding officer that the house was acting pursuant to the special session.

Once again, we decided to introduce identical bills in both houses simultaneously in hopes of speeding up the legislative process. On February 17, A.B. 1X (the "X" designates an extraordinary session) and S.B. 2X were introduced in their respective houses. They were identical bills; both would enact the Zenovich-Moscone-Chacon Housing and Home Financing Act. With the clear backing of both the governor and Democratic leadership of both legislative houses, there was virtually no doubt at all from the time it was introduced that this legislation would be enacted. But despite that assurance, and to some extent because of it, the next four months were not comfortable ones.

The principal respect in which the legislative process differed this time from what we had been through before was the role played by the Brown administration in contrast to that of Governor Reagan's. The personal administrative style of Ronald Reagan, as well as the fact that the opposing party controlled the Legislature, caused him to be rather aloof in his dealings with that body. Favors were sometimes exchanged with individual legislators of both parties and with the majority leadership, but there were relatively few instances in which legislative and administrative staff worked closely together to produce a mutually acceptable product. Certainly there was no such cooperation on our housing bill.

The new governor's appointee for secretary of business and transportation was Donald Burns, a lawyer from Washington, D.C., and a personal friend of Brown's. Burns brought with him from Washington Michael Elliott, an economist who was to become a deputy secretary and, later, the housing agency's first chairperson and acting president, and Arnold Sternberg, who was appointed director of the Department of Housing and Community Development (HCD). By early March it was clear that these three men had considerable interest in the housing bill and had some specific ideas in mind for it. The most substantial of these was to use it as a vehicle for reorganizing HCD and substantially increasing the scope and powers of that department. The strength of our bill made it attractive for this purpose; it might be used to accomplish changes in HCD which they would otherwise be unable to get through the Legislature.

Bob, Renée Franken, Bob Frank, and I met with Burns. Elliott, and Sternberg several times during March. Bob and I were interested principally in keeping the bill as much the way it had been introduced as possible. We were very conscious of the battles fought over its many provisions the year before and the accommodations that had been made with some difficulty among the three authors in arriving at a consolidated bill for the extraordinary session. The administration was quite persistent in its desire for amendments, though, especially those which would cause changes in HCD.

Bob and I had almost no substantive interest in what the administration wanted to do with HCD and we felt that Brown's people underestimated both the independence of the California Legislature and the scrutiny which the HCD amendments would receive. Our concern was that controversy over the HCD provisions might substantially delay, and possibly even jeopardize, creation of the housing finance agency. Politically, the administration had considerable strength, though, and we finally arrived at an accommodation which included provisions which made substantial organizational changes in HCD.

In its first committee hearings the amended bill ran into difficulty. The legislators were suspicious of the language relating to HCD. They recognized it as an attempt to carry out a major administrative reorganization by riding on the strength of the housing finance agency legislation. We took heat not only from the Republicans but also from the Democrats who had supported Moretti. Jerry Brown had beaten them in the primary and they were not about to let him come over and start pushing them around on their own turf. I recall, in particular, an exchange between Willie Brown and Don Burns during the first Assembly hearing in Chacon's committee. Brown came down on Burns very hard and fast with a flurry of questions and reprimands about the way in which the administration ought to behave in its relations with the Legislature. Burns is the only man I ever saw who could answer Willie Brown as quickly and as well as Brown could question. After ten minutes of firing back and forth Brown broke into a big grin and, turning to the committee member next to him, said loudly, "You know, this guy is good, he is really very good," and both members and audience broke into laughter.

This was the only light moment I remember. More than once during that spring we heard members grumbling about the bill and wondering aloud about three Easterners deciding after two month's time that they knew how California's housing department ought to be run. The conflict was ultimately resolved by a compromise under which the administration was permitted to retain some provisions relating to HCD, but those which would have made major changes in its organization and the extent of its powers were deleted.

Besides changes in the political context that had taken place at the end of 1974, we found ourselves facing a sudden weakening in confidence regarding the whole concept of housing finance agencies. On February 25, 1975, one week after A.B. 1X and S.B. 2X were introduced in the special session, the New York State Urban Development Corporation (UDC) failed to pay $104.5 million of notes due on that day. UDC had $1.1 billion in bonds outstanding and the default put it on the edge of financial collapse. UDC was not strictly a housing finance agency. It was an agency of the State of New York which financed not only housing but commercial and industrial development as well, and the way in which its financial base was structured differed significantly from that of a housing finance agency. Nonetheless, its troubles, which received considerable publicity, made the legislators very nervous, and they began to look for assurances that a similar thing could not happen to a California housing agency.

In January, Jesse Unruh, who was the new state treasurer, had told Zenovich, his former protégé in the Assembly, that he wanted some amendments in our housing bill. Pursuant to that request and before our discussions with Chacon and Moscone leading to the consolidated special session bill, Bob and I began a series of discussions with Unruh and his staff. What Unruh didn't like about Zenovich's bill, which was identical to S.B. 1633, was that it made the state treasurer a nonvoting ex-officio member of the agency's board. Unruh was very firm about wanting the treasurer to have control over the investment of any money held by the agency, and to serve as trustee for holders of the agency's bonds.

Bob and I were concerned about granting the state treasurer's office such a grip on agency finances that the agency would be able to operate only pursuant to the treasurer's express consent. We were not worried about Unruh personally, as we felt that he would be sympathetic to the goals we thought the agency should pursue. But the attitude of the former treasurer, Ivy Baker Priest, toward a housing agency was still very fresh in our minds and we did not wish to put the agency at the mercy of some like-minded treasurer who might be elected in the future. But there was little we could do, since this was one of the few issues in the bill about which we received explicit instructions from Zenovich, which were to give Unruh anything within reason that he asked for.

Then, as we began our discussions with the Brown administration in February, we found that they also didn't like the treasurer's proposed amendments. But the UDC collapse considerably strengthened Unruh's position. During hearings on the bills it became clear that the Legislature wanted a watchdog and figured the state treasurer was ideal for that role. As an elected official and directly accountable for the financial health of the state, he would have every incentive to assure that the agency was managed in a financially conservative manner. Despite the administration's efforts, Unruh got most of what he wanted.

While giving the state treasurer an oversight function, the Legislature decided to further its own influence over the agency as well. Provisions were included detailing specific information which the agency had to report annually to the Legislature, and the Joint Legislative Budget Committee was given review and comment powers over the agency's budget.

In addition, a number of amendments were offered by members of the policy and finance committees in both houses which heard A.B. 1X and S.B. 2X. None of the amendments was particularly significant in itself. They bore on specific, sometimes trivial, issues. Almost all sought to limit or prescribe agency activity in some highly particular way. The agency was required to provide services and publications in languages other than English. It was required to impose specified types of rent control on certain kinds of housing which it financed. Detailed requirements for supervising those who owned housing financed by the agency were prescribed. Quotas were established for different types of housing to be financed, such as units designed specifically for the elderly and for persons with orthopedic disabilities. Priorities were established for specific areas such as rural sections of the state, areas in which new construction was determined to be needed, areas in which rehabilitation was needed, and areas with credit shortages. Most of the concerns addressed seemed legitimate and, alone, none of the amendments troubled us. But as more were added in each hearing, Bob and I became increasingly concerned that, together, they would so confine the agency's activities that its ability to respond with flexibility to changing conditions in the housing and financial markets would be substantially impaired.

That sort of concern is difficult to express effectively. It is almost impossible to argue against including quotas for the elderly and handicapped without seeming as if you lack sympathy for the old and crippled. And among the legislators there appeared to be little concern for or even awareness of the administrative difficulties which such restrictions might impose. Individual legislators were most obviously concerned that they set some imprint of their own on the bill, not only to satisfy some part of their constituency, but I believe in many instances to satisfy their personal desire to feel a sense of involvement, of participation in this major legislative effort. To Bob and me it often seemed as if none of the legislators had any substantial interest in whether and how well this administrative apparatus, once created, would actually work. The legislative procedure itself seemed inadequate. Amendments were made sequentially, in four different committees in two different houses. There was no legislative forum in which attention was given to the overall coherence, symmetry, and internal consistency of the bill.

Despite these several difficulties A.B. 1X was finally passed and sent to the governor's desk on June 24, 1975. The bill included an authorization for the agency to issue up to $300 million in tax-exempt revenue bonds and also provided that Proposition 1 on the November 1976 ballot, if passed by majority vote, would authorize the state to issue an additional $500 million in general obligation bonds, backed by the state's credit, on behalf of the agency. After signing A.B. 1X into law on June 27, Governor Brown declared the extraordinary legislative session adjourned, and ninety-one days thereafter, on September 26, 1975, the California Housing Finance Agency became a reality.

By that time I had already moved to Washington, D.C., and was consulting for HUD in an attempt to get the Section 8 subsidy program on its feet. A year later I returned for three months to help the new agency structure its first bond issue, and in January 1977 came the culmination of our efforts. Jose and Carmelita de la Cruz, a young Filipino couple, ceased living with their relatives. Along with their three children, they moved into a house of their own in San Jose, purchased with the first mortgage loan made by the California Housing Finance Agency.

Though I can hardly imagine a happier conclusion to our efforts than what actually occurred, when I recall the two years we spent in Sacramento I confront a number of difficult and even disturbing questions. Some relate to the wisdom and even the legitimacy of government housing subsidies. But more pertinent are those questions bearing on the modern legislative process, the means by which our representative government arrives at public decisions.

One of the most striking aspects of legislative decision-making is that the basic, formative decisions which shape a major program are made before the formal legislative process ever begins. The single, most formative decision, which shaped and confined all of the legislative controversy over our bill, was that of structuring the legislation around the issue of housing. The reasons for this decision were a natural outgrowth of Bob's and my previous experience with subsidized housing and the fact that Zenovich was comfortable with the topic and believed it to have political value. So naturally did the topic of housing come to Bob and me, so much was it a part of our reasons for being in Sacramento in the first place, that we never seriously considered any alternatives. Yet it requires only a little thought to realize that housing was just one of at least several ways of approaching the problems which concerned us.

Housing—more housing, better housing, less costly housing—is not an end in itself. It is, rather, a means of achieving more fundamental public goals: reducing unemployment, assisting the poor, promoting racial integration, or whatever. Equally clear, I think, is that any one of these goals might be pursued in ways that have nothing directly to do with housing. Unemployment might be reduced by means of job skill training or placement services, for example; poverty can be alleviated by means of direct income supplements; racial integration can be furthered by more intensive efforts to enforce anti-discrimination statutes. But these, or the myriad other kinds of programs that might be conceived to accomplish such ends, we never considered.

Nor was this failure the peculiar result of Bob and me having especially limited vision. Before we arrived in Sacramento, housing subsidy bills had already been presented in previous sessions, drafted by the staff consultants to the Assembly Standing Committee on Urban Development and Housing and the Senate Select Committee on Housing and Urban Affairs. There was no evidence that these were the products of any comparative analysis of housing subsidies and other means of accomplishing specific public goals. It might be argued, I suppose, that such judgments are implied in whether or not a particular bill is passed. The failure of a housing bill to pass, for example, might indicate a collective legislative judgment not that the goals being sought are inappropriate, but that housing is not the best means of achieving them. But that reply is not persuasive because whether housing ought to be subsidized in order to reduce unemployment or to assist the poor can be answered only by an explicit comparison between the costs and benefits of housing assistance and those of some other kind or kinds of public programs directed toward the same end. It was apparent to me that such a comparison was never undertaken.

There exist obvious advantages in the committee system used by legislatures to screen bills before they are presented for a floor vote. Committees institutionalize specialization by legislators and staff in specific areas of public concern; this has become increasingly necessary as the number and complexity of issues with which government deals have increased. Unfortunately, legislatures have not institutionalized a structural or procedural apparatus to assure rigorous analysis which cuts across these specialties. Housing bills are usually drafted by the staff of a housing committee, sponsored by a member of such a committee, and then referred to that same committee for analysis; a bill which proposed cash income assistance for the poor would normally emanate from and be screened by the committee on welfare; a bill creating a network of public placement offices would have the same relationship with the committee on labor.

None of the specialized committees has the inclination, nor, usually, the competence, to weigh objectively in each case the relative benefits of approaching a particular problem by means of programs which fall within its province as opposed to accomplishing the same objective with an entirely different type of implement. A forum in which this might be done is the finance committee, which cuts across topical specialties in considering all bills which have financial implications before they go to the floor. In my experience, though, the finance committees viewed their role far more narrowly. They did not attempt any sort of cost-benefit comparisons to determine whether a particular housing bill, for example, was the best means of achieving some specific purpose; rather they attempted to confine their scope of inquiry to the kind and magnitude of impact each bill would have on the state's finances.

Between the time our bill was introduced and its final passage, all of the substantive legislative inquiry that occurred could be classified under one of two general questions. The first was whether housing was an appropriate area of government activity. This question was asked by only a small number of conservative legislators, who seemed to view it as largely an issue of political philosophy. The second was whether this particular housing bill was the best housing bill that could be devised. This question was by far the more prominent both in terms of the number of legislators to whom it was of concern and the amount of committee and floor debate consumed by it. One critical question was never considered: Assuming the goals sought by this housing bill are legitimate concerns of state government, is subsidizing housing the best means of pursuing them?

The scope of legislative inquiry was limited not only by such intellectual myopia, but also by political realities which narrowed the predominant question to an even greater extent than I have phrased it above—narrowed it from whether this bill was the best possible housing bill to whether it would create the best housing finance agency. There are an enormous variety of ways to subsidize housing besides creating a housing finance agency which sells bonds and uses the proceeds to make low-interest mortgage loans. Our decision to propose this particular kind of program was not made because it is necessarily the most cost-effective means of providing housing subsidies, but rather because it offered what we felt were crucial political advantages. The same type of program had been tried in other states, which would allow us to counter any charges that the program was unworkable; the budgetary cost was very low, most of the subsidy being "hidden" in the tax-exempt nature of the agency's bonds; and this type of program offered a means of involving the mortgage finance and home-building industries to the extent we believed necessary to gain their support. The fact that we were never called upon to provide a comparative analysis between the cost-effectiveness of our program and other types of subsidy designs may be some confirmation of our political judgment, but it does not speak particularly well for the thoroughness of legislative decision-making.

It is true that politics is the art of the possible, but this does not imply that success lies in choosing the path of least resistance. The legislative process is one of unceasing negotiation in which, as in any vigorous negotiation, no one gets all that he wants. The skillful negotiator is the one who demands as much as possible, short of queering the deal. Whether a deal is made is not necessarily an indication of success; if you set out to buy an automobile, the measure of your skill is not whether you buy one but how much you pay for it. The basic design of the agency which Bob and I included in our original bill endured and the bill finally passed, but maybe we didn't ask for enough. Maybe the tactical compromises which that original bill included were greater than necessary. Maybe we should have included, for example, the authority and funding to enable the agency to provide substantial amounts of direct rent subsidies to low-income tenants. The reason we did not include that was because we did not think we could get such a bill passed, but were we shrewd or overly timid?

The calculus of legislative negotiations is more complex than that involved in more common commercial transactions for two reasons. One is that a legislative deal is never final. Once you've bought a car, it's yours; you can't go back to the seller six months later and renegotiate the same transaction. Not so in a legislature, where each session signals the opportunity to rehash any issue decided in any previous session. This fact is of considerable strategic importance. For example, we received numerous signals from Governor Reagan's office during 1974 that we could avoid the threat of a veto if we included in the bill a provision which limited the agency to assisting only housing intended expressly for the elderly. Our refusal may have been a mistake. If we had included such a provision, the agency might have been created a year sooner and instead of having to wrestle the whole bill through the next legislative session as we did, all that would have been necessary was a tiny bill which struck out the limiting phrase from the agency's statute.

Brian Paddock used inter-session bargaining very shrewdly. For permitting us to leave out the requirement of good cause for tenant evictions, he got in exchange Zenovich's promise both to support a bill in the next session which would impose that requirement on the agency and, in addition, to assist Paddock with two other bills of his choosing. During the spring and summer of 1976, less than a year after the agency came into existence, a number of the most vigorous battles we fought during 1974 and 1975 were fought again with equal vigor by many of the same advocates in the context of bills introduced to amend specific provisions of the agency's statute.

The second distinguishing element of legislative negotiation is the number of parties and issues involved. A major bill such as ours attracts the active interest of a large number of legislators and lobbyists; this group does not break down neatly into those who are for and those against the bill. There may be a few, like Senators Cusanovich and Deukmejian in our case, who are so fundamentally opposed to what . the bill represents that they would not find it acceptable in any form. But far more common are those whose position is qualified; whether they vote aye or no depends on the inclusion or deletion of very particular provisions in the bill. The most time-consuming and agonizing work is trying to reconcile the myriad and frequently conflicting demands of those who are comfortable with, and even enthusiasts for, the basic aims of the legislation. It is usually impossible to please everyone entirely, but there are strong pressures to give each group at least enough to prevent their making noises in front of a committee. Five enthusiastic supporters may not be able to rectify the damage done by one disgruntled ally who tells a committee he has been mistreated.

It is often said that for an incumbent legislator to remain in office, it is not so important that he generate enthusiasm among his constituency as that a challenger have no issue with which to cultivate significant dissatisfaction. There are strong pressures which push a legislative proposal toward blandness, toward becoming a lowest common denominator or an untidy patchwork of conciliation. By the time our bill was signed by Governor Brown it was no longer the trim, symmetrical document with which we began. Bob and I tried very hard to retain the fundamental shape and powers of the agency throughout and were by and large successful, but the bill emerged considerably disheveled and disarranged with odd bits and pieces hanging about it here and there. This has made the bill frequently awkward to administer and caused considerable, though not insurmountable, difficulties in structuring the agency's first bond issues.

The capacity of the California Legislature to grapple with lengthy and complex legislation is particularly instructive because that legislature is considered to be so very good compared to the legislatures in most other states.

In 1969, with a grant from the Ford Foundation, the Citizens' Conference on State Legislatures undertook an evaluative survey of the fifty state legislatures. California's was judged the best state legislature in the country. Whether it would be considered so today might be debated, but its position is secure among the top five. Former members of the California Legislature who went on to serve in the U.S. Congress have implied that even the House of Representatives compares unfavorably to its counterpart in California. In 1969 U.S. Congressman Jerome Waldie, former majority leader of the California Assembly, challenged Congressional leadership by offering to the Democratic caucus a resolution of "no confidence" in the speaker of the House. The resolution failed but it was supported by several other Democratic congressmen from California. Later, Waldie told reporter Michael Green that he "would model the House after the body he knew [in California], with all the modern, up-to-date research facilities and other devices . . . introduced to strengthen the Assembly as an independent branch. . . ." Green commented: "For at least a few California congressmen, the contrast between their earlier service in the Assembly . . . and the system they have encountered in the Congress is a basis for much of their present disillusionment and zeal for House reform." And he quoted California Representative Robert Leggett: "In the Assembly, you really felt you could get something done if you had a good idea, and you didn't have to wait forever to do it."

Lou Cannon, now a reporter for the *Washington Post* and author of two books on California politics, observed the same dissatisfaction.

Many of the congressmen work incredibly long hours, far longer in fact than most of their legislative counterparts in Sacramento, but rarely do they possess the sense of achievement common to the able California state legislator. . . . One congressman, who has spent several sessions on the Hill after a single one in Sacramento, recalls with fondness a role he played in a then-major resources bill as a freshman assemblyman. "That was in my only term there," the congressman said, shaking his head. "Now, after all these years, I've been here long enough to get the committee schedules."

Whether the California Legislature is, or ever was, as Jesse Unruh used to say, "the best Legislature in the world" I do not know. But there is substantial evidence that it compares very well with the others. One of the attributes to which its relative position is ascribed is the quantity and quality of its staff. In ranking the California Legislature number one in the country, the Citizens' Conference stated:

The amount and quality, as well as the extensiveness of coverage and availability, of professional staff services is probably the outstanding feature of the California Legislature.

Staffing is widely thought to be the key ingredient for improving legislative process. Alan Rosenthal, as director of the Center for State Legislative Research and Service of the Eagleton Institute of Politics at Rutgers University, wrote in 1972:

If there is any wonder drug in this whole business, it is legislative staffing. Legislatures need greater professional assistance in gathering, processing, and assessing information. Without staff, legislatures cannot possibly arrive at competent judgments, independent of governors, bureaucracies, and interest groups. Without staff, there is little hope of redressing the contemporary imbalance between the power of the legislature on the one hand and that of governors and administrative bureaucracies on the other. Informed opinion is virtually unanimous. The report of the American Assembly, for example, recommends professional staff for majority and minority leaderships, legislative councils, major standing committees, and central services, such as bill drafting, law revision, and library and reference. A recent compilation of recommendations from various national and state reports, published by the Citizens' Conference, has more space devoted to staff than to any other subject. My own surveys of opinion among members in six legislatures indicate that staffing is thought to be the most important improvement.

The perceived need for legislators to have more staff assistance is not difficult to understand. The number of legislators has remained fairly constant over the years while the amount and complexity of decisions which both the national and state legislatures are called upon to make has increased rapidly during the past three decades.

The California Legislature has had professional staff resources since 1913, the year in which the legislative counsel's office was created. A legislative auditor was hired in 1941 to direct a small fiscal analysis staff which eventually became the legislative analyst's office, later headed by A. Alan Post. The staffs of these two central services had grown to a total of about sixty full-time professionals by 1955, when a third bureau, the Office of the Auditor General, was created to assure the Legislature that appropriated funds were being properly spent.

The real growth in staff, however, began with Jesse Unruh's election to the Assembly speakership in 1961. He recognized that knowledge was power and that without additional independent research capability, the Legislature would increasingly become the captive of outside sources of information. By 1963, at his urging, every Assembly committee had at least one consultant and some had more than one. The Senate, to maintain a comparable degree of competence, began staffing its committees as well. By 1963, all senators and assemblymen were allowed district offices in addition to both secretarial and professional staff. Each assemblyman is permitted one district office, three secretaries (two in the Capitol; one in the district office), one administrative assistant, and one field representative, while senators have a minimum of one district office, two administrative assistants, four secretaries (two in the Capitol; two in the district office), and one field representative. In 1964 the Assembly created what was to become the Office of Research and also initiated staffing of caucuses. The Senate followed both of these leads in 1969.

By 1970, when Unruh left the Legislature to run for governor, the total legislative staff had reached almost 1,500, including 500 professionals, with an annual payroll of $15 million. By 1974, when Bob and I were a part of it, the total staff had grown even larger, to a total of 1,875, with over 700 professionals and a payroll of $21 million.

From the standpoint of the Legislature as an institution there remains no question in my mind that a large staff is necessary to enable the legislative branch to maintain a vigorous and independent role as a public decision-maker. In this I am in agreement with Mr. Unruh and most other expert observers of the legislative process. Still, however necessary staff may be to maintaining the strength of a legislature in its relationship with the executive branch and lobbyists, the influence of legislative staff greatly alters the character of representative decision-making and may even affect its legitimacy.

I recall the first press conference on the housing bill, at which Zenovich and Chacon were unable to respond intelligently to the questions they received, and Bob, after frantically gesticulating from the back of the room, ended up sitting behind the two legislators in order to feed them answers. Whenever the bill was to be heard by a Senate committee, Zenovich would begin the testimony on it by making a brief introductory statement. The few times he tried to respond to questions from committee members which probed any deeper than the most general intent of the bill, he almost invariably gave an incorrect answer. I remember coming into the foyer of the Assembly floor just before the summer recess in 1974 and finding Bob and George Beattie frantic over misstatements Chacon had made on the floor which almost prevented passage of the constitutional amendment (A.C.A. 96).

To the best of my knowledge, there was not a single legislator who ever read any of the housing bills in its entirety. Certainly not one of them ever demonstrated in my presence any more than the vaguest understanding of what the bills as a whole contained. It may not surprise a constituent that his representative does not read every one of the thousands of bills introduced each session, or even not all those on which he votes. The housing bills were, however, among the major pieces of legislation introduced in 1974 and 1975. They were not read by the members or chairmen of the committees through which they passed, nor even by their authors.

In pointing this out, I do not mean to criticize either Zenovich or Chacon. Their lack of knowledge about the contents of the bill differed in no significant respect from what I observed to be the extent of familiarity which most legislators had with bills they authored. Nor do I think this implies, in turn, that the California Legislature is less competent than its counterparts elsewhere. Michael Malbin, writing in *The Public Interest,* tells a story about one of his first interviews with a U.S. Congressman:

When I first came to Washington, fresh from academe, I was assigned by *National Journal* to write a story about a conference committee that was deadlocked over the use of Highway Trust Fund money for mass transit. The $23 billion authorization bill was the most significant piece of legislation to come out of the House Public Works Subcommittee on Transportation that year (1973), so I decided to interview its chairman, the late John Klucyznski, from Chicago.

When I arrived at his office, the receptionist said that the Congressman would be glad to see me in a few minutes. While I waited, she telephoned one of the committee-staff professionals working on the bill: the Congressman wanted him to sit in on the interview, she said, in case I asked any technical questions. This seemed like a routine procedure until we got to some of those "technical questions."

I began the interview with what I thought was an easy question (generally a good way to get an interview going): "What makes this issue important?"

"This is a tremendously important bill. It involves millions of dollars." Klucyznski began to answer, and then paused. "No—billions isn't it?" he asked, turning to the staff aide.

The considerable amount of influence which staff has on legislative decision-making to a large extent reflects how very necessary legislators find it. California is one of the few states with a full-time legislature. But, alone, even a full-time legislator cannot possibly give thoughtful consideration to the myriad decisions he is called upon to make during a session, let alone do that plus attend to his formal duties in the legislature, handle the many individual constituent requests he receives, and continue to cultivate his constituency at large so that it will not have forgotten him by the next election. Legislators are forced to rely heavily on all the assistance they have available to them.

The relative size of legislative staff compared to the legislators is important to keep in mind. For every legislator there are over fifteen staff members, six of whom are professionals and the rest clerical. In the case of each assemblyman, at least one of those six professionals and, in the case of each senator, two of them, are under the individual member's direct control. The way in which members use their administrative assistants varies a good deal. Some use them more for strictly political work, while others prefer keeping them occupied drafting and analyzing legislation, preparing committee testimony, and performing other tasks related to the substance of legislative business. From my casual observation over about two years I would guess that generally half the time of administrative assistants is spent on substantive business. Aside from the some sixty consultants working directly for the leadership and caucuses in both houses, the remainder of the Assembly and Senate staffs, such as the committee consultants and the two offices of research, spend considerably more than half their time on the substance of legislative activity. The centralized staffs, such as legislative counsel, are devoted almost entirely to non-partisan tasks.

A formal survey of how legislative staff spends its time would be very useful. My guess is that two-thirds of the total business hours of professional legislative staff are spent on matters substantially related to legislative decision-making. In 1974, this was the equivalent of 470 professionals engaged full time in legislative research, investigation, drafting, and related activities—four times the number of legislators. But the calculation understates the staff's predominance, because legislators themselves spend a considerable amount of their time engaged in purely partisan activities. What a legislator actually accomplishes can assist in his re-election only to the extent his constituents are aware of those accomplishments. Doing, on the one hand, and telling voters what he has done or will do, on the other, are two very different kinds of activity. The large amount of time a legislator must spend advertising himself is time which is not spent on substantive legislative business.

The most remarkable discovery I made during my tenure as a staff member was the amount of power I had over the bills on which I worked. The members relied almost entirely on staff to accurately summarize the legislation and also to develop compromises among the many interests which were brought into conflict by these bills. Zenovich was drawn into the issue of whether good cause was to be required for eviction of tenants, and Chacon sat in on a meeting with Emma Gunterman and Sharon English concerning late charges and prepayment penalties. In the context of legislation of such size and complexity these were hardly major issues, and Bob and I found that even the accommodation reached in the Chacon meeting had to be reversed the next day, to avoid a serious confrontation with the savings and loans.

Legislative staffs are, of course, not autonomous. Legislative counsel is most distant from the Legislature, being the only part of the staff services whose positions are filled by civil service examination. The legislative analyst and auditor general offices are accountable to the rules committees of both houses. The remainder of the staff—two-thirds of the total—work directly for committees or individual legislators and are controlled by the members in the sense that they are hired and fired by them. But this does not vitiate the influence they have nor the extent to which legislation bears their own ethical and administrative judgments. Staff members themselves become a very significant part of the political calculus involved in passing legislation. They are, by necessity, at the fulcrum of that balance between substance and raw political influence which constitutes the guts of legislative decision-making. Staff members not only know considerably more than any member about the substance of a bill but also possess a far more refined knowledge of how each concerned interest group is positioned with respect to the provisions it contains. At the same time, because they work on a daily and often intimate basis with the members, they are in a far better position than anyone outside the Legislature to assess its ever-shifting political geography.

In order to achieve independence from lobbyists and oversee an increasingly large executive bureaucracy, the Legislature has by hiring an increasingly large staff, created its own bureaucracy.

The Citizens' Conference on State Legislatures in its book *The Sometime Governments* urges the need for independence:

> The problem, then, is not so much that lobbyists buy legislators as that lobbyists have, by legislative default, cornered the market on some of the important resources that a legislator needs to do his job. Public policy, as a result, tends to reflect unduly the desires and ideas of the interests these lobbyists represent. It is the convergence, or sometimes the clash, of these interests that often determines public policy. Other interests, including the overall public interest, tend by comparison to have little impact on that policy. The surest and quickest way to reduce the influence of special interest lobbyists upon our legislatures is to raise the level of competence in those legislatures to the point where they can compete with lobbyists on even terms on behalf of the citizens.

The implication is that by developing independent sources of information within the Legislature by means such as more and better staff, the members will be less reliant on lobbyists and in this way better represent the public as opposed to special interests. Such a view seems too simplistic to me. In negotiating with the many lobbyists who were interested in the housing bills, I was never aware of any particular position on any given issue which was "best," which in some abstract way was above the petty squabblings of parochial spokesmen, which represented something called "the overall public interest." Recall the kinds of issues with which we dealt: Should or should not landlords be required to show good cause before evicting tenants? Should public deposits be held only by banks? What percentage of units financed annually by a state housing finance agency should be designed specifically for the elderly and handicapped? Should the state treasurer sit on the board of directors of such an agency, should all the members be chosen by the governor, or should the Legislature as well as the governor participate in the selection? To what extent should local governments have discretion over whether the state is permitted to finance low- and moderate-income housing within its jurisdiction?

The "public interest" is merely the aggregate of all the individual and institutional biases in the state. Anyone representing a particular viewpoint claims that he represents the "public interest" in hopes that such rubric will gild his particular request with an inference above that of mere self-interest. The apartment owners, for example, claim they serve the "public interest" because their position strengthens the institution of private property and guards the fiscal integrity of rental housing generally. The tenants imply that they serve the public interest by trying to protect the state's citizenry from heartless and arbitrary evictions by rapacious owners. Who can honestly say that either claim is either wholly wrong or wholly right?

To some extent conflicts such as these are resolved by the raw political pressure lobbyists can bring to bear. But within the constraint of getting enough support for passage, there are many issues—many significant issues—which a staff member is free to resolve himself. With respect to some of these, lobbyists may try to persuade him one way or another. If there is conflict between different interest groups, either the staff member acts as an arbitrator and tries to determine the fairest compromise or he may simply base his decision on his own preferences. Some issues may be overlooked by affected interests or simply not be sufficiently important to any one group to make legislative advocacy worthwhile. Again, the staff member is free to exert his own preferences.

Bob and I were constantly aware of the substantial extent to which the basic structure of the housing finance agency—its position outside the Business and Transportation Agency, the breadth of its financing authority, the selection of its board of directors— was shaped by our own concept of how a housing finance agency should work. And as our sophistication in working within the Legislature increased, we became more careful in providing information to members. In part this care was encouraged by Zenovich, who chided us several times for talking too much—telling too much about the bill—in committee hearings. But much of it was an instinctive reaction. The less everyone else knew about the bill—both members and lobbyists—the less chance there was they would find something objectionable in it and the less disturbed the provisions we put into the original draft of the bill would be.

Legislative staff substantially reduces the dependency of a legislature on lobbyists. No longer must legislators rely upon special interests to draft bills and supply them with information by which to evaluate the bills on which they vote; they now have staff to perform these functions. But it is essential to recognize that, to a significant degree, this exchange has merely replaced the known bias of some particular group for the more individual, more personal, but not necessarily less prejudicial views of legislative staff. And the preconceptions of a staff member are far more difficult to discover because they do not announce them publicly, as lobbyists do. When Doug Gillies of the California Real Estate Association testifies that requiring good cause for eviction will wreak havoc in residential rental real estate, a member knows very well that the apartment owners, whom Gillies represents, believe it could reduce their income. If a staff member represents the same thing, it is much more difficult to tell whether the origin of his concern is that the owners will lose money, that the requirement will jeopardize the peace and safety of "good" tenants, that he himself owns or lives in an apartment house containing tenants he wants removed, or that he is merely relying on what Doug Gillies told him. Does the fact that the lobbyist expresses the views of some very particular constituency make him less credible than a staff member because of the bias it implies, or does it increase the legitimacy of his input because he represents at least some portion—indeed, sometimes a very large portion—of the state's voters while the staff member has no constituency at all?

In assessing the influence of legislative staff it is important also to consider the role it can play in initiating legislation. Michael Malbin discusses what David Price has referred to as "entrepreneurial" staff members in Congress, who develop legislation around an issue which they believe may be of political value to a committee chairman, in the case of committee staff, or in the case of an administrative assistant, to the member for whom they work. The staff-developed legislation is a "product" which is "marketed" to a potential "buyer." The "buyer" is the member who presumably then sponsors the legislation.

Bob and I carried the entrepreneurial paradigm a step further by coming from outside the Legislature and making our sales pitch to several members before finding a "buyer" in Zenovich and working with him to create an entirely new committee devoted almost exclusively to marketing our public policy "product" to the entire Legislature. Our case may have been unusual, but the proprietary enthusiasm with which we pushed "our" bill was not. Malbin states that "not all partisan staffs are entrepreneurial, but all entrepreneurial staffs are partisan." If by this he means that entrepreneurial activity is limited to instances in which staff members wish to further the interests of a particular member or political party, he believes it to be a more limited phenomenon in Congress than I found it in the California Legislature.

Bob and I were not seeking to further Zenovich's or Chacon's political aspirations. We believed that California should have a housing finance agency. That conviction, plus our enjoyment of the political negotiations involved and the satisfaction we hoped to obtain in seeing what we considered *our* ideas ultimately become law, kept us working fifty to sixty hours per week. And I do not think our motivations were dissimilar from those of a number of the other staff members with whom we worked. The personal satisfaction of identifying what one believes is a problem requiring public attention, designing a legislative solution, and working to see it ultimately effected can be considerable. A staff member must be able to demonstrate to some legislator that it is in his interest to author the bill and lend it whatever support he can, but this is only the first of many political hurdles the staff originator has to jump on the way to implementing his own ideas as public policy.

The increasing role of legislative staff reflects the pressures for more government, the need, or at least the demand, that an increased amount of economic and social decisions be made by the public rather than the private sector. The size of the staff bureaucracy in the U.S. Congress has increased over the past thirty years in tandem with the influence of the federal government. The growth of government at the national level has generally not taken place at the expense of state government in the sense that the former has not poached in areas where the states were effectively involved. Rather, as the demand for public decision-making expanded, the federal government moved more aggressively than the states to fill that demand. But as Senator Moynihan has pointed out, the federal government, while very good at collecting revenues, has turned out to be rather bad at disbursing services.

It was what Bob and I felt to be the failure of the federal government in providing housing assistance that initially prompted us to go to Sacramento. In doing so we tried a solution to federal adiposity which has been frequently proposed over the last decade: transfer significant amounts of responsibility from the national government to the states. That suggestion has usually been made along with the recognition that before the states can exercise that responsibility, their governmental institutions—particularly the legislatures—must be improved. Such a realignment of responsibility within the federal system might very well improve the responsiveness and quality of public decision-making and administration. But what impressed me while working with a state legislature which is a model of reform was the extent to which its strongest feature—a large and competent staff—had insulated the elected representatives from the guts of legislative decision-making.

This dilution of the representative nature of our government is not the result of incompetent legislators nor power-hungry legislative staffs. It will not be cured by throwing any rascals out. There is, quite simply, more governing demanded of the California Legislature than the 120 individuals of which it is comprised can accomplish without delegating far more of the responsibility for decision-making than is generally known. Occasionally a legislator will be candid on the issue. I recall one of the hearings on our housing bill during the spring of 1975. Zenovich stood at the witness podium and gave his usual short general introductory statement. He was then asked several questions by a committee member, to which he gave what were clearly inadequate answers. Finally, he pointed to Bob and me who were seated at the witness table, and said, "Hell, if you want to know about the bill, ask them. They're the ones who wrote it."

But such candor is rare among California legislators. Many do not, I believe, wish to admit the extent of staff influence, even to themselves. To do so would damage their personal sense of self-esteem. And certainly a strong inhibitor is concern that their constituents might be alarmed. This refusal to acknowledge staff influence produces the "love/hate" which George Beattie referred to as characterizing the attitude of members toward staff generally. Legislative staff become increasingly embarrassing as they become more necessary.

There is inevitable tension between the capacity of a legislature to grapple competently with the volume and complexity of issues it is called upon to address and the extent to which it can retain the representative nature of its decision-making process. I hope that, in whatever other ways this narrative may further an understanding of legislative procedure, it at least implies the existence of this conflict. To legislators, it may suggest that their role is changing from that of policy-maker to one which is largely that of a manager—overseeing a cadre of professional staff. Certainly the way in which such a conflict can be resolved or alleviated institutionally deserves attention from political scientists. The public at large should understand the way in which staff members function in a modern legislature. Constituents are, increasingly, represented not by a single individual, but by a team, only one member of which is elected. Constituents' knowledge of that fact may affect the character of the decisions they entrust to the public sector and the extent to which our representative government is relied upon to address the social, economic, and ethical issues confronting society.

Afterword

Eugene Bardach

DESPITE MANY CONTRARY APPEARANCES, POLITICAL SCIENTISTS do not often grapple in a serious way with legislative "dynamics" or legislative "process." The many books, articles, and course names that contain the words "process" and "dynamics" are for the most part simply misleading. They are about institutions, about structure, about roles, about rules, about behavior—but they are usually, except in certain superficial ways, not about "process" or "dynamics." These latter words connote a phenomenon that has at its center the passage of time and the regular succession of system states; and such phenomena, at least in the realm of politics and policy-making, are, as it turns out, extremely hard to conceptualize and to study empirically. Political scientists have intuitively grasped the nature of "process" phenomena and have pursued this intuition diligently and often insightfully. But clear, deep comprehension has so far been elusive.

Legislative Statics: Some Premises

I believe a fruitful beginning would be to construe the legislative process as a contest in which support waxes and wanes on behalf of some legislative proposal. A central objective of political science should therefore be to describe, and implicitly to explain, how this waxing and waning occurs. In doing so, we may be aided by the following premises about legislative institutions, strategies, and practices that have already been reasonably well established in the political science literature.

1. Calculating, strategic, opportunistic behavior is extremely widespread, even though not universal.

2. Interests are quite various, but generally fall into four major categories: economic, bureaucratic, "ideological" or "policy-
oriented," and careerist (especially in a "partisan" or "political"
sense). In most situations careerism probably explains behavior
better than any other single motivational hypothesis; but the
structure of the institutions that shape careers and determine role
requirements reflects underlying economic, bureaucratic, and Constitutional relationships. "Ideological" or "policy-oriented" interests are expressed relatively infrequently, but when they are
prominent, they can profoundly influence the way an issue is
defined and the way any contest over the issue shapes up.

3. Most permanent participants in the world of legislative
politics specialize by issue area. This means that most issues being
contested in legislative arenas at any given moment are not salient
to most participants. It means, furthermore, that the potentially
mobilizable allies for any given issue or contest are usually a small
and finite subset of the total number of persons and organizations
routinely active in legislative politics.

4. Even when an issue or contest is salient to a participant, it
is only intermittently so, as it is usually only one of several salient
issues or contests requiring attention.

5. The general strategic objective of a policy-oriented entre-
preneur in the legislative process is to achieve "sufficient consensus" among interested parties, including legislators themselves, so
as to outweigh opponents of the proposed policy. Procedural rules
determine that "outweighing" is often operationalized as "attain-
ing a majority of the votes." But this is not always the case inas-
much as certain interests or individuals are sometimes accorded
extraordinary weight, either by custom or by virtue of their institutional position or for some other reason. "Broad," as opposed
to "sufficient," consensus usually threatens excessive dilution of
the substantive policy being proposed, and almost always requires
the expenditure of much time and effort as well.

6. The internal structure of legislative bodies—especially
those rules that affect the routing of bills through the committee
system and the scheduling of hearings and key votes—furnishes resources, opportunities, and incentives to participants on all sides
to maneuver against each other for tactical advantage.

7. Most communication among participants takes place among presumptive allies, and communication with presumptively incorrigible opponents is relatively infrequent. However, much attention is devoted to interests whom it is thought important to neutralize and to neutrals whom it is thought important to win over. The content of most communications is exhortative an informative. Although communications involving bargaining and negotiations are relatively infrequent overall, they are usually disproportionately significant to the outcome of the consensus-building process.

Legislative Dynamics: A Model

The accompanying figure displays a sort of longitudinal section of a certain common type of legislative process.[1]

FIGURE 1

Dynamic Model of a Legislative Contest

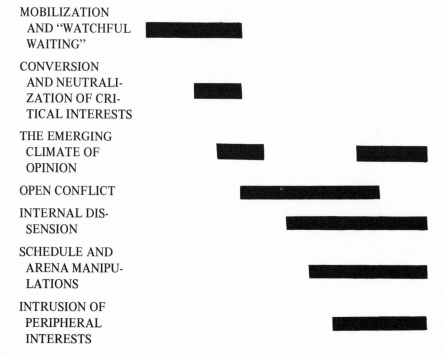

MOBILIZATION
   AND "WATCHFUL
   WAITING"

CONVERSION
   AND NEUTRALI-
   ZATION OF CRI-
   TICAL INTERESTS

THE EMERGING
   CLIMATE OF
   OPINION

OPEN CONFLICT

INTERNAL DIS-
   SENSION

SCHEDULE AND
   ARENA MANIPU-
   LATIONS

INTRUSION OF
   PERIPHERAL
   INTERESTS

Actually, "the process" being modeled here is a series of partially sequential but partially overlapping sub-processes. They are integrated by virtue of the fact that sub-processes which occur earlier in the sequence create the political conditions that give impetus to sub-processes which come later. (For convenience in presentation I have indicated roughly when each process begins and how long it might ordinarily be expected to last. Obviously such indications are meant to be illustrative only.) The model is based partly on my reading of the case study literature in political science and partly on an analysis that I have published elsewhere of a legislative contest over mental health policy reform in California which seems to me fairly typical of a large set of contests.[2] It is also based on the case history reported in this book, and I shall elaborate some of the reasoning behind the model displayed in the chart with reference to this case.

1. **Mobilization and "watchful waiting."** During this early phase of the process, policy-oriented and more politically oriented staff entrepreneurs seek each other out and establish a provisional alliance. An "office" with some sort of political legitimacy emerges to serve as an operations center. Interests within the policy area's routinely attentive public—especially middle-level bureaucrats, interest group leaders, staffs to professional associations, and paid lobbyists—are sounded out. Based on speculations that the emerging venture will have a good political payoff and entail minimal risks, a few prominent politicos (from either the legislature or the executive branch or both) agree to act as patrons to the proposal in their official capacities. At this stage, presumptive opponents and skeptical neutrals remain relatively passive. They reason that since most new political (and policy) ventures die simply for want of sufficient enthusiasm among the nominal allies and supporters, there is no reason to risk being viewed as an obstructionist or to expend any time, energy, or money on active opposition.

In the present case, BeVier and his associate Bob Klein were the policy-oriented entrepreneurs who established a working relationship with certain legislators, and with William Hauck, a staff assistant to the speaker of the California State Assembly. They touched base with numerous organized interests in the housing field in connection with their proposal to involve the state as a supplier and/or a guarantor of mortgage loans to low- and middle-income persons. Senator Zenovich and Assemblyman Chacon enlisted as patrons. A Joint Committee on Community Development and Housing Needs was set up, with BeVier and Klein as the committee staff. The main opposition was expected to be the administration of Governor Ronald Reagan, but the administration did nothing during this period to block any of the proponents' political moves.

2. **Conversion and neutralization of critical interests.** The first line of defense by political opponents is the argument that "it can't work." Entrepreneurial energies on the proponents' side are therefore directed towards establishing a record of testimony that "it can work." Interests identified as critical to the subsequent implementation of the proposal are coaxed and prodded—and strategic concessions are sometimes made in order to buy promises of subsequent cooperation and immediate verbal support.[3] If support is not possible, the objective of such negotiations is neutrality or at least continued temporizing. If this too is not achievable, it is necessary to mobilize one's own "experts" to counteract the adverse testimony of opponents.

In the contest described by BeVier, the interests defined as critical from this point of view were the savings and loan associations ("s & l's"). In most cases, any bureaucratic objections that "this proposal will create an administrative nightmare" would have to be neutralized during this phase: there were none in this case, however, probably because no existing state agency was occupying the "housing" turf at all in 1973-74.

3. **The emerging climate of opinion.** Surrounding every proposal is a "climate of opinion" concerning its political prospects and its general advisability as public policy. People come to talk about "the issue" and begin to say things like, "It's a hot one" or "It's a winner" or "It's a turkey." A number of individuals and/or organized interests develop political stakes in just how they are seen to be related to the developing contest. Bandwagon effects, for instance, attract people to "winners" (and, conversely, repel

them from "losers"). Controversial issues attract some people
but repel others. Of particular significance to the development of
the political process at this point is the emerging belief that
"something is going to happen" in the policy area. This growing
belief stimulates people to come forward with counter-proposals.
Some counter-proposals are intended to undercut the original proposal entirely. At the other extreme are attempts by rival politicos
to steal credit by advancing essentially identical proposals under
their own banners.

In the present case, Paul McCarron, lobbyist for the California
Builders Council, came forward during this period with a housing
bill more favorable to the building interests than the concept then
being pushed by BeVier and his allies. BeVier's speculation about
McCarron's motives, while scanty and unsupported by data, nevertheless throws light on the general phenomenon: "We never felt
as though he was particularly comfortable with us. He had, I
think, little confidence in his ability to influence us. We surmised
[also] that . . . he was attempting to demonstrate [to his em-
ployers] a more assertive role."

4. **Open conflict.** At some point after the opposition has crys-
tallized and has begun serious counter-attack, the proponents
suffer what they and others regard as "a major setback." This perceived "setback" jars loose some interests that had attached themselves in the most recent period and threatens to detach even some
of those interests that had come into the coalition in the early
days. Provided the inner circle of managers of the proponents' side
is even minimally competent, at this point they typically invent
means to effect some sort of "comeback." This in turn triggers renewed opposition, and the contest settles into a period of open
conflict, full of rhetorical attacks and counter-attacks, and occasionally punctuated by the public affirmations of various interests,
hitherto neutral, that now endorse, or repudiate, one or the other
side to the conflict.

This period of open conflict, though usually the most visible
as well as one of the more lengthy phases of the legislative process,
was atypically brief and undramatic in the California housing
finance case. It consisted mainly of a four-week period from late

May to late June 1974, in which a few extra "conservative" votes were being pursued by both sides in the Senate. The major interest that "tipped" during this period was the California Real Estate Association.

5. **Internal dissension.** The inner circle among the proponents' coalition usually has to make concessions during the period of open conflict (and thereafter too) that are strongly disliked by some of the coalition participants. For this reason, and lesser ones too numerous to describe, the inner circle of managers spends a lot of time and energy keeping the peace, and beating back challenges to their own leadership positions. The policy proposal might have to be modified to accommodate new (or old, but hitherto unsatisfied) demands by allies. But modifications might jeopardize existing understandings with opponents and powerful neutrals. Hence this period is marked by imputations of false dealing and by heightened suspiciousness and defensiveness all around.

In the present case, "liberal" members of the proponents' coalition stopped allowing themselves to be taken for granted by the inner circle. They demanded certain amendments that were anathema to both the s & l's and the real estate interests. It is apparent from BeVier's account (if one reads between the lines ever so slightly) that the "pro-tenant" reformers were viewed by the inner-circle professional types as quixotic and irresponsible, and that the reformers felt the professionals were duplicitous trimmers or worse. Personal feelings—usually negative ones—constantly threaten to intrude. Interestingly enough, intra-coalition politics was more dramatic, and more critical, than the politicking against the opposition—in which respect this case is also probably somewhat atypical.

6. **Schedule and arena manipulations.** Eventually the contest must get channeled through formal legislative routes, e.g., subcommittees, policy committees, finance committees, the lower chamber, the upper chamber, a conference committee, the desk of the chief executive. And it must pass from one arena to the next according to a schedule determined in large measure by internal legislative rules and decisions. To the extent that schedules and routes can be manipulated by contest participants, political re-

sources are invested in doing so, and in preventing opponents (and sometimes certain allies) from succeeding in their own attempts at manipulation.

In the case history at hand, relatively slight attention seems to have been paid to the routing of the package of housing bills through the committee structure: the bills went through the most advantageous route conceivable under the circumstances, and the bill's managers did not have to do much to arrange it. Scheduling was another matter, however. For rather complicated reasons, the California primary elections in early June created unexpected urgency for the managers of the housing bill package, who were forced to expend a great deal of time and energy on pushing forward certain ostensible "deadlines" and on advancing the schedule of committee consideration of their bills. Exactly how—or whether—opponents or disgruntled allies used these conditions of urgency to increase their bargaining leverage is not clear from the BeVier account, though there are intimations that the bill's managers were very aware of their vulnerability in this respect.

7. **Intrusion of peripheral interests.** Outside the boundaries (however loosely or strictly defined) of the issue area's routinely attentive public are (1) the "general public," which is usually apolitical, and (2) the publics routinely attentive to other policy areas. The "general public" and the "peripheral interests" in these latter publics can intrude at any point in the contest, of course, but it is likely that their activities (if they occur at all) will tend to be concentrated towards the final stages. The primary reason is that involvement by the governor (or in national politics, the president) and by legislators from outside the routinely attentive public is usually not formally prescribed until near the end of the contest, and their involvement often pulls with it the attention and the participation of special interests that had remained on the periphery. Another reason for relatively late intrusion by these interests is that the volatile conditions created as a result of intra-coalition dissension, last-minute concessions to opponents and neutrals, and the crash-effort mobilization to deal with surprise shifts in routing and scheduling tend to alter the "objective" stakes for many contestants, including the interests at the peri-

phery. Their participation, of course, merely increases the volatility of the contest as it moves towards its resolution.

The California State Employees Association entered the housing bills debate only in mid-June 1974, after most of the committee hearings had been concluded. The commercial banks waited until then as well. In neither case, unfortunately, is it clear why they did not move earlier. Also showing up towards the final days were the *Los Angeles Times* and the California Republican party convention. These were attracted to the issue because Governor Reagan's national political ambitions made him particularly vulnerable to influences from such quarters at that time, and these interests wished somehow to take advantage of the fact.

Some Methodological Observations

Whatever its virtues or defects, the above model should be considered of limited generality, at least pending a good deal more conceptual and empirical investigation. I believe first that it should prove most useful in illuminating contests that begin and then remain, essentially two-sided. There was momentarily a chance that the California housing policy contest would develop a third side (the California Builders Council bill). Had this occurred, the contest would surely have become a great deal more complicated; and one wonders if the rather simple processes described above in stages 4-7 would have done justice to its complexity. Secondly, the model is probably not applicable to contests in which the general public is heavily involved, that is, contests in which the climate of opinion is highly sensitive to media treatment of the issue, to the results of public opinion surveys, and/or to the mobilization of electoral constituencies. In such contests, the propensity of many key players to strut and posture makes negotiations—indeed, all political communications—harder to carry out and probably introduces more random elements into the process.

I should further warn the reader that the foregoing model has deliberately excluded a certain type of political skill, namely, the ability to foresee future political developments and to take measures in advance to prevent or hasten them or to maximize or minimize their potential. BeVier and Klein, for instance, antici-

pated from the first the possibility of having to make concessions
to the Reagan administration and packaged their policy proposal
in several different bills so as to give themselves the option of jet-
tisoning some bills to save the others. They also decided to introduce identical legislative packages in each legislative chamber
separately, largely in order to avoid delays in the later stages of
the contest. Who can say how these early decisions altered later
phases of the process—or even earlier phases, for that matter?
Similarly, one wonders what BeVier and Klein would have done in
November and December 1973 had they foreseen the trouble that
their more "liberal" allies would cause them in May and June
1974. Perhaps other legislative entrepreneurs, more experienced
than BeVier and Klein, would have taken greater pains to nurture
bonds of loyalty and trust with these allies. In that case the sub-
process I call "internal dissension" might not have occurred at all.

The logical implications of this last possibility are unsettling.
In order to gain insight into the legislative process we apparently
must exclude from the definition of "the process" the use of high-
level skills aimed at understanding, predicting, and controlling the
underlying process; for if these skills are assumed to be at work,
they cause the underlying process to take on an entirely different
form than it might otherwise have taken. But in order to recognize
such anticipatory skills, so that we may exclude their effects from
our interpretation of the underlying process, we need to have arrived at some understanding of the process already. Otherwise we
would not be able to distinguish genuine anticipatory skills from
just any sort of prognosticating behavior. Unfortunately, empirical
observation cannot help much to cut this logical knot, for the
events of any actual contest must be assumed to reflect some combination of both the underlying process and those anticipatory
skills that in effect contradict that process.[4]

If there is a clear-cut solution to this problem, I do not have it.
Of course, the very fact that I have attempted above (and in my
earlier *Skill Factor*) to construct a "skill-free" model of the underlying process suggests that I must have found some palliative for
the problem if not a solution. Perhaps the key lies in the possibility of making inferences from the subjective experiences in politi-

cal problem-solving of political entrepreneurs such as BeVier and Klein. From the point of view of political entrepreneurs trying to put together a winning coalition in a real contest, the underlying process registers as a succession of problems: they must mobilize allies, neutralize opponents, shape the climate of opinion, still internal dissension, manipulate legislative schedules, orchestrate last-minute policy shifts, and so on. If we could understand when and how these problems enter the cognitive map of such entrepreneurs, and what they look like *before* they are reshaped by skillful anticipatory strategies and tactics, we would have quite a lot of useful data with which to construct both a model of the underlying process and an inventory of certain important entrepreneurial skills.[5]

It would behoove us to understand, in particular, one of the least remarked upon, but also one of the most revealing, behavior patterns in the legislative process—what might be called "watchful waiting." Watchful waiting at the "micro" level of individual behavior reflects unusually well the underlying dynamics of the legislative process that are unfolding at the "macro" level.

Let us see how this reflection comes about. For what are participants waiting? "For others to make their moves," "for events to unfold," "for so-and-so to state his terms," "for the opportunity to ripen," etc. They are often waiting, in other words, for what we called "sub-processes" to begin. Why are they watching instead of acting? Because they understand, at least implicitly, that there is an internal logic to the whole process, a developmental or dialectical logic if you will, that tends to cause the process to open up in a relatively orderly and therefore predictable way.[6] Contest participants who are vouchsafed such understanding, therefore, can act as "informants," much in the same way that certain native tribesmen function as "informants" to visiting anthropologists. Admittedly, if we must crawl in this fashion through the minds of the participants on the way to our own, more detached, understanding of the dynamics of the legislative process, the route is bound to be somewhat complicated. On the other hand, I believe this route will in fact work, which is more than can be said for other routes that have been tried or proposed. Where can we obtain data furnished by such "informants"? One obvious source is the written records furnished by reflective, intelligent participants such as Michael BeVier and his recent predecessor in this genre, Eric Redman, in *The Dance of Legislation.*[7]

Unfortunately this source is limited by the rare occurrence of that mix of talent, opportunity, and motivation required to produce accounts of useably high quality. Political scientists, therefore, will have to rely on their own field work. Moreover, the field work will have to be of a certain kind. Observations and interviews carried out as the process unfolds are likely to be far more useful than *ex post* reconstructions, for these latter accounts are not so likely to convey the uncertainties and ambiguities that beset political actors in actual problematic situations, much less the pattern of "watchful waiting." It would be premature, however, to claim clear superiority for any one approach to data collection over another. In the end, experience will tell. So long as the analytic objectives are clear, the methodological issues will present only minor difficulties.

Jerusalem, Israel
September 1978

NOTES

1. We shall say more below about the features of the contest that restrict the applicability of this model. Briefly, they are the aggregation of the interests into no more than two main contending parties, the absence of sustained participation by the "general public," and the absence of extraordinary "anticipatory skills" among the players.

2. *The Skill Factor in Politics: Repealing the Mental Commitment Laws in California* (Berkeley: University of California Press, 1972).

3. Unfortunately, the analysis of potential implementation problems is rarely broad or deep enough. See my book, *The Implementation Game: What Happens after a Bill Becomes a Law* (Cambridge, Mass.: MIT Press, 1977). From BeVier's account in Chapters 3 and 4, he and Klein appear to have been unusually astute implementation analysts.

4. One could conceivably argue that the definition of process ought to include the effects of these skills. But this is not a solution. If such skills are applied only by unusually talented entrepreneurs and even by them relatively infrequently—as I believe is the case—we would face the very difficult task of framing postulates for our model about exotic and hard-to-calibrate phe-

nomena. The postulates would be inescapably arbitrary. On the other hand, if such skills are in fact applied quite routinely, "the process" cannot, by definition, occur—since all contingencies are foreseen and prevented. The only thing left would be the interplay of random elements and steps governed by rules of formal procedure—hardly an interesting subject to study.

5. This was essentially the approach I followed in *The Skill Factor in Politics*, although I did not explain it there. For an account of some of the more important anticipatory skills, see chapter 12 therein, especially pp. 241-260.

6. But if they do rely on such an implicit order, one might ask why participants are watching the events linked to still-distant sub-processes instead of paying no attention at all. It is because they understand that these developmental tendencies are often disrupted either by accident or by someone else's strategic design—and because they themselves may wish to disrupt them with strategic designs of their own.

7. New York: Simon and Schuster, 1973.

Appendix A

Individuals Referred to Frequently
in the Text

NAME	POSITION (1974-1975) (Districts are before 1974 election.)
Bagley, William T.	assemblyman (R) 7th District, Marin, Sonoma Counties; ran for state controller in 1974, defeated by Kenneth Cory
Beattie, George	principal consultant, Assembly Committee on Urban Development and Housing; replaced in 1975 by Renée Franken, associate consultant
BeVier, Michael J.	consultant, Joint Committee on Community Development and Housing Needs
Biddle, Craig W.	senator (R) 36th District, Riverside, San Bernardino Counties; defeated in 1974 by Robert Presley
Bradley, Clark L.	senator (R) 14th District, Santa Clara, Alameda Counties; defeated in 1974 by Jerry Smith
Brown, Edmund G. Jr. (Jerry)	secretary of state; elected governor in 1974
Brown, Willie L., Jr.	assemblyman (D) 18th District, San Francisco, chairman of Committee on Ways and Means until defeated by Leo T. McCarthy in contest for assembly speakership, June 1974
Burns, Donald E.	secretary of the Business and Transportation Agency, appointed by Governor Brown, January 1975
Cannon, W. Dean, Jr.	executive vice-president and legislative advocate, California Savings and Loan League

251

Carpenter, Dennis E.

senator (R) 34th District, Orange County, chairman of Republican Caucus

Chacon, Peter R.

assemblyman (D) 79th District, San Diego, chairman of Committee on Urban Development and Housing (in 1975 the committee's name was changed to Housing and Community Development)

Collier, Randolph

senator (D) 1st District, Del Norte, Humboldt, Lake, Mendocino, Siskiyou, Sonoma, and Trinity Counties; chairman of Finance Committee

Connerly, Wardell A.

private consultant retained by the California Builders Council; formerly deputy director of the Department of Housing and Community Development (resigned in 1973)

Cusanovich, Lou

senator (R) 23rd District, Los Angeles

DeMonte, Robert C.

director of the Office of Planning and Development; formerly director of the Department of Housing and Community Development (replaced in January 1974)

Deukmejian, George

senator (R) 37th District, Los Angeles; replaced Fred Marler as Republican floor leader in May 1974

Dills, Ralph C.

senator (D) 32nd District, Los Angeles, chairman of Committee on Government Organization

Elliott, S. Michael

deputy secretary of the Business and Transportation Agency, appointed by Governor Brown, January 1975; chairperson and acting president, California Housing Finance Agency, 1975

English, Sharon J.

legislative advocate, California Housing Coalition

Flournoy, Houston I.

state controller; defeated in 1974 gubernatorial election by Edmund G. Brown, Jr.

Frank, Robert H.

consultant, Senate Select Committee on Housing and Urban Affairs

Gillies, Dugald

vice-president and legislative advocate, California Real Estate Association

Glikbarg, William K.

president, OGO, Inc.

Greene, Bill	assemblyman (D) 53rd District, Los Angeles; elected to serve 29th Senatorial District on April 1, 1975
Grunsky, Donald L.	senator (R) 17th District, Monterey, San Benito, San Luis Obispo, Santa Cruz Counties
Gunterman, Emma E.	legislative advocate, National Senior Citizens Law Center
Hardin, Kathryn	analyst, Office of the Legislative Analyst
Hauck, R. William	director, Assembly Office of Research; formerly administrative assistant to Assembly Speaker Robert Moretti
Holoman, Frank	assemblyman (D) 65th District, Los Angeles, chairman of Subcommittee on Community Development of the Joint Committee on Community Development and Housing Needs
Honse, Stuart	consultant, Subcommittee on Community Development of the Joint Committee on Community Development and Housing Needs
Kapiloff, Lawrence	assemblyman (D) 78th District, San Diego
Keiser, William H.	assistant legal counsel and legislative advocate, League of California Cities
Kersten, Elisabeth	associate consultant, Assembly Committee on Ways and Means
Klein, Robert N., Jr.	consultant, Joint Committee on Community Development and Housing Needs
Knox, John T.	assemblyman (D) 11th District, Contra Costa County
Livingston, Donald G.	assistant to Governor Reagan and director of programs and policy
Marler, Fred W., Jr.	senator (R) 2nd District, Shasta, Tehama, Glenn, Colusa, Butte, Yuba, Sutter, Yolo, and Solano Counties; appointed by Governor Reagan to superior court judgeship in May 1974
McCarron, Paul N.	legislative advocate, California Builders Council
Melnicoe, Peter	deputy legislative counsel
Mikell, Bernard J., Jr.	assistant vice-president and legislative advocate, California Savings and Loan League

Mills, James R.	senator (D) 40th District, Imperial, San Diego Counties, president pro tempore of the Senate
Moretti, Bob	assemblyman (D) 42nd District, Los Angeles, assembly speaker until June 1974 when he was defeated in Democratic gubernatorial primary
Moscone, George R.	senator (D) 10th District, San Francisco
Oschin, Samuel	chairman, OGO, Inc.
Paddock, Brian	legislative advocate, Western Center on Law and Poverty
Petris, Nicholas C.	senator (D) 11th District, Alameda County, chairman, Senate Select Committee on Housing and Urban Affairs
Post, A. Alan	legislative analyst
Pownall, Frederick M.	legislative advocate, California Bankers Association
Priest, Ivy Baker	state treasurer; did not run for reelection in 1974
Ratcliff, Richard E.	legislative advocate, California Bankers Association
St. Lezin, Richard	executive vice-president, Bay View Federal Savings and Loan Association
Shelby, Jack	legislative associate and legislative advocate, California Real Estate Association
Steinkamp, Alex D.	deputy state treasurer
Stern, Robert M.	associate counsel, Office of Secretary of State
Sternberg, Arnold C.	director, Department of Housing and Community Development, appointed by Governor Brown, January 1975
Teague, Elwood (Woody)	chairman, United Financial Corporation; chairman, Commission of Housing and Community Development
Unruh, Jesse M.	state treasurer, elected in 1974
Vasconcellos, John	assemblyman (D) 24th District, Santa Clara County
Walton, Frank J.	secretary of business and transportation (appointed by Governor Reagan)

Welch, Keith R.   legislative advocate, California State Employ-
                             ees' Association

Welch, Michelle   secretary, Joint Committee on Community De-
                             velopment and Housing Needs

Young, Casey L.   administrative assistant to Senator George
                             Zenovich

Zenovich, George N.   senator (D) 16th District, Fresno County,
                             chairman, Joint Committee on Community De-
                             velopment and Housing Needs

Appendix B

Legislative Process in the
California Legislature

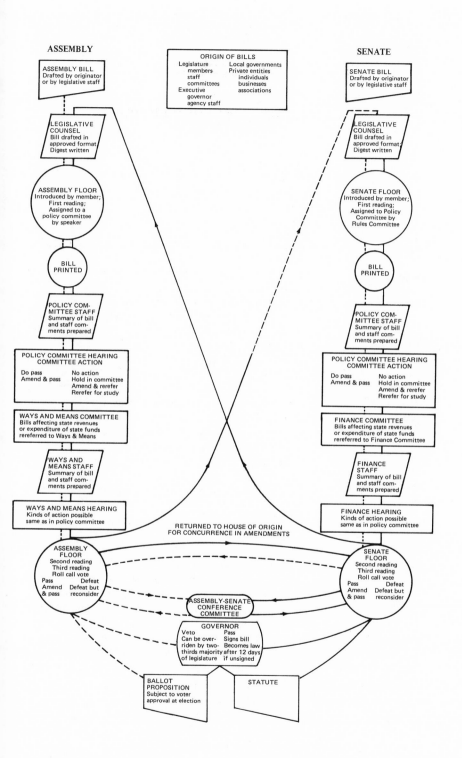

ASSEMBLY

ASSEMBLY BILL
Drafted by originator
or by legislative staff

LEGISLATIVE
COUNSEL
Bill drafted in
approved format;
Digest written

ASSEMBLY FLOOR
Introduced by member;
First reading;
Assigned to a
policy committee
by speaker

BILL
PRINTED

POLICY COM-
MITTEE STAFF
Summary of bill
and staff com-
ments prepared

POLICY COMMITTEE HEARING
COMMITTEE ACTION

Do pass   No action
Amend & pass   Hold in committee
                 Amend & rerefer
                 Rerefer for study

WAYS AND MEANS COMMITTEE
Bills affecting state revenues
or expenditure of state funds
rereferred to Ways & Means

WAYS AND
MEANS STAFF
Summary of bill
and staff com-
ments prepared

WAYS AND MEANS HEARING
Kinds of action possible
same as in policy committee

ASSEMBLY
FLOOR
Second reading
Third reading
Roll call vote
Pass   Defeat
Amend   Defeat but
& pass   reconsider

ORIGIN OF BILLS

Legislature   Local governments
  members   Private entities
  staff   individuals
  committees   businesses
Executive   associations
  governor
  agency staff

RETURNED TO HOUSE OF ORIGIN
FOR CONCURRENCE IN AMENDMENTS

ASSEMBLY-SENATE
CONFERENCE
COMMITTEE

GOVERNOR
Veto   Pass
Can be over-   Signs bill
riden by two-   Becomes law
thirds majority   after 12 days
of legislature   if unsigned

BALLOT
PROPOSITION
Subject to voter
approval at election

STATUTE

SENATE

SENATE BILL
Drafted by originator
or by legislative staff

LEGISLATIVE
COUNSEL
Bill drafted in
approved format;
Digest written

SENATE FLOOR
Introduced by member;
First reading;
Assigned to Policy
Committee by
Rules Committee

BILL
PRINTED

POLICY COM-
MITTEE STAFF
Summary of bill
and staff com-
ments prepared

POLICY COMMITTEE HEARING
COMMITTEE ACTION

Do pass   No action
Amend & pass   Hold in committee
                 Amend & rerefer
                 Rerefer for study

FINANCE COMMITTEE
Bills affecting state revenues
or expenditure of state funds
rereferred to Finance Committee

FINANCE
STAFF
Summary of bill
and staff com-
ments prepared

FINANCE HEARING
Kinds of action possible
same as in policy committee

SENATE
FLOOR
Second reading
Third reading
Roll call vote
Pass   Defeat
Amend   Defeat but
& pass   reconsider

Appendix C

Chronology and Voting Record

	1973
January 5	President Nixon suspends all federal housing subsidy activity.
January 17	BeVier and Klein meet with William Hauck of the Assembly Office of Research, Senator George Zenovich, and others to propose study of state assistance to housing.
February to August	BeVier and Klein work in tandem with Senator Zenovich's staff to obtain passage of Senate Concurrent Resolution No. 45, creating the Joint Committee on Community Development and Housing Needs.
September 1	BeVier and Klein are hired as consultants to the newly created Joint Committee on Community Development and Housing Needs.
November 14	First Public hearing of joint committee is held in San Francisco.
December 11	Second public hearing of joint committee is held in Sacramento.
December 17	Third public hearing of joint committee is held in San Francisco.
	1974
January 28	a legislative package to create a California housing finance agency is introduced by Senator Zenovich in the Senate. The package consists of three bills: S.B. 1633, S.B. 1634, S.B. 1635, and one constitutional amendment, S.C.A. 40.
January 30	A legislative package identical to that introduced by Zenovich is introduced by Assemblyman Chacon in the Assembly: A.B. 2966, A.B. 2967, A.B.2968, A.C.A. 96.

258

April 3

S.B. 1633, introduced in January as a "spot" bill, is amended by the author to include the full enabling legislation for a housing finance agency.

April 4

A.B. 2966, also introduced in January as a "spot" bill, is amended by the author to make it identical to S.B. 1633. At the Assembly Committee on Urban Development and Housing hearing on A.B. 2967, the committee votes "Do Pass and rerefer to Committee on Ways and Means" (ayes 5, noes 0).

April 17

At the Assembly Committee on Urban Development and Housing hearing on A.B. 2966, A.B. 2968, A.C.A. 96 the committee decides to continue the hearing at later date.

May 1

At the Assembly Committee on Urban Development and Housing hearing the committee votes: A.B. 2966, "Do pass and rerefer to Committee on Ways and Means" (ayes 5, noes 1); A.B. 2968, "Do pass and rerefer to Committee on Ways and Means" (ayes 4, noes 2): A.C.A. 96, "Amend and be adopted as amended and rerefer to Committee on Constitutional Amendments" (ayes, 5, noes 1).

May 2

At the Senate Committee on Governmental Organization hearing the committee votes: S.B. 1633, "Amend and pass as amended, and rerefer to Committee on Finance" (ayes 7, noes 1); S.B. 1634, "Do pass and rerefer to Committee on Finance" (ayes 7, noes 1); S.B. 1635, "Do pass and rerefer to Committee on Finance" (ayes 7, noes 1); S.C.A. 40, "Be adopted but first amend and rerefer to Committee on Finance" (ayes 7, noes 1).

May 8

At the Assembly Committee on Ways and Means hearing the chairman appoints a subcommittee, chaired by Assemblyman Knox to hold hearings on A.B. 2966, A.B. 2967, A.B. 2968.

May 20

At the Senate Committee on Finance hearing. S.B. 1635 is held in committee with consent of the author; the committee votes: S.B. 1633, "Amend and pass as amended" (ayes 8, noes 2); S.B. 1634, "Do pass" (ayes 8, noes 2); S.C.A. 40 "Be adopted" (ayes 9, noes 0).

May 20

At the Assembly Committee on Constitutional Amendments hearing on A.C.A. 96 the committee votes: "Amend and be adopted as amended" (ayes 6, noes 0).

May 21   The assembly Committee on Ways and Means ad hoc
                   subcommittee, chaired by Assemblyman Knox holds
                   a hearing on A.B. 2966, A.B. 2967, A.B. 2968. The
                   subcommittee requests certain amendments and
                   adopts recommendation to full committee that A.B.
                   2966 and A.B. 2967 be passed as amended.

May 29   Senate floor vote on S.B. 1633. Passage is refused
                   (ayes 18, noes 10) but reconsideration is granted; roll
                   call:

Ayes (18)		Noes (10)
Alquist	Marks	Berryhill
Ayala	Mills	Bradley
Beilenson	Nejedly	Carpenter
Biddle	Robbins	Collier
Dymally	Rodda	Cusanovich
Gregorio	Schrade	Deukmejian
Grunsky	Short	Marler
Holmdahl	Song	Stevens
Kennick	Zenovich	Stull
		Whetmore

June 5   At the Assembly Committee on Ways and Means
                   hearing A.B. 2968 is held in committee with consent
                   of the author; committee votes: A.B. 2966, "Do
                   pass" (ayes 11, noes 0); A.B. 2967, "Do pass" (ayes
                   11, noes 0).

June 6   Assembly floor vote on A.C.A. 96. It is adopted and
                   sent to the Senate (ayes 56, noes 11).

June 14   Assembly floor vote on A.B. 2966. It is passed and
                   sent to the Senate (ayes 57, noes 13). A.B. 2967 is
                   also passed and sent to the Senate (ayes 64, noes 3).

June 18   Senate floor vote on S.B. 1633. It is passed and sent
                   to the Assembly (ayes, 29, noes 8); roll call:

Ayes (29)		Noes (8)
Alquist	Moscone	Berryhill
Ayala	Nejedly	Bradley
Behr	Petris	Carpenter
Beilenson	Robbins	Cusanovich
Biddle	Roberti	Deukmejian
Collier	Rodda	Richardson
Dills	Schrade	Way
Dymally	Short	Whetmore
Gregorio	Song	
Grunsky	Stevens	
Holmdahl	Stiern	
Kennick	Stull	
Marks	Wedworth	
Marler	Zenovich	
Mills		

S.B. 1634 is also passed and sent to the Assembly (ayes 29, noes 8). S.C.A. 40 is adopted and sent to the Assembly (ayes 29, noes 8).

June 20 At the Assembly Committee on Urban Development and Housing hearing the committee votes: S.B. 1633, "Amend and be adopted as amended and rerefer to Committee on Ways and Means (ayes 4, noes 0); S.B. 1634, "Do pass and rerefer to Committee on Ways and Means (ayes 4, noes 0); S.C.A. 40, "Amend and be adopted as amended and rerefer to Committee on Constitutional Amendments (ayes 4, noes 0).

June 24 At the Assembly Committee on Constitutional Amendments hearing on S.C.A. 40 the committee votes: "Amend and be adopted as amended" (ayes 4, noes 2).

June 26 The Assembly Committee on Ways and Means hearing on S.B. 1633 is postponed. Committee votes on S.B. 1634: "Do pass" (ayes 11, noes 2).

June 27 Assembly floor vote on S.C.A 40. It is adopted and sent to the Senate (ayes 58, noes 14). S.B. 1634 is passed and sent to the Senate (ayes 61, noes 7).

June 27 Senate floor vote on S.C.A. 40. Senate concurs in Assembly amendment (ayes 27, noes 7).

June 28 Legislature begins summer recess.

August 5 Legislature reconvenes.

August 5 At the Assembly Committee on Ways and Means hearing on S.B. 1633 the committee votes "Do pass" (ayes 12, noes 2).

August 5	Assembly floor vote on S.B. 1633. It passes and is sent to the Senate (ayes 62, noes 8).
August 5	Senate floor vote on S.B. 1633. Senate concurs in Assembly amendment (ayes 27, noes 11); roll call:

Ayes (27)		Noes (11)
Alquist	Nejedly	Berryhill
Ayala	Petris	Bradley
Behr	Rains	Carpenter
Beilenson	Robbins	Collier
Biddle	Roberti	Cusanovich
Dills	Rodda	Deukmejian
Dymally	Schrade	Richardson
Gregorio	Short	Stiern
Grunsky	Song	Stull
Holmdahl	Stevens	Way
Kennick	Walsh	Whetmore
Marks	Wedworth	
Mills	Zenovich	
Moscone		

	Vote on S.B. 1634: Senate concurs in Assembly amendment (ayes 29, noes 10).
August 8	Senator Zenovich receives telephone call from Governor Reagan saying he will veto the housing bills.
August 9	Senate receives veto messages on S.B. 1633 and S.B. 1634.
August 12	Governor Reagan's veto of S.B. 1633 is sustained on Senate floor (ayes 24, noes 13); roll call:

Ayes (24)		Noes (13)
Alquist	Nejedly	Berryhill
Ayala	Petris	Biddle
Behr	Rains	Bradley
Beilenson	Roberti	Collier
Dymally	Rodda	Cusanovich
Gregorio	Short	Deukmejian
Grunsky	Song	Harmer
Holmdahl	Stevens	Marler
Kennick	Stiern	Richardson
Marks	Walsh	Schrade
Mills	Wedworth	Stull
Moscone	Zenovich	Way
		Whetmore

Governor's veto of S.B. 1634 is sustained (ayes 24, noes 12). Reconsideration is granted on both votes.

August 13	Governor Reagan's veto of S.B. 1633 is sustained upon reconsideration. (ayes 24, noes 13); roll call:

Ayes (24)		Noes (13)
Alquist	Moscone	Berryhill
Ayala	Petris	Biddle
Behr	Rains	Bradley
Beilenson	Robbins	Carpenter
Dills	Roberti	Collier
Dymally	Rodda	Cusanovich
Gregorio	Song	Deukmejian
Grunsky	Stevens	Marler
Holmdahl	Stiern	Richardson
Kennick	Walsh	Schrade
Marks	Wedworth	Stull
Mills	Zenovich	Way
		Whetmore

November 5	General election.
December 2	Start of new two-year legislative session.
December 2	Senator Zenovich introduces S.B. 29, which is virtually identical to S.B. 1633, incorporating S.B. 1634.
December 3	Assemblyman Chacon introduces A.B. 116, a housing finance agency bill; Senator Moscone introduces S.B. 50, a housing finance agency bill.
	1975
January 6	Edmund G. (Jerry) Brown, Jr. assumes the governorship of California.
February 17	Governor Brown declares the 1975-1976 First Extraordinary Legislative Session for the purpose of considering legislation related to housing.
February 17	Assemblyman Chacon introduces A.B. 1X and Senator Zenovich introduces S.B. 2X. Both bills are identical to each other and similar to S.B. 29.
June 27	Governor signs A.B. 1X, enacting the Zenovich-Moscone-Chacon Housing and House Finance Act, creating the California Housing Finance Agency.
January 1977	The first home to be financed with a loan from the California Housing Finance Agency is purchased.

Appendix D

Summary Descriptions of Topic Legislation as Prepared by Legislative Counsel

---

This appendix includes summaries of the topic legislation prepared by legislative counsel. Such descriptions are prepared for every bill introduced in the Legislature and amended whenever significant changes are made in a bill as it moves through the Legislature. These summary descriptions, called the *Legislative Counsel's Digest,* are included in every bill printed and serve as an introduction to the legislation. Along with committee staff reports, they serve the legislator as a formal interpretation of a bill's content. The following are excerpts from the *Legislative Counsel's Digest* which describe the final version of each of the designated bills as it was enrolled and sent to the governor.

1973-1974 SESSION

Senate Bill No. 1633 (enrolled and sent to the governor on August 6, 1974)

Enacts the Zenovich-Chacon California Housing Finance Act providing for the creation of the California Housing Finance Corporation, to be administered by a board with prescribed membership. Prescribes conflict-of-interest standards for board members and officers and employees of the corporation. Requires the board to select a president of the corporation to manage the daily affairs of the corporation. Empowers the president to employ staff personnel as prescribed. Authorizes the board to appoint an attorney for the corporation, but requires the Attorney General to represent and appear for the people of the State of California and the corporation in prescribed court proceedings.

Designates the corporation as the sole state agency to receive and allocate federal assistance for subsidizing housing for persons and families of low or moderate income, and vests the corporation with responsibility for coordinating federal-state relationships affecting subsidy of housing for such persons and families. Authorizes the corporation to exercise the powers of a housing authority, as prescribed, for the sole purpose of receiving federal funds pursuant to specified provisions of federal law.

Authorizes the corporation to make loans, through specified intermediaries and intermediary devices, or to qualified mortgage lenders, as defined, for housing developments, as defined. Authorizes the corporation to make loans for such purpose directly, to the ultimate borrower only if the housing development to be financed is aided by a government housing subsidy. Provides that the corporation may restrict loans for the construction, rehabilitation, or acquisition of rental housing under the act made with the proceeds of tax-exempt securities, whether made directly or indirectly through a qualified mortgage lender, to limited-dividend housing sponsors, nonprofit housing sponsors, and local public entities, as defined. Requires the corporation to fix and alter a schedule of rents for all rental housing developments. Requires the corporation to establish maximum sale prices for single-family residential housing developments, as prescribed, with respect to initial sales and sales to buyers receiving mortgage loans from the corporation. Authorizes the corporation to contract with public agencies and private parties for specified purposes.

Requires the corporation, upon application, to designate any city, county, city and county, or combination of such entities acting jointly as a local housing agent if it meets specified criteria and requires applications for loans for housing developments made or assisted under the act to be reviewed by the local housing agent, if any, for the area. Authorizes any such city, county, city and county, or combination thereof to delegate the functions of the local housing agent, as prescribed. Provides that no such loan shall be made unless the housing development is approved by the local housing agent as complying with prescribed requirements.

Creates the California Housing Finance Fund which is not within the State Treasury and which is under the sole custody and control of the corporation. Continuously appropriates moneys in the fund to the corporation for the purposes of the act. Provides, however, that if neither SCA 40 nor ACA 96 is approved by the voters, the California Housing Finance Fund shall be created in the State Treasury and moneys in the fund shall be deposited with such depositories and withdrawn therefrom as prescribed by the general law.

Requires the corporation to make prescribed annual reports to the Governor, State Treasurer, Legislature, Joint Legislative Audit Committee, and Joint Legislative Budget Committee. Requires the Joint Legislative Audit Committee and Joint Legislative Budget Committee to submit a report to the Legislature on the corporation's activities within 90 days following receipt of the corporation's annual report.

Requires the corporation to provide an opportunity to review and comment to councils of government or cooperative metropolitan planning organizations created pursuant to specified provisions or other provisions of law with respect to housing developments within their respective jurisdictions.

Appropriates $750,000 to the State Housing Finance Fund to be used for the initial expenses of the corporation, and requires such moneys to be repaid to the State Treasury not later than 10 years from the date of their deposit in the fund.

Provides that the act shall become operative January 1, 1975, if the Housing Finance Bond Law of 1974 is approved by the voters at the November 1974 election, and provides that the act shall not be operative if the Housing Finance Bond Law of 1974 is not approved by the voters at such election.

Senate Bill No. 1634 (enrolled and sent to governor on August 6, 1974)

Provides, conditioned upon the approval of the state electorate, for the issuance of state bonds in a total amount not exceeding $500,000,000, the proceeds of which are authorized for use by the California Housing Finance Corporation in financing housing developments pursuant to prescribed provisions. Creates the California Housing Finance Committee with prescribed membership and functions. Provides that the act shall not become operative unless SB 1633 or AB 2966, or both, are enacted creating a California Housing Finance Corporation with the power to finance housing developments, and specifies that the act shall become operative on the date the first of such bills becomes operative.

Provides for submission of the bond proposal to the electors at the 1974 general election.

Senate Constitutional Amendment No. 40 (enrolled and sent to the secretary of state on June 28, 1974)

Declares that the use of public funds or credit to provide decent, safe, and sanitary housing serves a public purpose. Exempts housing financed by any agency or public corporation of the state, other than housing developed, acquired, constructed, or rehabilitated for the purpose of providing publicly owned and operated housing, from the provisions of the Constitution which require voter approval of low-rent housing projects, and from any local referendum.

Authorizes granting of sole custody and control of public moneys to any agency or public corporation of the state financing housing, and provides that such moneys may be deposited in the same manner as other moneys belonging to the state. Authorizes moneys advanced by such an agency or public corporation for financing housing to be transferred to the construction lender at the time the construction loan for the housing is recorded, pursuant to such requirements and conditions as the Legislature determines.

Exempts from civil service the members of the board of directors of the California Housing Finance Corporation and not more than an aggregate of 6 officers, attorneys, and employees of the corporation as may be designated by the Legislature or, if not, by the board of the corporation. . . .

Provides that the Secretary of State shall not submit this measure to the voters unless SB 1633 or AB 2967, or both, are also chaptered.

1975-1976 FIRST EXTRAORDINARY SESSION

Assembly Bill No. 1 (enrolled and sent to governor on June 24, 1975)

Present law creates and provides for the organization and functions of the Department of Housing and Community Development and the Commission of Housing and Community Development. However, present law specifies that the provisions creating the department and commission shall be operative only until the 61st day after final adjournment of the 1976 Regular Sesssion of the Legislature and that as of such date functions transferred to the department shall be retransferred to the agency from which they were removed.

Under present law neither the department nor any other state agency is empowered to conduct programs of housing finance specifically for persons and families of low or moderate income, and the department is specifically prohibited from engaging in direct loan or grant programs. However, cities, counties, cities and counties, housing authorities, and redevelopment agencies are authorized to finance residential rehabilitation, as specified, and to issue revenue bonds for such purpose under the Marks-Foran Residential Rehabilitation Act of 1973.

This bill would repeal current provisions relating to the organization of the department and commission and relating to certain of their functions, and would enact new provisions continuing the department and commission in existence and prescribing the organization and certain of the functions thereof. The bill would establish three divisions within the department. The bill would delete provisions which would eliminate the department and commission and retransfer the functions of the department at a time subsequent to adjournment of the 1976 Regular Sesssion of the Legislature.

This bill would create a Housing Finance Agency in the Business and Transportation Agency and would prescribe the organization and functions thereof. Specified regulations of the agency would be subject to approval by the department, the Secretary of the Business and Transportation Agency, or his representative. The agency would be empowered to lend moneys through specified intermediaries and intermediary devices, including the creation of secondary mortgage markets, directly to the ultimate borrower, or to qualified mortgage lenders, for the purpose of financing the construction, rehabilitation, or acquisition of housing for persons and families of low or moderate income, as defined. The bill would authorize the agency to grant money and property to housing sponsors and local agencies, as defined, for prescribed purposes.

The bill would empower the agency to enter into agreements with local public entities, as defined, for the conduct by the agency of programs of rehabilitation loans and housing finance, as prescribed, in areas designated by the department as participating concentrated rehabilitation areas. The bill would alternatively authorize the department to enter into agreements for the administration of such programs by the local public entity. The bill would alternatively authorize the agency to purchase bonds and notes issued by the city, county, city and county, housing authority, or redevelopment agency pursuant to the Marks-Foran Residential Rehabilitation Act of 1973. The bill would also permit the agency to enter into agreements with local public entities to provide specified assistance in connection with a citywide or countywide program of enforcement of housing standards.

The bill would authorize the agency to provide staffing for the Farmers Home Administration of the United States Department of Agriculture for loan-guarantee and grant programs conducted in the state.

The bill would authorize any city or county or combination thereof acting jointly or the governing body of an Indian reservation or rancheria, which meets specified criteria and which has been approved by the department, to review and approve or reject proposals for housing to be financed under the bill within the jurisdiction thereof, in accordance with specified criteria. Delegation of such review function to another local public entity would be permitted. The agency would also be required to provide specified areawide clearinghouses with opportunity for comment and review respecting proposed housing developments to be financed under the bill within the jurisdiction thereof.

The bill would empower the agency to contract with local public entities for the provision by such local public entity of specified services or property in connection with a development financed under the bill. The bill would permit state agencies authorized to convey real property of the state and local public entities to sell, lease, grant, or convey real property and appurtenances to the agency, or to a housing sponsor designated by the agency.

The bill would create the California Housing Finance Fund, which would be continuously appropriated to the agency for financing housing developments and rehabilitation of residential structures, as defined, pursuant to the bill and for servicing or retiring specified revenue bonds and obligations of the agency authorized by the bill. All moneys accruing to the agency would be required to be deposited in the fund. The agency would be empowered to direct the investment of moneys in the fund not required for its current needs and any interest or increment resulting from such investment would accrue to the fund. Moneys in the fund declared by the agency to be surplus and not necessary for specified purposes would be required to be used by the agency to provide special interest reduction programs, financial assistance or subsidies for housing financed under the bill, or prescribed counseling programs.

The bill would authorize the agency, for the purpose of financing housing developments under the bill and other specified purposes, to issue and refund, or renew, as specified, revenue bonds or other obligations secured by prescribed revenues or property of the agency, but which would not be a debt or liability of the state. The bill would require establishment of primary and secondary bond reserve accounts to secure each issuance of such bonds, as specified. The amount of such bonds would be limited to $300,000,000 of bonds not guaranteed by the federal government and $150,000,000 additional of bonds so guaranteed. The State Treasurer would be required to act as trustee for the agency and bondholders for prescribed purposes.

The bill would provide that the Secretary of the Business and Transportation Agency shall be responsible for allocating federal financial aid for subsidizing housing for persons and families of low or moderate income and gives the agency priority in receipt of such housing subsidies. Under the bill the department would be the principal state department for coordinating federal-state relationships in housing, except for housing finance. The bill would make the California Housing Finance Agency a state representative for receipt and allocation of federal financial aid for subsidizing housing for persons of low and moderate income and the agency would be required to receive priority as to such funds to the extent units financed under the bill are eligible for such assistance.

The bill would provide, conditioned upon the approval of the state electorate, for the issuance of state bonds in a total amount not exceeding $500,000,000, the proceeds of which are authorized for use in financing housing developments pursuant to the bill. The bill would provide for submission of the bond proposal to the electors in NOvember of 1976.

The bill would appropriate $10,750,000 for transfer to the California Housing Finance Fund to be used according to a prescribed schedule for the initial expenses of the agency and for the establishment of supplementary bond reserve accounts to secure issuance of the agency's revenues bonds, and would require such moneys to be repaid to the General Fund from specified revenues of the agency. The bill would require repayment of $750,000 of such amount not later than January 1, 1986, from such revenues. The bill would appropriate $599,817 to the Department of Housing and Community Development for its expenses under the bill. If the issuance of state general obligation bonds proposed by the bill is approved by the voters, the bill would require retransfer to the General Fund of moneys which would be appropriated by the bill for the establishment of supplementary bond reserve accounts of an amount equal to such moneys from the first proceeds of such state general obligation bonds.

Index

271